SAVING OLD BUILDINGS

SAVING OLD BUILDINGS

Sherban Cantacuzino and Susan Brandt

THE ARCHITECTURAL PRESS · LONDON

First published in 1980 by The Architectural Press Limited : London

© Sherban Cantacuzino and Susan Brandt 1980

British Library Cataloguing in Publication Data

Cantacuzino, Sherban
  Saving old buildings.
    1. Buildings—Remodelling for other
    use
    2. Architecture—Conservation and
    restoration
    I. Title   II. Brandt, Susan
    720   NA2793

ISBN 0-85139-498-1

Filmset and printed in Great Britain by BAS Printers Limited, Over Wallop, Hampshire

Contents

General introduction   ix

PART I   THE CITY

1 Case study: the restoration of Bologna's historic centre   3

2 Conversions to cultural uses   20
Convent, Urbino   *University faculty*   21
Various buildings at Buckingham   *University College*   25
Pavillon Baltard, Nogent-sur-Marne, France   *Multi-purpose hall*   28
Royal Exchange, Manchester   *Theatre*   30
Bank and Warehouse, Louisville   *Theatre*   33
The Old Patent Office, Washington D.C.   *Art Gallery*   35
Halifax Piece Hall, Halifax, Yorkshire   *Centre of tourism, culture and entertainment*   37
Carnegie Mansion, New York   *Museum*   39
Police Station, Boston   *Art Gallery*   41
Bush Warehouse, Bristol   *Art Gallery, theatre, restaurant and offices*   42
Gamul House, Chester   *Exhibition and lecture hall*   44
Old Speech Room, Harrow School, Middlesex   *Gallery*   45
School Hall, Sevenoaks, Kent   *School library*   46
Southern Alleghenies College Gymnasium, Pennsylvania   *Art Museum*   48

3 Conversions to commercial use
Introduction   51
Laundry, Santa Barbara, California   *Restaurant*   52
Laundry, Karlsruhe-Dammerstock, Germany   *Architects' office*   54
Central Market Buildings, Covent Garden   *Shops, cafes, offices etc*   56
Faneuil Hall Market, Boston   *Market, restaurant, shops and offices*   60
Cement Factory, Barcelona   *Architects' offices*   63
Warehouse, Toronto   *Offices and restaurant*   66
Warehouse, Copenhagen   *Hotel*   68
St Paul's House, Leeds   *Offices*   69
Industrial Building, Camden Town, London   *Architects' offices*   71
Students' Union, Copenhagen   *Showrooms and offices*   73
American Surety Building, New York   *Offices for the Bank of Tokyo*   75
Sweet Factory, New York City   *Artists' apartments and studios*   77
Police Station, St Louis, Missouri   *Design studio and offices*   79
Hospital Buildings, St Louis, Missouri   *Offices and studio*   81

4 Conversions to housing

Introduction	84
Three Warehouses in Amsterdam, Holland *Housing and a shop*	85
The Blue Warehouse, Copenhagen *Flats*	87
Tannery Complex, Peabody, Massachusetts *Residential complex, with park and pond*	89
Bell Telephone Laboratories, New York *Flats and studios for artists*	91
Mercantile Wharf Building, Boston *Shops, restaurants and flats*	93
Riverhead Granaries, Driffield, Humberside *Flats*	95
Warehouse loft, New York City *Apartment and artist's studio*	97
Piano factory, Boston *Artists' housing*	98

5 Churches

Introduction	100
St Leonard's Church, Streatham *Religious services, concerts, plays, conferences*	109
St Matthias Church, Richmond, Surrey *Religious services and community centre*	111
First Church of Christ Scientist, Daisy Bank, Manchester *Arts centre*	114
Holy Trinity Church, Colchester *Agricultural museum*	116
Synagogue, Houston, Texas *Theatre*	117
All Saints' Church, Oxford *Library*	119
Holy Trinity, Southwark, London *Orchestra rehearsal hall*	122

6 Railway stations

Introduction	124
Pocklington Railway Station, Yorkshire *Sports centre*	126
Darlington North Road Railway Station, Yorkshire *Station and railway museum*	128
Monkwearmouth Station, Tyne and Wear *Transport museum*	130
Union Railway station, New London, Connecticut *Railway station plus offices and restaurant*	131
Richmond Station, Yorkshire *Part of recreation centre*	133

PART II   THE COUNTRYSIDE

7 Case study: the changing village	137

8 Small buildings converted to a new use

Watermill, Wadenhoe, Northamptonshire *House*	146
Lower Trevollard Farm, Cornwall *Two houses*	148
Lacock Barn, Lacock, Wiltshire *Photographic museum*	150
Curtis Mill, Lower Kilcott, Gloucestershire *House*	152
Wharf, Warehouse and China Works, near Telford, Shropshire *Museum*	154
No. 34 High Street, Ironbridge, Shropshire *Shop and flats*	158
Barn, Friesland, Holland *House*	159
Tithe Barn, Dersingham, Norfolk *Store for salvaged historic building materials*	160
St Faith, Newton in the Willows, Northants *Field studies centre*	161
New Melleray Abbey, Dubuque, Iowa *Church, chapter house and chapel*	163
Old All Saints, Langdon Hills, Essex *House*	165
Tintern Railway Station, Gwent *Visitors' centre*	167

9 Case study: the Landmark Trust and the Little Houses of the National Trust for Scotland

Introduction	169
Margells, Branscombe, Devon *Holiday house*	175
The Egyptian House, Penzance, Cornwall *Holiday house*	176
The Music Room, Lancaster *Bookshop and holiday flat*	177
The New Inn, Peasenhall, Suffolk *Permanent and holiday accommodation*	179

Appleton Water Tower, Norfolk *Holiday house*   181
Tixall Gatehouse, Staffordshire *Holiday house*   182
The Pineapple, Dunmore, Stirlingshire *Holiday house*   184

10 Case study: the paradores of Spain   186

11 Large country houses and castles
Saddell Castle, Argyll *Holiday house*   196
Prince-Bishops' Summer Palace, Eichstätt, Bavaria *Administrative centre*
for polytechnic   198
Willibaldsburg, Eichstätt, Bavaria *Natural history museum and archives*   200
Clytha Castle, near Raglan, Wales *Holiday house*   202
Parnham House, Beaminster, Dorset *Workshops, school, exhibition centre*
and residential accommodation   204
Stable Block, Great Fosters, Egham, Surrey *Conference centre*   206
Baranov Castle, Poland *Cultural centre*   208
Niedzica Castle, Poland *Conference centre, guest house, museum*   210
Farm Buildings, Culzean Castle, Ayrshire *Country park reception centre*   211
Wortham Manor, Lifton, Devon *Holiday house*   213

Appendix: Found space   215

General introduction

Conservation has by now taken such a grip on the public mind that another book on the subject requires a brief explanation. In an earlier book, *New Uses for Old Buildings* (Architectural Press, 1975), which is now sold out, we emphasised the building type before conversion because we felt that the single most important aim in adapting an old building to a new use must be to preserve as much of its original character as possible. This we still believe to be the case, but we also acknowledge the emergence of important strategic issues. That is why this new book is divided, broadly speaking, into the complementary problems of the inner city and the village, and why the chapters are arranged to take the reader from the urban scene of cultural, commercial and housing facilities, through building types which bridge both areas, to buildings in the village and the countryside. It follows that the emphasis must be on the new use. Exceptions to this pattern are churches and railway stations, for which there is a chapter each. Such specific building types, we felt, justified the change of emphasis to their original use, especially as among both types there were examples in which the original use was partly preserved after conversion.

The book hinges on two major case studies—Bologna for the inner city and the future of the English village. For a long time Bologna has been held up as an exemplar of conservation policy and, if the results have not yet lived up to expectations, if some of the principles themselves may be challenged by a more empirical Anglo-Saxon approach, the theory as a whole is the most advanced of any city in our experience. The first four chapters support the case for inner city regeneration, the last three for village and countryside renewal. In the second half there are subsidiary studies on the Landmark Trust, the Little Houses scheme of the National Trust for Scotland, and the *paradores* of Spain. In between are two chapters which span the two halves, railways stations and 'found space'. The latter in particular marks another change from the earlier book by emphasising the importance of finding short-life uses at minimum cost, rather than quality of design.

Apart from some 20 examples which illustrate the major case studies and subsidiary subjects, the book includes 75 jobs, of which 43 are in Britain, 18 in the United States, three each in Germany and Denmark, two each in Holland and Poland and one each in France, Italy, Spain and Canada. Three examples only—Holy Trinity, Southwark, All Saints, Oxford and the School of Education, Urbino—illustrated as projects in the earlier book, are included again as executed conversions. The drop in the number of British examples may also explain why there are fewer buildings belonging to that 'functional tradition' of the Industrial Revolution in which Britain is particularly rich.

In the earlier book we pointed to the fact that only in one-third of the examples was the client a public authority spending public money, and we forecast a reversal of this trend. Because of a general economic retrenchment this has not come about, though there are now many more examples of joint public and private funding. In the earlier book we referred to the Faneuil Hall market buildings in Boston as an encouraging example of large-scale rehabilitation which was then under way. This work has since been completed and is fully illustrated in Chapter 2, together with its recently finished parallel in London, the Central Market buildings in Covent Garden. On the other hand our optimism about the Albert Dock in Liverpool, which was to have been taken over by the Polytechnic, has been proved unfounded, and this vast and wonderful group of buildings continues to lie empty and mouldering. The earlier book also mentioned without illustrating the policy of the Spanish Government of converting castles and monasteries into a chain of tourist hotels called *paradores*. Some of these are now included in a chapter which concentrates on large building piles associated with country towns and villages, and includes examples of the smaller country house, a type which proliferates in Britain and which is now particularly at risk.

In the earlier book we included conversions that were 10–12 years old. Even the later examples had barely been touched by inflation, so that the cost of the work, given in almost every case, was in general substantially less than that of an equivalent new building. But even as the earlier book was being written, this relationship was rapidly being reversed and the economic justification for converting an old building increasingly had to include the unquantifiable values of age, character and architectural quality. These values have since become paramount in the equation and have acquired currency as a result of a climate of opinion which often forces a developer and architect to make the most of an existing building. Most of the examples in this book are no more than five or six years old and we have again included costs wherever possible, though it seems to us that these are becoming increasingly meaningless as the value of our available resources is becoming understood.

PART I
THE CITY

1. Fillippo Gnudi's great plan of Bologna (1702), done like an aerial view. North is pointing downwards, so it is upside down compared to all the other plans illustrating this section.

2

1 Case study: the restoration of Bologna's historic centre

Bologna demonstrates a systematic approach to the conservation of an historic centre which, when it was first undertaken in the early 1960s, was probably without rival. That it has not entirely fulfilled its promise in terms of achievement in no way detracts from the solid theory on which it is based, though that, too, can be criticised in certain respects. It is, as we shall explain, both authoritarian and rigidly conservative, reflecting the long and continuous reign of the Communist Party in the government of the city.

Bologna is the capital of Emilia as well as an important commercial and industrial centre. Its university, most of which is still housed in the historic centre, is one of the oldest and most famous in Europe. The city lies on the southern edge of the fertile Emilian plain against the foothills of the Apennines, the valleys of the Reno and Savena having always provided natural routes southwards through the mountains to Florence and to Rome. Its form is that of an irregular hexagon, nowadays described by a ring road that follows the line of the town walls, of which parts survive. Within this hexagon, which is roughly 2 km across, the road pattern reveals a grid-iron Roman town surrounded by a radial medieval town. Inevitably expansion has taken the line of least resistance into the agricultural plain to the east, west and north of the city, though sporadic development of a privileged kind has also occurred in the hills to the south. Bologna's population in 1881, before any major expansion had taken place, was 120,000. Today there are 500,000 inhabitants, 80,000 of whom live in the historic centre.

The nineteenth century was characterised by an accelerating pattern of change similar to other European cities. The Baroque legacy of the royal park was the modest Montagnola public gardens laid out in 1806 on the site of the former Galliera Castle in the northern part of the city. The southern part had to wait until 1875, when a large private garden between the Castiglione and S. Stefano gates was made into the Giardini Margherita. The railway station was opened in 1858 and Bologna, whose very existence had sprung out of an intersection of important roads, now became the centre of an elaborate railway network. The Via dell' Independenza, linking the station to the centre, was started soon after but not completed until 1888. An old medieval lane was widened into the Via Farini (1860–70) and the new

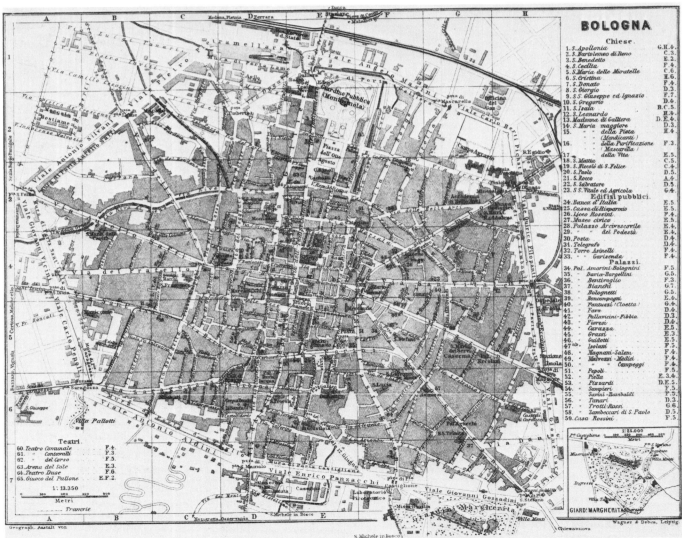

BOLOGNA

Chiese.

1.	S. Apollonia	G.H.4.
2.	S. Bartolomeo di Reno	C.3.
3.	S. Benedetto	E.2.
4.	S. Cecilia	F.4.
5.	S. Maria delle Muratelle	C.6.
6.	S. Cristina	H.6.
7.	S. Donato	F.4.
8.	S. Giorgio	D.3.
9.	SS. Giuseppe ed Ignazio	F.7.
10.	S. Gregorio	D.4.
11.	S. Isaia	B.C.5.
12.	S. Leonardo	H.4.
13.	Madonna di Galliera	D.E.4.
14.	S. Maria maggiore	D.3.
15.	" della Pietà	H.4
16.	" (Mendicanti) della Purificazione	F.3.
	" (Mascarella) della Vita	
17.	S. Mattia	E.5.
18.	S. Niccolò di S. Felice	C.5.
19.	"	C.4.
20.	S. Paolo	D.5.
21.	S. Rocco	A.4.
22.	S. Salvatore	D.5.
23.	SS. Vitale ed Agricola	G.4.

Edifizi pubblici.

24.	Banca d'Italia	E.5.
25.	Cassa di Risparmio	E.5.
26.	Liceo Rossini	F.4.
27.	Museo civico	E.5.
28.	Palazzo Arcivescovile	E.4.
29.	" del Podestà	E.4.
30.	Posta	D.4.
31.	Telegrafo	D.E.4.
32.	Torre Asinelli	F.4.
33.	" Garisenda	F.4.

Palazzi.

34.	Pal. Amorini-Bolognini	F.5.
35.	" Davia-Bargellini	G.5.
36.	" Bentivoglio	F.3.
37.	" Bianchi	G.7.
38.	" Bolognetti	G.5.
39.	" Boncompagni	E.4.
40.	" Fantuzzi (Cloetta)	G.4.
41.	" Faru	D.4.
42.	" Pallavicini-Fibbia	D.3.
43.	" Fioresi	D.4.
44.	" Caprara	E.5.
45.	" Grassi	E.3.
46.	" Guidotti	D.5.
47.ab.	" Isolani	F.5.
48.	" Magnani-Salem	F.4.
49.	" Malvezzi-Medici	F.4.
50.	" Campeggi	
51.	" Pepoli	F.5.
52.	" Piella	E.3.4.
53.	" Pizzardi	D.E.5.
54.	" Sampieri	F.5.
55.	" Surini-Banbaldi	
56.	" Tanari	D.3.
57.	" Trotti-Rossi	G.6.
58.	" Zambeccari di S. Paolo	D.5.
59.	Casa Rossini	F.5.

Teatri.

60.	Teatro Comunale	F.4.
61.	" Contavalli	F.3.
62.	" del Corso	F.5.
63.	Arena del Sole	E.3.
64.	Teatro Duse	F.6.
65.	Giuoco del Pallone	E.F.2.

1 : 13.350

Metri

Tranvie

Geograph. Anstalt von

Wagner & Debes, Leipzig.

GIARD. MARGHERITA

1 : 25.000

Metri

S. Michele in Bosco

4

2. Birds-eye view of Bologna, from a late nineteenth-century print. The bulk of the cathedral of S. Petronio rises in the centre and beyond are the southern hills. The radial street which runs to the bottom left-hand corner is the Via Zamboni. The other radial streets clearly visible beyond are the Via San Vitale, the Strada Maggiore, and the Via Santo Stefano. Further still, and just discernible, is the Via Castiglione. All these radials meet at the Asinelli and Garisenda towers, the only two of a group which survive today.

Piazza Cavour formed off this street (begun 1868). Accompanying this urban reconstruction were a number of monumental buildings, among them the Banca d'Italia (A. Cipolla, 1864), the Palazzo Guidotti (Coriolano Monti, 1866) and the Cassa di Risparmio (Giuseppe Mengoni, 1868–76), all three in the Via Farini and all three of considerable architectural quality.

The policy of site clearance and road widening, which had been practised for some 25 years, was not legally endorsed until the first master plan in 1889. This established the need to cut new roads and to enlarge both major and minor existing ones. Among the many so-called improvements that followed were the widening of the city's *decumanus*, the Vias Rizzoli and Ugo Bassi; the cutting of a new road between the Zambone and Lame gates and the formation of a second square off the Via Farini, the Piazza Minghetti (1893). The master plan was a licence for the straight line and right-angle, and only the economic crisis after the First World War prevented further planned destruction, notably in the Vias D'Azeglio and S. Stefano, both major streets of great architectural importance.

The master plan of 1889 also foresaw the need for expansion outside the walls, and proposed a grid-iron layout which wrapped tightly round the city on the east, west and north sides. In the event the population explosion, which made this necessary, did not occur until after the First World War, when an agricultural slump caused massive immigration to the cities and, in the case of Bologna, a rise in the population to 200,000. But the principles of the 1889 plan were not followed. Instead of the earlier, compact layout, which included a generous provision of green open space, the city began to spread haphazardly first to the north and later to the east and west along the direction of the Via Emilia, using up good agricultural land. The existing industry, mainly on an artisanal scale and concerned with traditional activities such as textile manufacture, food processing and warehousing, which at first could not provide employment for all the newcomers, both expanded and diversified into engineering and chemical works as well as war manufacture.

In the historic centre the major physical changes since the First World War occurred first in 1931, when whole areas were destroyed in the north-eastern quarter to make way for a new 'university city'; and, second, after the last war, when much of the north-western quarter, which had been destroyed by bombs, was rebuilt in a manner largely unsympathetic to the city's building traditions. It was then, too, that the canals, which had always characterised this proto-industrial part of the town, were covered in or built over. Despite a new master plan in 1955, new building was mainly of a speculative nature. Nothing, for instance, was done to keep two large convent gardens (of S. Domenico and S. Mattia), which had survived in the centre of the city, from the hands of the developer.

It was not until after 1960 that attitudes and policies began to change. At an architectural and planning level the 1960 plan for Gubbio, prepared by Idolosalire and Leonardo Benevolo, became the model for Bologna and for its architect-planner, Pier Luigi Cervellati. At a political level the ruling Communist Party adopted the Christian Democrats' policy of decentralising the city's power structure, and set up 18 neighbourhood councils, four of them in the historic centre. Though still not elected, these councils have in fact represented the community in all local planning matters and have given Bologna an enviable reputation in democratic government.

3. Plan of Bologna from Baedeker's Northern Italy (1913). It shows the new Via dell'Independenza and Via Farini.

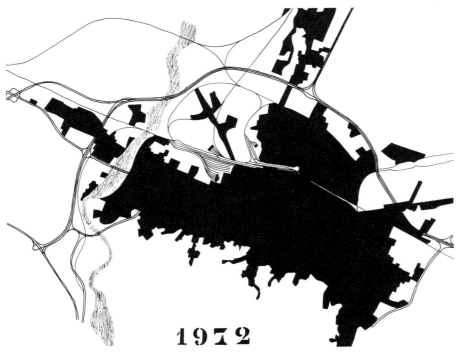

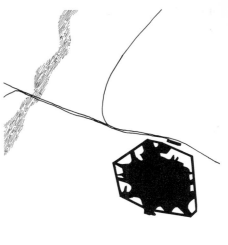

1889

5

6

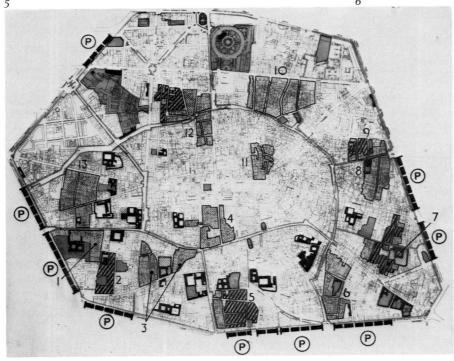

4. The development of Bologna in less than 100 years, 1889–1972.

5. The Canale di Reno with S. Bartolomeo di Reno in the middle. The church survives but the canal has been filled in.

6. As a result of the 1889 master plan the three towers in the foreground and the houses between the Via Orefici and the Via Rizzoli were pulled down. The Torre Garisenda and Torre Asinelli in the background survive.

7. Plan showing the 13 areas selected for rehabilitation. Five of these became pilot projects (2, 5, 7, 9 and 12)

  1. SANT'ISAIA
  2. S. CATERINA
  3. VIA DEL FOSSATO AND VIA DEL RICCIO
  4. VIA D'AZEGLIO
  5. SOLFERINO
  6. VIA RIALTO AND VIA DEI COTTELLI
  7. FONDAZZA
  8. VIA BROCCAINDOSSO
  9. S. LEONARDO
10. VIA MASCARELLA
11. VIA INFERNO
12. S. CARLO
13. VIA PIETRALATA

8. Demolishing the walls by the Porta Castiglione.

Symbolic of the early struggle was the battle over the demolition of S. Giorgio, which was won by the conservationists in 1962. The following year began the research into the principles that were later incorporated into the 1969 plan for the historic centre. Any conservationist plan at that moment in Italy was bound to draw not only on immediate precedent, like the plan for Gubbio, but also on a legal framework that goes back to the general principles laid down in the laws of 1931 and 1938. These stated that later additions to a monument must be respected for their historic or aesthetic value; the use of monuments must be compatible with their structures; all restoration must be the minimum necessary and as simple as possible; and all existing building around monuments must be retained. These principles show a concern for careful restoration and a respect for the minor architecture which plays such an important part in the total fabric of a town.

The 1969 plan, approved by central government in 1973, involved nothing less than the total regeneration of the existing built fabric, adequately integrated by social services and equipment. This kind of urban renewal was posed as an alternative to new speculative development. The plan proposed two main lines of action: to rehabilitate so as to maintain the local working-class population and to appropriate and convert some of the city's monuments for community use.

Rehabilitation was to proceed on the basis of the 1971 law, the 'Legge sulla Casa', which was passed to enable authorities to expropriate unbuilt and built-up real estate at indemnities far below market values. Increases in the value of land due to planning measures or improvements in the infrastructure were not to be considered in the assessment. All the land in the centre of Bologna would be expropriated by the Municipality and, in effect, leased back to the citizens after being restored. Central funds previously used for new public housing could now be used to improve old property. But these funds, when they eventually reached Bologna in the autumn of 1974, proved wholly inadequate for the purpose of expropriation (even at rural prices), let alone renovation. The neighbourhood councils, moreover, turned against their creators and political masters, as democratic institutions are apt to do. Real estate in the centre of Bologna is mainly in the hands of small landowners who make a living by letting rooms to students. The councils threatened massive desertion of the Communist Party if these landowners were deprived of their livelihood by the expropriation of their urban property at rural prices. They added for good measure that the Italian Government would first have to expropriate the Pirelli building in Milan before similar action on the small capitalist could even be considered.

If the idea of total public ownership was unacceptable, how else could the Municipality guarantee rehabilitation, protection of tenancies and control of rents? The proposals which were eventually agreed also required more money than was available. But they were politically acceptable and the tentative start which had been made on property already owned by the Municipality could now be transformed into a continuous process which would eventually result in the rehabilitation of all the housing in the historic centre. The agreement reached between the Municipality and private owners guaranteed a municipal subsidy for rehabilitation, the amount being regulated according to the means of each owner. In return the owner undertook to protect existing tenants and to control rents.

The 1969 plan identifies thirteen areas which had become over-built

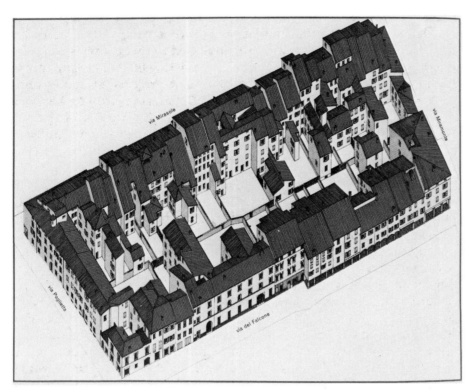

9. One of the blocks off the Solferino area 5 as it will be after rehabilitation. The axonometric shows many of the accretions at the back removed and a gap in the Via Falcone filled in.

10. The rebuilt garden party walls at the back of a block in the S. Leonardo area converted into flats.

11. *An example of* ristauro *in the Solferino area.*

12. *An example of* ristauro conservativo *in the S. Leonardo area 9. These are new houses built on traditional lines and filling a gap in the Via S. Leonardo.*

and unattractive for private investment but, some would argue, ripe for demolition and redevelopment. Together these areas totalled a population of some 32,000 and, rehabilitated in the manner proposed, would go a long way to maintaining the existing 80,000 inhabitants in the historic centre. To begin with five pilot projects, affecting some 6,000 people, were selected—in the Via S. Caterina (area 2); between the Vias Paglietta and Savenella (area 5); on both sides of the Via Fondazza (area 7); north of the Via San Vitale (area 9); and on both sides of the Via S. Carlo (area 12). All these were put in hand between 1976 and 1977.

The plan's second line of action, to appropriate and convert some of the city's monuments for community use, has also been put in hand. Surveys were undertaken to determine the need for public institutions, schools and green spaces. The first example (see photographs 13–15), was a small palace in the Via Pietralata, which was converted into a community centre of the Malpighi neighbourhood in the western part of the city. It provided a library, a lecture hall, a crêche, medical services and a landscaped courtyard. A number of other important buildings, some of which are also illustrated, have been either partly converted or planned for conversion as money becomes available. The convent of S. Leonardo in the Via S. Vitale will house a neighbourhood centre, a professional institute, a nursery school and, inside the church itself, a theatre. The wedge-shaped block between the church and the street has been converted into students' accommodation. The Baraccano complex in the south-east corner of the city already operates as a students' union. It too will become a neighbourhood centre with library and nursery school, as well as a theatre, a museum and an exhibition hall. Its large garden will become public. The former Jesuit church, Santa Lucia, in the Via Castiglione, will be converted into a centre for the performing arts for the use of the University, the Municipality and the City Theatre. The monastic buildings will house a secondary school and a library. In the adjacent eighteenth-century Collegio San Luigi work is proceeding apace to provide student accommodation and a home for the State Institute of Arts; and there are elaborate plans to convert the disused friary of S. Mattia (the church is used as a garage) into another neighbourhood centre, museum and elementary school. An example of methodical restoration rather than conversion is the Palazzo Ghisilardi-Fava in the Via Manzoni, where a museum of medieval and Renaissance art may be installed. The intention is to restore first and find a new use second.

The 1969 plan was based on a long and thorough survey of the city's buildings and open spaces. Not only did this show customary information such as use, structural condition and architectural importance, but it provided a typological analysis which identified four major categories, each with a number of sub-categories. This analysis has been of undoubted benefit to Bologna's architects in so far as it has helped to prevent some of the aberrations committed, say, in Venice where no comparable study has taken place. But it has also trapped the architects in their deep-rooted conservatism. In housing, for example, they claim that appropriate typology is carefully observed both in restoration and rebuilding. Yet the fact that rehabilitation and reconstruction has turned most of the houses into flats and that the carefully rebuilt garden party walls are now quite meaningless does not strike them as inconsistent. The restoration of existing houses is called *ristauro tipologico* and reconstruction of empty plots or when the house is beyond repair *ristauro conservativo,*

13. *The community centre for the Malpighi neighbourhood in the Via Pietralata, housed in a modest seventeenth-century palace.*

10

14. *The courtyard, which is used as a playground.*

15. *The library of the community centre.*

even though it is not a restoration but a completely new building. By elevating typological exactitude to a matter of principle, by insisting on slavish imitation and reproduction, the Municipality of Bologna has denied architects the opportunity of creative experiment in housing, of responding both to tradition and to contemporary needs.

If the 1969 plan is architecturally unimaginative, it is certainly one of the soundest conservationist documents in existence. The Piazza Maggiore has been a pedestrian zone for some ten years and there are proposals for restricting vehicular traffic in the historic centre by 'feeder' roads off perimeter roads; for developing public transport, which is already free during rush hours; and for extending the pedestrian network by opening up private courtyards, passages and gardens. Restoration, rehabilitation and new building are under the strict control of the Municipality which has laid down six principles: with absolute restrictions; with partial restrictions; allowing the renovation of the interior but preserving its functional and structural characteristics; allowing the renovation of the interior, but respecting rather than preserving its functional and structural characteristics; demolition and reconstruction; and demolition with restrictions on reconstruction (building rights may sometimes be transferred to another part of the city). In the plan the historic centre is seen as a whole, as an area for housing, university activities, cultural and tourist functions, small trades and business. Any concentration of administrative and bureaucratic institutions, department stores, warehouses, or anything requiring large plots and attracting a large amount of traffic is forbidden. Instead the small shopkeepers have been encouraged to band together in cooperatives to enable them to survive. In recognising this totality, the plan also recognises Bologna's special character which is derived from its arcades. Still required today under a fifteenth-century law, they give the whole city a sense of unity behind which the individual monument fades into relative insignificance.

16. *Ground floor plan of the convent of S. Leonardo showing the beginning of the wedge-shaped block between the church and the street.*

17. *The arcaded Via San Vitale with the convent of S. Leonardo behind the street façade.*

18. *The cloister of S. Leonardo is to be the focus of another neighbourhood centre* (PHOTOGRAPH: ENRICO PASQUALI).

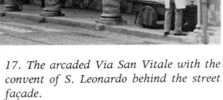

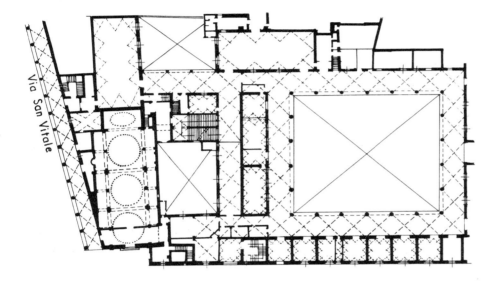

Via San Vitale

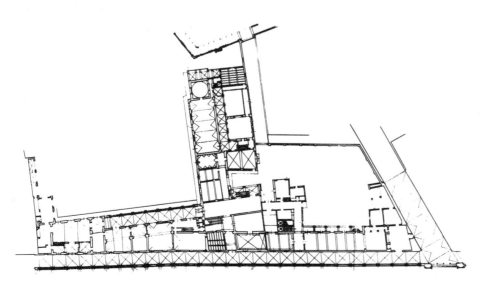

19. *Ground floor plan of the Baraccano complex.*

What, then, are Bologna's failures and successes, and what needs to be done? The historic centre of Bologna today is a service town. What industry there was has moved, and new industry has developed outside. This has been the result of land speculation and not, as the Municipality would like to believe, of sound planning measures. Industrialists quite simply grasped the opportunity of selling urban land at urban prices and buying agricultural land at agricultural prices in the outskirts. Industrial workers were therefore attracted to the municipalities all around Bologna rather than to the historic centre, which thus avoided the congestion of so many other Italian towns. The population in the centre has remained steady and consists mainly of elderly people, students, artisans, and a shifting group of immigrant workers. Speculation, on the whole, has been thwarted, though landlords let individual rooms to students for a high rent. These 'rich' students are from the 60,000 strong university which is well subsidised by the government. One possibility, though unacceptable to Cervellati and the Municipality (who would like the size of the university reduced by creating new universities), is for Bologna to become a university town in which major restoration projects, for use by the university, are jointly financed by the university and the Municipality. Another possibility, and a familiar one, is to attract industry back to the centre, and so investment to aid its renewal.

The financial predicament of Bologna and all Italian cities is due to local authorities having no income from local rates. All their finance, for building and otherwise, comes not only by permission of central government but in wholly inadequate amounts. It is generally accepted that the only real solution to this problem is to give local authorities tax autonomy so that they can manage their own budget.

In the absence of adequate government funds, even the ruling Communist Party now accepts and admits the need of private investment. In fact a large number of buildings in the historic centre—offices, banks, boutiques—have been restored with private capital, and we have already seen how the method of rehabilitating houses had to be modified in the face of strong opposition. Cervellati himself has spoken in support of a mixed economy: 'The economic climate prevents us from realising our plans except with the help of private capital—but no private capital with speculative ends or involved with the typical urban development, but to help restore the quality of life in the *centro storico*'.*

As a service town with a lively university Bologna has a viable future. It is wrong to pretend, as some of Cervellati's critics have pretended, that Bologna is already dead like a museum town. It is also wrong to suggest that nothing more is happening there in the way of building and restoration. The Municipality alone is involved in some eight sites, each of which represents a major, long-term commitment, and it has plans that will keep it busy for at least ten years. It commands the respect of the public because it has allowed the public to participate through the revolutionary and highly effective neighbourhood councils and because its administrators have been honest and dedicated men for whom serving the Party has been synonymous with serving the people.

20. The vaulted passage with the church of the Baraccano beyond.
21. The garden of the Baraccano already functions as a playground for a nursery school.

*'What is *really* happening in Bologna?' Talk presented by John Donat on BBC Radio 3, 1 August 1977.

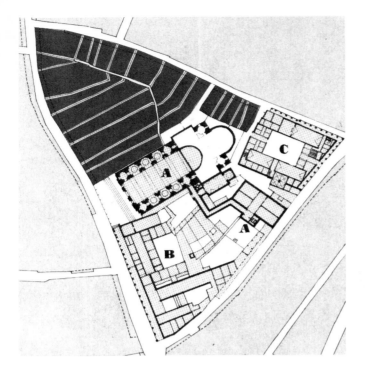

22. Plan of the former Jesuit church of Santa Lucia in the Via Castiglione with its school in the Via Cartoleria (A), the convent of Santa Lucia (B) and the College of S. Luigi (C).

23. The entrance tower seen from the courtyard.

24. Section through the grand staircase and courtyard.

27. A staircase in the College of S. Luigi (PHOTOGRAPH: ENRICO PASQUALI).

26. Elevation of the College of S. Luigi to the Via Cartoleria.

25. Ground floor plan of the College of S. Luigi.

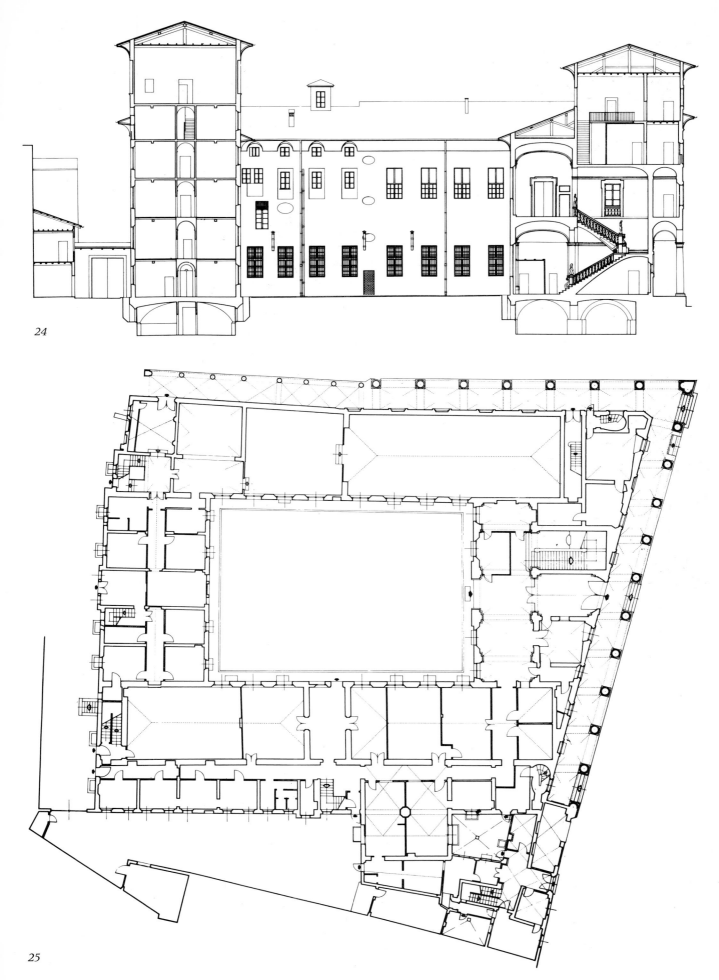

24

25

28. The interior of Santa Lucia, to be used as a theatre.
29. Aerial view of S. Mattia with post-war development (right) which destroyed the large garden of the monastery.

30. The cloister of S. Mattia, now used as a school playground (PHOTOGRAPH: PAULO MONTI).
31. The entrance to the cloister from the street.

32. The Piazza Maggiore at the turn of the century. Except for the far end, it has been pedestrianised for some 12 years.

33, 34. *Private gardens and* trompe l'oeil (PHOTOGRAPH: PAULO MONTI).

35. Bologna's streets are not suited to modern traffic conditions. There are proposals to restrict traffic in the centre and to improve public transport which is already free. (PHOTOGRAPH: PAULO MONTI)

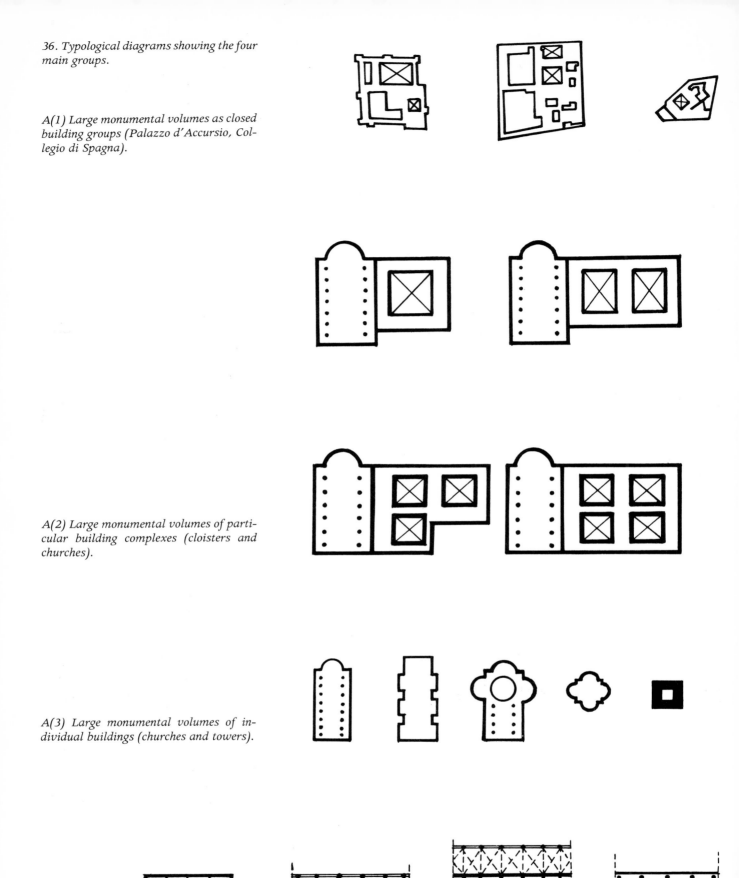

36. *Typological diagrams showing the four main groups.*

A(1) Large monumental volumes as closed building groups (Palazzo d'Accursio, Collegio di Spagna).

A(2) Large monumental volumes of particular building complexes (cloisters and churches).

A(3) Large monumental volumes of individual buildings (churches and towers).

A(4) Large monumental volumes in serial form (Palazzo Archiginnasio).

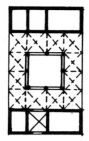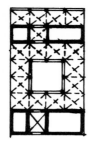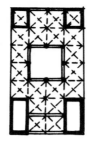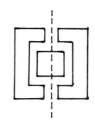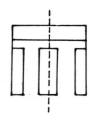

B(1) Former noblemen's houses with a front 20m to 50m wide and with a court enclosed on all four sides.

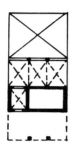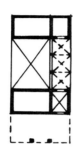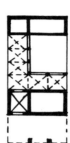

B(2) Residential buildings of the former nobility with a front 10m to 20m wide and a courtyard that is bounded laterally by a wall on at least one side.

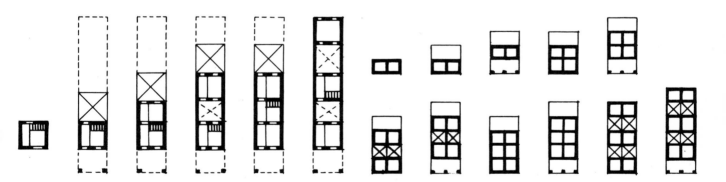

C. Small private houses on narrow and deep lots, with arcades on the street and a succession of courts and gardens behind.

D. Small private houses which do not fit into category C; they have so many peculiarities that they defy classification.

2 Conversions to cultural uses

Introduction

The examples which follow are all from buildings adapted to a cultural use. There are seven from England, five from America and one each from France and Italy. In every case the new use has a parallel in Bologna, though most of the examples there are still only in project form or at best under construction. Thus the conversion in Bologna of former ecclesiastical buildings to university use is matched exactly by Giancarlo De Carlo's rehabilitation work in Urbino. Both are old universities that want to retain a substantial presence in the city centre. Buckingham on the other hand is an unusual example of a small English country town which has become the seat for a new university, several of its existing buildings being adapted for the purpose.

Equally common seems to be the conversion of redundant buildings to museums, art galleries and exhibition centres. Counting the Old Speech Room at Harrow School with its small museum and the Piece Hall at Halifax with its mixed cultural and commercial uses, there are no less than seven in the chapter, four of which are in America. In Bologna there is the Palazzo Ghisilardi-Fava which will probably become a museum of medieval art. It demonstrates the principle, which is common in Italy but which was also applied in the conversion of Gamul House at Chester, of restoring first and finding a new use afterwards. In this way the restoration need not be inhibited by the practical considerations which a new use might impose.

With the exception of a school hall converted into a library, the remaining examples are all places where performances can take place and have their Bolognese parallel in the project for Santa Lucia. Two are straight theatres, though no one could describe the remarkable steel structure inserted into the vast Neo-Classical space of the Royal Exchange at Manchester as in any way ordinary or conventional. Remarkable too is the salvage operation which saved one of Baltard's cast-iron pavilions at Les Halles. Dismantled and re-erected in a Paris suburb, it serves as a multi-purpose hall and provides the local community with an unusual and magnificent centre.

The examples which follow, however, only deal with one aspect of inner city regeneration through the adaptation of redundant buildings. The subsequent chapters on commercial use, housing, churches, railway stations and 'found space' form an essential part of this theme. Indeed the reader will have to turn to the chapter on converted churches to find anything comparable to Bologna's 'centri civici di quartiere', which have made such an important social contribution to the urban community.

CONVENT, URBINO

New use University faculty (School of Education)

Architect Giancarlo De Carlo

Client University of Urbino

Site A roughly rectangular but tapering site at the southern end of the town near the walls. Bounded by Via Saffi to the west, Via S. Girolamo to the north and Via S. Maria to the south and east, the site slopes sharply down to the south and the existing buildings on Via Saffi step down with the slope. The buildings on the site are roughly L-shaped, with a walled garden making up the rectangle. On the corner of Via Saffi and Via S. Girolamo stand two private houses, and on the opposite side of Via S. Girolamo a redundant church bearing the same name as the street forms part of the project.

The site is one of several earmarked for, or already converted to, university use (see the *Architectural Review*, October 1972) in the southern part of the city where there are a large number of

1. Site plan showing university buildings in the historic centre.
1. ADMINISTRATION AND LIBRARY
2. SCHOOL OF SCIENCE
3. SCHOOL OF EDUCATION
4. SCHOOL OF LAW

convents and palaces half-abandoned and difficult to convert to residential use. The policy of concentrating the university in one part of the city, which is of long standing, suffered a shift of emphasis when it was decided a few years ago to move the student residences to new buildings outside the city and to use the old convents and palaces for university departments only.

History In origin the building was a convent, probably constructed in the eighteenth century but subsequently much altered. Towards the end of the nineteenth century the founding order moved elsewhere and the building became an orphanage which was first run by a religious order and later by a semi-lay organisation. In the latter period widespread alterations were carried out to the main building and the garden became a dump for rubble. When the university acquired the building in the early 1960s it was in such a dilapidated state that it would have been tempting to demolish it had it not formed, together with the brick walls enclosing the site, an indispensable element in Urbino's fabric.

Character The brick walls facing outwards on to the streets are generally massive—three and four storeys high— with small rectangular openings for doors and windows, and the remains of arches which must once have surmounted wide openings. The roofs are covered with Roman tiles and provide deep overhangs at the eaves, except at the north end of Via Saffi, where an attractive pediment and three symmetrically placed windows with stone surrounds introduce a semblance of order. The best preserved parts are at the west end of the site and the worst preserved around the garden, which has provided space for piecemeal additions over the years. Of the interiors, only the church offers a space of distinct character worthy of preservation. Generally the spaces within the building were too small to be suitable for collective activities, though on the corner of the Via Saffi and the Via S. Gerolamo there was a substantial shell—formerly a church—which could be used for this purpose.

Work done The School of Education, for which the old convent was destined, already existed but was divided among a number of buildings in different parts of the city. Although the building after conversion is considerably greater in volume than the old convent, it is no higher, thanks to an excavation of 15m which allowed expansion below ground. The stepped section of the

building, the courtyard and the great skylight all ensure that daylight reaches even the deepest point. Much of the roof is covered with planted tubs so that anyone looking at the building from the surrounding hills would see no interruption in the fabric of gardens and buildings which is characteristic of Urbino's historic centre.

The plan is organised around two focal points: the circular courtyard and the semi-circular theatre. Facing the courtyard are studies for the professors and their assistants stacked on four levels which are connected by a spiral staircase. The generous circulation space surrounding these acts as a foyer to the teaching rooms which are housed in the restored shell of the old building along the Via Saffi. At the junction of the Via Saffi and the Via S. Gerolamo the volume of the former church was divided to provide an experimental cinema (for another faculty) at the lower level, and a library which could also be used for university ceremonies.

Around the theatre, also on four levels, are rows of lecture rooms, all of which are lit by the great skylight. On the two lower levels all the lecture rooms can be used together, making a large hall for 1500 with stalls and balcony. This hall can be subdivided with manually operated sliding partitions into two and six parts. Another lecture room, always separate, is suspended from the skylight structure above the semi-circular stage of the theatre. Above the four levels of lecture rooms a fifth level accommodates a café with access to the roof garden.

Of the three entrances to the building one is the main entrance from the Via Saffi, and the other two, from the Via S. Girolamo, give direct access to the cinema and café. This is to encourage anyone in Urbino to use these amenities when the School is closed. Even the theatre is intended for community use and is already helping in the integration of city and university.

Accommodation Basement—lecture rooms, theatre, foyer, lavatories.
Lower ground floor—lecture rooms, theatre balcony, foyer, lavatories, cinema, cinema foyer, studies, teaching rooms.
Ground floor—lecture rooms, foyer, lavatories, roof garden, studies, teaching rooms, offices, projector room.
First floor—lecture rooms, foyer, lavatories, roof garden, students' common room, studies, teaching rooms, library, entrances from the Via S. Gerolamo.
Second floor—café, roof garden, lavatories, studies, teaching rooms, library.

Date of completion: 1978

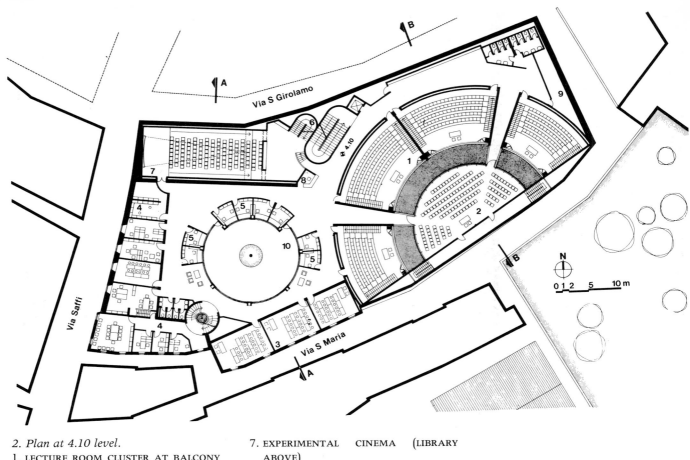

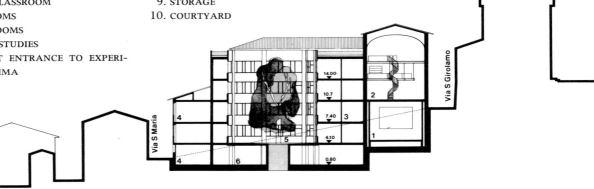

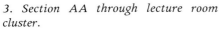

2. Plan at 4.10 level.

1. LECTURE ROOM CLUSTER AT BALCONY LEVEL
2. SUSPENDED CLASSROOM
3. SEMINAR ROOMS
4. TEACHING ROOMS
5. PROFESSORS' STUDIES
6. INDEPENDENT ENTRANCE TO EXPERIMENTAL CINEMA

7. EXPERIMENTAL CINEMA (LIBRARY ABOVE)
8. JANITOR
9. STORAGE
10. COURTYARD

3. Section AA through lecture room cluster.

1. LECTURE ROOM CLUSTER
2. SUSPENDED CLASSROOM
3. CLASSROOM
4. CAFE
5. SKYLIGHT
6. ROOF GARDEN

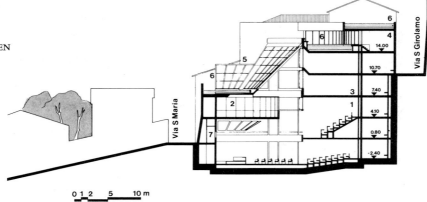

4. Section BB through courtyard.

1. EXPERIMENTAL CINEMA
2. LECTURE HALL AND LIBRARY
3. PROFESSORS' STUDIES
4. SEMINARS
5. COURTYARD
6. PLANT
7. BOOKS FOR SIMULTANEOUS TRANSLATION

5. *The School of Education with its great
skylight seen in its urban setting.*

7. *The skylight over the lecture room
cluster, the roof gardens and the church of
S. Girolamo in the background.*

6. *Looking down the Via Saffi from the
corner with the Via S. Girolamo.*

8. The corridor on the top level. On the left the 'key' window extending through two storeys. On the right the courtyard.

9. The lecture room cluster. Sliding partitions subdivide the space into several lecture rooms.

10. The lecture hall and library above. The spiral staircase connects all three levels.

VARIOUS BUILDINGS AT BUCKINGHAM

New use University College at Buckingham

Architect Stillman & Eastwick-Field; Darnton Holister, consultant to the University

Site Buckingham is an ancient city which was once a county capital. Its fortunes declined when it ceased to act as a market town, yet failed to promote any significant substitute industries. The university buildings are numerous and situated here and there in the Prebend End quarter of the town. The site, of about seven acres, and on either side of Hunter Street, is embraced by a curve of the River Ouse.

History The buildings, not all owned by the university, were previously owned by Unigate Dairies and used as their depôt. When they moved to Bedford, they sold the buildings to the Buckingham Borough Development Company, The buildings remained unoccupied, though the site was used as a coalyard and store. When in 1973 the company sold the site to the university as part of its scheme to revitalise the town, the buildings had fallen into a bad state of repair. To the west of Hunter Street are Yeomanry House and Yeomanry Barracks, eighteenth-century buildings which were formerly used by the Royal Bucks Huzzars. Attached to the barracks is an old single-storey brick storage shed. Further north, on the same side of the street, is a row of stone cottages. On the opposite side of the street stands the remnant of an old dairy, which had been extended to form a depôt.

Character The buildings, typically for a town centre such as this, vary considerably in character. Yeomanry House is an imposing three-storey house with a stuccoed Georgian façade, Ionic pilasters, moulded cornice and pedimented doorcase, tacked on to an earlier and humbler structure. The barracks and stables are two-and-a-half storey brick buildings of the early nineteenth century with slated roofs, and the dairy is similar in character.

1. Site plan.

2. Ground floor (bottom); first floor (middle); second floor and section (top) of former Yeomanry Barracks, converted into common room, refectory and library.

25

3. *Ground floor plan (bottom); first floor (middle); second floor and section (top) of houses in Hunter Street, converted into students study bedrooms, with shared kitchens and bathrooms.*

4. *The two-storey houses in Hunter Street, converted into student study bedrooms, with the three-storey Yeomanry House at the end, which is used as university offices.* (PHOTOGRAPH: HENRY LAW).

The oldest buildings are Nos. 2–3 Hunter Street, two-storey cottages dating from the seventeenth and early eighteenth century. These cottages are constructed of local coursed rubble limestone and, fronting directly on to the street, are a characteristic ingredient of the old town. Other buildings included a modern weights office in unsympathetic orange-buff brick with a projecting flat roof, a timber-framed, weatherboarded store of the mid-nineteenth century, and some small barns, stores, tannery sheds and pigsties.

Work done Because of its poor condition, unsuitability for the university's immediate purposes, and to improve the daylighting for the adjacent cottages, the timber-framed store has unfortunately been demolished. Derelict and useless buildings, such as lean-to sheds, pigsties etc, were also demolished. The western part of the site has been graded and levelled, and now has a tennis court and grassed areas. Access to the river bank has been improved by the removal of unsightly vegetation. In restoring the remaining buildings, the architects aimed to define and retain the essential

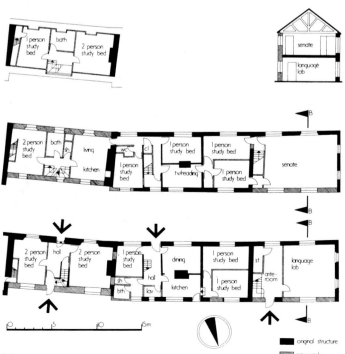

original structure

new work

26

character of the buildings without resorting to conjectural restoration. New work is simple and unashamedly contemporary, but the materials used are traditional, and where possible, second-hand. The architects, mainly for economic reasons, have replaced decayed elements rather than repaired them, but the quality of these semi-industrial buildings is such that the new elements harmonise quite well. In some cases, unwanted nineteenth-century additions have been carefully stripped away to reveal previously hidden elevations. Timber was treated against dry-rot and insects, and damp-proof courses were inserted using an electro-osmosis system. Brickwork has been sandblasted to erase the patchwork contrast between old and new.

The main contractor is a local builder, with a small team of traditional craftsmen whose sensitivity to the character of these old buildings has made a great contribution to the quality of the conversion.

5. *The back of the houses in Hunter Street.* (PHOTOGRAPH: HENRY LAW).

Accommodation Yeomanry House—offices for principal and other staff. There is a small paved garden at the back on the site of two demolished outbuildings.

Yeomanry Barracks and single-storey extension
Ground floor—refectory, kitchen and services, common room, librarian's offices.
First floor—teaching accommodation, reading room and senior common room
Second floor—library

Nos. 2–3 Hunter Street and carpenter's workshop
Ground floor—study/bedrooms, dining room, kitchen and language laboratory.
First floor—study/bedrooms, senate
Second floor (attic)—study/bedrooms

Dairy Life-sciences laboratories including main teaching lab, staff labs, and greenhouse

Weights office (until demolition) Law school, containing three lecturers' rooms and a seminar room.

Date of completion The University College was opened by Margaret Thatcher in February 1976, but only part of the original plans for the college have been completed.

Costs Yeomanry House—total cost £62,759; rate per m² £143.94
Barracks (library)—total cost £32,094; rate per m² £133.72

Nos. 2–3 Hunter Street and carpenter's workshop—total cost £67,587; rate per m² £158.65
Barracks and extension—total cost £63,305; rate per m² £190.11
Dairy—total cost £76,710; rate per m² £205.10.

6. *The former Yeomanry Barracks, converted into the library, with the single-storey building in the foreground housing the refectory and common room.* (PHOTOGRAPH: HENRY LAW).

7. *The common room.* (PHOTOGRAPH: HENRY LAW).

PAVILLON BALTARD, NOGENT-SUR-MARNE, FRANCE

New use Multi-purpose hall

Architect Claude Guillemin, local authority architect

Client Town of Nogent-sur-Marne

Site In the centre of Nogent, a small town on the Marne river, not far from Paris. Access to the pavilion is through a planted court known as 'le square du vieux Paris' in which several nineteenth-century artifacts are permanently exhibited.

History The 'pavillon' is one of several built by Victor Baltard (1853–7) in the Halles district of Paris where the daily flower and fruit markets took place. In 1969 the markets were transferred to a new site at Rungis, outside Paris, and the pavilions stood empty and deteriorating for some years, much to the dismay of Parisians who at the same time discovered their interior beauty and made use of them for sales, exhibitions and all manner of performances. The government responded to public pressure and decided to save them, so in 1972 a circular was sent to every French town offering them a 'pavillon' which would be dismantled, transported and re-erected all at the expense of the state. Any conversion work needed would also be paid for. Nogent took up this offer, and in 1976 the pavilion began to be rebuilt on its new site.

2. Despite its considerable size, the building fits comfortably into its suburban setting.

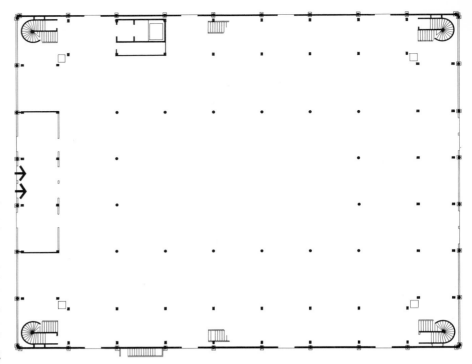

1. Ground floor plan.

Character 'Almost a basilica in iron and glass' is how the pavilion has been described. It was originally built over vaulted cellars which served as stores for the fruit and vegetables. The plan is rectangular (55 × 43m) with a single high-roofed space surrounded on all four sides by a continuous aisle covered with a lower roof. The walls are completely glazed and a clerestory lets in additional light to the central space. The slender iron pillars rise to Corinthian capitals and the trusses are elaborately decorated with wrought ironwork. The whole impression is one of grace and light.

Work done In the first place, the building was dismantled and re-erected on its present site over a reinforced concrete basement supported on piles. Fire-resisting insulation was applied to the roof, and the old cast-iron structure and new steel elements were protected by fire-resisting paint. The colours are green, light brown and cream. (The authentic colours are not known.)

A continuous gallery was built all around the walls as an independent steel supporting structure with a reinforced

3. Detail of the façade. The dark, anti-solar glass gives the building a slickness which Baltard never intended.
4, 5. Interior views. The gallery is a modern addition.

concrete floor. It helps the stability of a building which was formerly surrounded by other similar buildings but now stands exposed on its own. It also provides a neat means of tucking away services such as recording rooms. Gallery railings and lamps are new, but closely follow Baltard's designs.

Other changes to the original structure are the wide entrance doors in the centre of each of the four sides, and the dark anti-solar glass which replaces the original clear glass. A ducted air system round the perimeter of the building and electric elements buried in the concrete ground floor provide winter heating.

A stage was placed at one end of the central space, and stacking chairs provide the seating. To improve visibility for those furthest from the stage, the chairs are placed on a stepped wooden structure. Two steel frames for stage lights have been suspended from the pillars—one at one end of the central space and one across the middle. A huge cinema organ has found a new home here on the gallery behind the stage.

Accommodation Conferences, concerts, theatre, exhibitions, music-hall etc., for a maximum audience of 3,000. Basement (another 2,300m²) has parking, service access and dressing rooms.

Date of completion 1977

Cost 8 million francs (£940,000 approx.)

ROYAL EXCHANGE, MANCHESTER

New use Theatre

Architect Levitt, Bernstein Associates

Client Royal Exchange Theatre Trust Limited

Site A large urban site in central Manchester between two of the city's busiest streets and facing on to St Anne's Square.

History Manchester is the centre of the Lancashire cotton industry, and the Royal Exchange was once the world's most important market place for cotton. Although designed in the late nineteenth century, the existing building was not completed until 1921. It was bombed in 1940, repaired after the war and re-opened in 1953 with half the original Great Hall rebuilt as offices. Trading ceased in 1968, since when the remains of the Great Hall, measuring 52 × 40m, remained unused.

In 1968, the 69 Theatre Company was formed and for some years produced plays at the Manchester University Theatre. After trying, and failing, to get a new theatre built in Manchester, they found the Royal Exchange, launched an appeal, and in 1973, for the Manchester Festival, started productions in a temporary tent inside the Exchange. In 1974 the building was 'listed' as of architectural and historical merit, and the conversion to a permanent new use became desirable.

Character The Exchange is of classical design with monumental proportions reflecting the wealth and power of the Lancashire cotton kings who once did their business there. A massive arched doorway leads into a huge echoing hall lit by three glazed domes supported by scagliola-clad brick piers.

Work done The idea of a module within the Exchange building was conceived by one of the theatre's artistic directors, Richard Negri, and inspired by the temporary tent which Theatre 69 had used in 1973. It served a dual purpose: first, it preserved intact the monumental, spacious character of the Exchange building, and second, it is sufficiently enclosed to be acoustically sealed from the 11.5 second reverberation time of the Exchange hall, although special flaps can be opened to take advantage of this, if required.

The new open-stage theatre is seven-sided in plan. At the level of the Exchange floor it contains seating for 448 people and a stage, which was the greatest load the existing floor was capable of bearing. The 'roof' (contain-

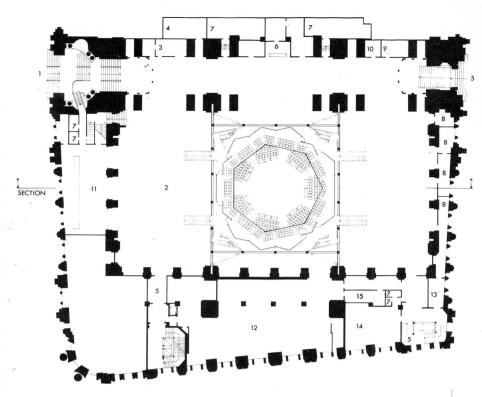

1. Plan at first gallery level. The new auditorium is shown in the context of the Great Hall of the Cotton Exchange.

2. Section through auditorium and Great Hall.

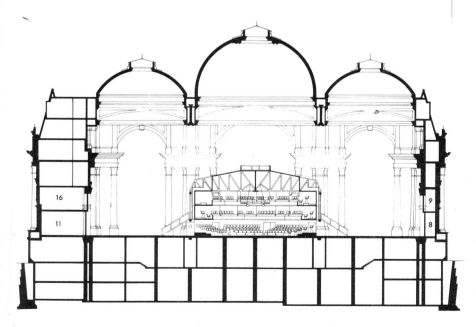

1. ENTRANCE	9. OFFICES
2. FOYER	10. DISABLEDS' WC
3. BOX OFFICE	11. CAFE BAR
4. COATS	12. WORKSHOPS
5. EXITS	13. STAGE DOOR
6. INTERNAL BAR	14. GREEN ROOM
7. WCS	15. BREAKDOWN ROOM
8. STORES	16. RESTAURANT

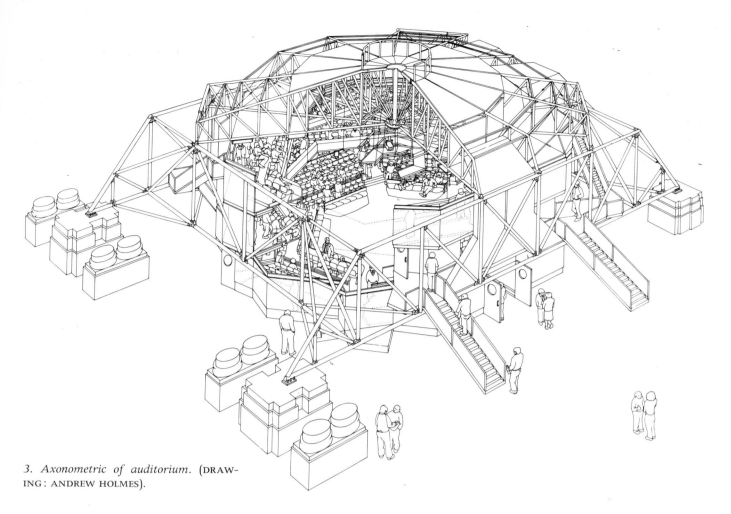

3. Axonometric of auditorium. (DRAW-ING: ANDREW HOLMES).

ing the lighting structure) and the two upper seating galleries, for 150 people each, were suspended from tubular steel trusses inserted into the four massive piers supporting the central dome. The seats in these upper galleries can easily be removed if required.

Because of weight restrictions and sight line requirements, relaxation of fire regulations was required in order to permit the use of an exposed steel structure. This relaxation was given in return for a design in which low combustible materials only have been used. Special escape routes have been designed from the auditorium. Other spaces in the Exchange hall have all been converted to uses required by the theatre.

4. The Great Hall before the building of the auditorium. (PHOTOGRAPH: PHOTOCALL, MANCHESTER).

Accommodation Ground floor (first gallery level)—seven-sided stage, seating for 448, foyer, box office, restaurant, cafeteria, bar, workshops, lavatories, offices, stores.

First floor (second gallery level)—seating for 300, rehearsal rooms, dressing rooms, lavatories, offices, etc.

Date of completion 1976

Cost £775,000 (excluding professional fees)

5. *The Great Hall after the building of the auditorium.*

6. *A light tubular steel canopy immediately identifies the new theatre and provides an effective contrast with the monumental archway (below).*

7. *Inside the new auditorium during a performance (right).*

BANK AND WAREHOUSE, LOUISVILLE, KENTUCKY

New use Theatre

Architect Harry Weese & Associates

Client The Actors' Theatre of Louisville

Site A narrow city lot between two nineteenth-century commercial buildings on West Main Street, Louisville.

History Built originally to house the Bank of Louisville, the main building dates from 1836, and is traditionally thought to be the work of Gideon Shryock. Recent research, however, indicates that it was designed in part by James H. Dakin, a New Orleans architect, with Shryock supervising the construction. Recently the bank was vacated and bought by the Actors' Theatre. The warehouse building to the left has also been taken over by the Actors' Theatre.

Character The bank building, in Greek Revival style, has a fine distyle-in-antis stone portico with Ionic columns rising to a cast-iron parapet with anthemion cresting. The double doors are surmounted and flanked by windows and are decorated with an Egyptian-style motif which echoes the crest over the parapet and is continued throughout the interior. The main banking hall is a large double-height space, surmounted by an oval dome decorated with graduated coffering and lit by a skylight. Pilasters and four free-standing columns support the dome. The structure of the bank building is of brick over a concrete frame, with steel roof trusses.

The four-storey brick warehouse on the left is a worthy companion to the bank building with its regularly spaced large window-openings and Florentine decoration.

Work done The façade was cleaned and restored. The banking hall has been cleared and is now in use as a foyer. The warehouse building has been remodelled for use by the theatre, openings having been cut through the dividing walls, and the building now contains a shop, storage space, offices and a 200-seat rehearsal room. In the space at the back of both buildings, a theatre has been created, with the main floor and cantilevered balcony focusing on to a slightly raised stage, equipped with traps which can be raised or lowered. Pierced brick walls form the rear wall of the auditorium and help absorb sound. The roof is supported by two 72ft long steel trusses which allow a column-free interior.

The basement of the bank was exca-

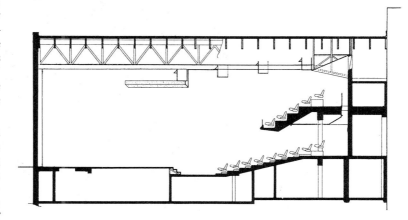

1. Ground floor plan.

2. Section through theatre.

3. The two faces of the Actors' Theatre on West Main Street. On the left, a mid-eighties' warehouse converted to office space, shop and storage areas, and a second, 200-seat auditorium; on the right, the Actors' Theatre entrance foyer, built as a bank in 1836.

vated to make a members' lounge, and its brick walls and ceiling timbers make it a cosy space. The basement also houses a gas-fired hot-water boiler and coolers. The public spaces are provided with a code-controlled sprinkler system.

Accommodation Basement of bank building—members' lounge, services.
Ground floor—foyer, shop, offices, lavatories, stage and auditorium (seating 649).
Mezzanine—offices, rehearsal room, balcony seating (auditorium).
Upper floors of warehouse—offices.

Date of completion October 1972

Cost $1,065,603

4. *The Actors' Theatre foyer and box office.*

5. *The auditorium of the Actors' Theatre.*

THE OLD PATENT OFFICE, WASHINGTON D.C.

New use Art gallery

Architect Faulkner, Stenhouse, Fryer & Faulkner, and from 1970 to 1973 Faulkner, Fryer & Vanderpool

Client Smithsonian Institution

Site The building occupies two entire blocks in the centre of downtown Washington's commercial district, at F and 8th Streets, North-west. It is located half-way between the Capitol and the White House.

History The Patent Office, a temple dedicated to the 'useful arts', took 31 years to build, between 1836 and 1867, and several architects had a hand in its construction. The Patent Office and the Treasury Building (initiated in the same month) were the first major federal structures following the Capitol and the President's House.

William P. Elliot was responsible for the first design. Then Robert Mills was appointed to oversee the building, to Elliot's disgust, who claimed Mills had ruined his design. In 1851, Thomas Ustick Walter took over, and his assistant, Edward Clarke, finished the work.

A fire in 1877 severely damaged part of the interior which was rebuilt during the following decade, but in a more grandiose style than before. In 1932, the Civil Service Commission took over the building, and remained there for thirty years. Two attempts to demolish the building failed (the second time through presidential intervention) and in 1965 the building was transferred to the Smithsonian Institution who restored it, and then used it to house the National Collection of Fine Arts and the National Portrait Gallery.

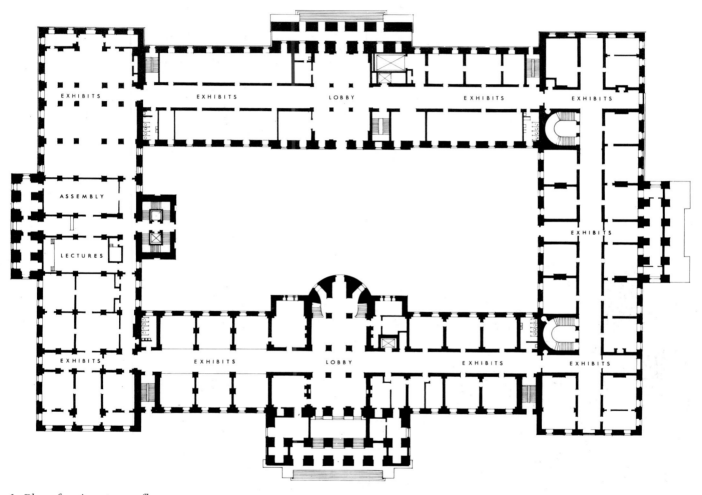

1. Plan of main entrance floor.

2. East-west section.

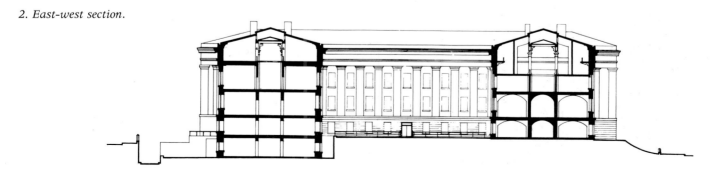

3. The corner of F Street and 9th Street.
4. The National Collection of Fine Arts in the Lincoln Gallery on the top floor.

Character This was one of the largest Greek Revival public buildings undertaken by the government in the early nineteenth century. The plan is rectangular, with a central courtyard. Each front is dominated by a large pedimented Doric portico. Window openings, regularly spaced along all four fronts, are separated by stonework simulating pilasters. The south façade is of Aquia sandstone, while the rest are of marble, which accounts for the considerable variation in colour. The interior is of brick with marble and granite piers, and in some parts has iron floor and ceiling beams. Inside the original south entrance, Mills's superb cantilevered double staircase sweeps up to the second floor where a long gallery with a groin-vaulted ceiling, supported by 32 marble pillars, runs the entire length of the east wing.

Work done The building was restored as far as possible to its original condition, which involved removing partitions and government green paint, and additions and changes from the time the building was in use as offices. Entirely new mechanical and electrical systems were installed throughout the building. The use of many old chimney flues as risers for air-conditioning ducts facilit-ated the installation of this otherwise costly and difficult operation. A small number of parking spaces were provided in the basement of the building.

Accommodation Galleries for the National Collection of Fine Arts and the National Portrait Gallery.
Offices, small café, libraries, shop, lavatories, lecture halls and assembly rooms.

Cost $6,120,000

Date of completion March 1967. Later remodelling and completion of certain galleries and a third floor of the National Portrait Gallery, 1970–1973.

HALIFAX PIECE HALL, HALIFAX, YORKSHIRE

New use Centre of tourism, culture and entertainment

Architect Architect's Department, Metropolitan Borough of Calderdale (Chief Architect: W. A. Clarke)

Client Metropolitan Borough of Calderdale

Site An urban site off Westgate in the central area of Halifax.

History The Piece Hall was erected as an exchange for manufacturers and merchants of woollen cloth and opened for business in January 1779. Its name came from the lengths of cloth, called 'pieces' which were bought and sold here. It was believed to have been designed by Thomas Bradley, about whom little is known except that his other major work was Crow Nest Hall, Lightcliffe (now demolished). Others now credit John Hope of Liverpool with the Piece Hall. The Hall was used every Saturday for trading until powered looms in factories replaced the wide-spread cottage industry and there was no further need for a central exchange. Soon after the beginning of the last century the Hall began to be used for activities other than cloth-trading—public meetings, agricultural shows, firework displays, Sunday School meetings, etc, and in 1868 the Trustees, for whom the Hall was no longer a viable proposition, gave it to the Halifax Corporation. It then became a wholesale fruit, vegetable and fish market and a number of alterations were made. These included three buildings inside and additional lean-to structures around the court, and the building of the south, or Horton Street, gate with massive decorated cast-iron doors, which broke into the colonnade above it.

The Piece Hall was declared an Ancient Monument in 1928. The Halifax Corporation decided in 1971 to restore the Piece Hall, which in 1972 was listed by the Department of the Environment as a grade I building of historical and architectural interest.

Character In his *Buildings of England*** series Nikolaus Pevsner writes: 'These piece-halls or cloth-halls were a feature of the wool towns of Yorkshire. They were either simply rectangles, as the cloth halls of Flanders had been in the late Middle-Ages, or open quadrangles for stalls enclosed by four ranges of building. Such is that at Halifax'.

*Nikolaus Pevsner, *The Buildings of England, Yorkshire*, 2nd edition, Penguin Books, Harmondsworth, 1967.

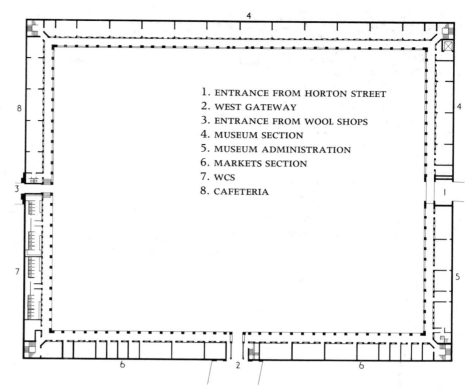

1. Ground floor plan.

1. ENTRANCE FROM HORTON STREET
2. WEST GATEWAY
3. ENTRANCE FROM WOOL SHOPS
4. MUSEUM SECTION
5. MUSEUM ADMINISTRATION
6. MARKETS SECTION
7. WCS
8. CAFETERIA

The building stands on a sloping site and to maintain a constant roof level, the west side has a ground floor and one upper storey whereas the east side has a ground floor and two upper storeys with a basement beneath.

There is an arcade at the lower ground level on the east side, extending partly on the north and south sides which taper away towards the west. Above this level and on all four sides is a gallery of rusticated pillars surmounted by another of Tuscan columns at the third level. At each corner there is an internal staircase and on the north, west and south sides there are gates, each with a semi-circular arch. The massive oak door of the original entrance still survives on the north side. Over the west gateway is a classical cupola on wooden columns surmounted by a Golden Fleece and a weather vane. The exterior walls have no windows or decorative features except on the north face where pilasters and arches imitate those of the arcade. The interior was surrounded by a cobbled roadway with two transverse roads. The rest of the courtyard was grassed over. The galleries provide 315 rooms, each with a window and panelled door.

Work done The Calderdale Council took advantage of a Government grant to restore the property. Buildings added since the nineteenth century were demolished, the stonework was cleaned and repaired, the courtyard re-laid with new grassed areas. A new electric drawbridge was built over the south gate, which can be raised for tall vehicles to pass through. The building was re-wired and plumbed and lavatories were installed.

2. The west gateway with cupola and weather vane. (PHOTOGRAPH: HUDDERSFIELD EXAMINER).

Accommodation Colonnade level—craft and antique shops with four of the original rooms left unaltered as a record of the Piece Hall's wool trading days. Rusticated level—East side: industrial textile museums; south side; art gallery

Court—open-air market operating twice weekly.

Date of completion 1977

Cost £300,000

3. *The three-storey east wing of the quadrangle.* (PHOTOGRAPH: KEITH GIBSON).
4. *Market stalls with two-storey west wing behind.* (PHOTOGRAPH: KEITH GIBSON).

CARNEGIE MANSION, NEW YORK

New use Museum

Architect Hardy Holzman Pfeiffer Associates

Client The Cooper Hewitt Museum, the Smithsonian Institution's national Museum of Design

Site The house was built in 1901, a year after the founding of the Carnegie Institute in Pittsburgh, by Andrew Carnegie, the steel magnate, for his own private use. The architects were Babb, Cook and Willard. The building was used for a time by Columbia University's School of Social Work, and was later donated by the Carnegie Corporation to house the very fine Cooper-Hewitt collection of decorative arts and design, which was threatened with public sale through shortage of cash. Instead, the Smithsonian Institute adopted the collection and a completely new museum was established.

Character The 64 interior rooms are arranged on an axial plan with each level of the building surrounding a large central hall, set slightly off-centre so that the south-facing rooms are larger than those facing north. On the upper floors the rooms were small and numerous. The most interesting features of the house are the devices used to heat, cool and control the humidity of the rooms—the utilities basement, looking like a steamship engine room is, in itself, a museum of turn-of-the-century technology. The interior décor is a stylistic jumble (much in fashion at the time of building). Finishes are of high quality, for example parquet flooring, oak ceilings carved by Scottish craftsmen and teak panelling by Indian joiners, wrought bronze grilles, quartered oak panelling, and stained glass by Tiffany.

Work done Financial restraints did not permit a total restoration of some of the elaborately crafted ingredients of the interior. Instead an 'interpretative restoration' (as the architects describe it) has been carried out. Cleaning and restoration has brought ornate ceilings back to life and, where this was not possible, surfaces are painted a neutral grey or beige. Recent fire partitions around the main staircase have been removed to reveal the original design. An ornate iron and glass entrance canopy to the main door, probably by Tiffany, has been restored. A hydraulic lift has been inserted into the main hall as unobtrusively as possible. The bed-rooms on the south side of the second floor have been eliminated and made into one, simply detailed long gallery where the structure of steel beams and concrete arches is exposed. Recessed lighting has been introduced, and is supplemented by period wall sconces which, although not original to the house, recreate the warmth which was once provided by a miscellany of floor lamps.

Accommodation Basement—maintenance, storage and meeting rooms.

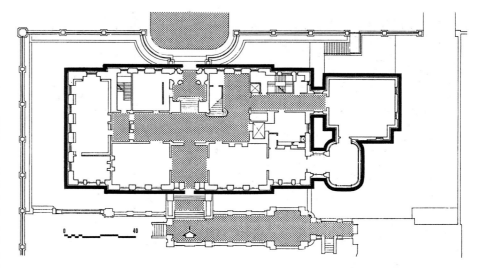

1. Ground floor plan.　　2. The garden front.

Ground floor—staff entrance, small gallery, lecture and class rooms, conservation labs, offices.
First Floor—public entrance, exhibition galleries, museum shop.
Second floor—exhibition galleries, administrative offices.
Third floor—library, registrar.
Fourth floor—departments of drawings and prints, and of textiles.

Date of completion October 1976

Cost $2,000,000

3. The central hall on the ground floor seen from the main street entrance. (PHOTO-GRAPH: NORMAN MCGRATH).

4. The Buckminster Fuller exhibition in the former Carnegie Library on the ground floor. (PHOTOGRAPH: NORMAN MCGRATH).

5. The Palladio exhibition in the same room.

40

POLICE STATION, BOSTON

New use Art gallery

Architect Graham Gund Associates Inc.

Client Institute of Contemporary Art

Site Fronting on to Boylston Street in the Back Bay quarter of Boston, the building is flanked by another, smaller building of the same type, which is still used as the headquarters of Ladder Co 15 of the Fire Department. The two face the vast modern Prudential Center on the other side of the street.

History The building was designed by the prominent Boston architect Arthur H. Vinal, and built in 1886 as 'Station 16'. Made redundant after the construction of new central facilities in 1973 it was left almost derelict until the Institute of Contemporary Art, which

3. Renovated façade to Boylston Street. (PHOTOGRAPH: STEVE ROSENTHAL).

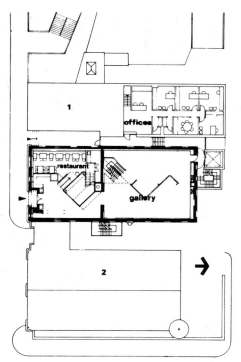

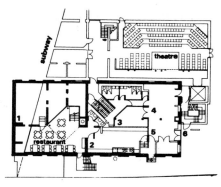

1. Ground floor plan.   *2. Basement plan.*
1. POLICE SUB-STATION   1. MECHANICAL
2. FIRE STATION   2. KITCHEN
                          3. STORAGE
                          4. SHOP
                          5. RECEIVING
                          6. LOADING

4. Looking down on to the two-level restaurant. On the left is the entrance from Boylston Street. (PHOTOGRAPH: STEVE ROSENTHAL).

had for some time been looking for a suitable building, took an 80-year lease on it from the city.

Character The two adjoining neo-Romanesque 'castles', are characteristic of nineteenth-century Boston and impressive examples of Richardsonian architecture. On the left side of the police station were stables, and the interior was a warren of guard rooms, prison cells, coal rooms and a drill hall. The ground floor had (and still has) a slope of 8in back to front and 4in side to side, the result of water table disruption during excavations for a subway tunnel below the Boylston Street façade.

Work done The exterior brickwork was cleaned, but otherwise unaltered. The interior was virtually gutted, some loads being transferred to two new steel columns, and an open, three-storey stairwell inserted in the middle of the entrance space, with the exhibition spaces and restaurant made accessible from its landings. The advantage of the open stairwell is that it makes the most of what is quite restricted space (the building's dimensions are 40 × 90ft) by opening up diagonal views in several directions. The old stables have been converted into a theatre and offices by another architect. The job won the American Institute of Architects' Honor Award in spring 1978.

Accommodation Main building—ground floor: shop, restaurant (lower part), kitchen, services and storerooms.
First floor—lobby, restaurant (upper part), gallery space.
Second floor—gallery space.
Third floor—offices and conference room.
Stable block—Ground floor: theatre.

First floor: theatre offices.

Date of completion The conversion was phased. An interim gallery in the stable was opened early in 1973. The restaurant was in use before the gallery which was opened to the public in May 1974. The theatre block was finished last, in 1976.

Cost $796,000 including conversion of police station and initial work on theatre.

BUSH WAREHOUSE, BRISTOL

New use Art gallery, theatre, restaurant and offices

Designers Building Partnership (Bristol) Limited

Job architect M. E. Duckering

Client Arnolfini Gallery Ltd. and J. T. Group Limited

Site The warehouse is situated on the waterfront in Bristol's dockland, which is close to the city centre. The area, once the scene of buzzing activity, is now, like so many of Britain's sea ports, silent and decaying. There are some new office buildings, but most of the warehouses stand empty and disused.

History The warehouse was built in the early 1830s to store tea. Later the building became a granary and then a bonded warehouse. In 1973 it was empty and its structure was deteriorating. The insurance company who owned it agreed to lease it to the J. T. Group who, together with the Arnolfini Gallery, converted it into a permanent home for both organisations.

Character This solid, five-storey warehouse is a fine example of early nineteenth-century industrial architecture in a stripped classical style. Its bold round arches and recesses, which take in three floors, anticipate H. H. Richardson's Romanesque revival in America. The exterior elevations are listed as being of special architectural interest. The walls are of stone, but the internal structure is of cast iron and timber with massive internal dividing walls of stone.

Work done The design brief required complete separation between the premises of the two users. Arnolfini took over the first and second floors as public spaces and offices, and the J. T. Group took the remaining four floors and converted them to offices. For this reason the building's interior layout was unsuitable for adaptation and had to be completely gutted. A new concrete structure supported on 50ft concrete piles was then erected within the perimeter walls. Work on the exterior has preserved the original appearance except for a new steel and grey glass sixth storey, partly concealed behind the parapet. Otherwise the stonework was cleaned and repaired, and new windows inserted. Inside, finishes were kept simple, to harmonise with the robust character of the building. In the galleries, concrete coffered slabs, cast in fibreglass moulds, were left exposed and painted. In the offices, the walls were cleaned and painted. The offices and the theatre are air-conditioned and conform to stringent standards in acoustics, lighting, public safety and security.

Accommodation Basement (below water level)—services.
Ground floor—entrance area, bookshop, exhibition gallery and associated workshop/store. Restaurant, bar and kitchen. Lavatories and cloakroom. Double-height performance area with retractable seating for 180–280, according to layout.

First floor—bar/foyer, exhibition gallery and associated store, three dressing rooms, darkroom, offices, projection and light/sound control room, lavatories and showers for staff and performers.

Date of completion Gallery—October 1975, offices—April 1976

Cost Approximately £1·1 million, including design costs; rate—£18 per sq ft.

1. Ground floor plan.

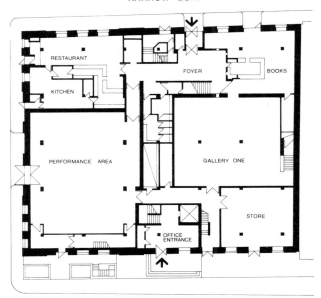

2. Section.

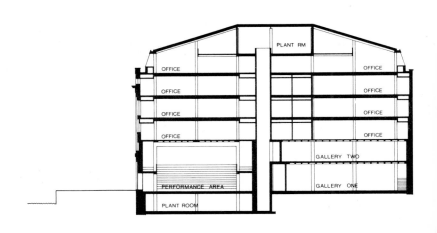

3. The Bush Warehouse after conversion, showing the new roof.

4. Gallery One on the ground floor.

5. The bookshop on the ground floor.

GAMUL HOUSE, CHESTER

New use Exhibition and lecture hall

Architect Donald W. Insall & Associates

Client The Council of the City of Chester

Site Gamul House occupies a prominent position in the street-scape of Bridge-gate, Chester's Conservation Action Area and a national exemplar during European Architectural Heritage Year in 1975. It has a stepped approach, which also serves Gamul Terrace beyond and backs on to Gamul Place, a terrace of small nineteenth-century cottages, also rescued during Heritage Year.

History Gamul House is said to have been built by Sir Francis Gamul, royalist mayor of Chester during the Civil War. Evidence suggests, however, that the hall may have been added to an existing building (possibly by infilling a court-yard), and that other parts of the town house, as Sir Francis knew it, have subsequently disappeared. The remaining first-floor hall and three-storey section adjacent have in the last 50 years served as an organ-builder's workshop, antique showroom warehouse, and brief-ly as an architect's studio, but they then fell into severe disrepair. It was pur-chased by the City of Chester, with the aid of the City's Conservation Fund, backed by contributions from the His-toric Buildings Council, who also gave financial assistance towards essential repairs. After use as an exhibition and lecture hall during Heritage Year, Gamul House has now been let to a private tenant.

Character The building is typical of Chester in being of many levels and dates. During its repair, original wattle and daub partitioning was uncovered, as well as the earlier mullioned windows, complete with their leaded diamond glazing. The present tall street windows were no doubt inserted in the mid-nineteenth century, when the building served for a while as a chapel. The handsome street door case concealed an earlier nail-studded door, now re-positioned in an inner doorway. An extremely handsome carved stone fire-place forms the focus of the interior, which has a tall plaster-vaulted ceiling with remarkable carved brackets. These may perhaps have been re-used, and set vertically rather than horizontally. The principle behind this restoration re-sembles an approach common in Italy where a building is first restored and a use is found afterwards.

Work done The essential repair of Gamul House included complete re-

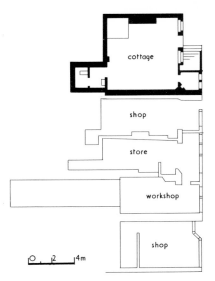

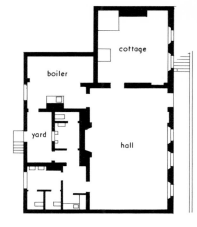

1. Ground floor plan.

2. First floor plan.

3. The street front after restoration with shops at pavement level. The windows left of the pedimented door light the hall.

4. The hall before and, 5, after restoration.

newal of the roof timbers, together with re-slating, and re-leading of roof fin-ishes, rebuilding of the front wall above the string course, and the com-plete refurbishing of the interior. A modern gallery and partition wall were removed, and the main hall was restored to its original fine proportions. The floor was re-finished in local clay tiles, sal-vaged from the cottages in Gamul Place. Two cottages at the back were converted to provide toilet and kitchen accom-modation. The three-storey 'Gamul Cot-tage' at the north end of the hall was also repaired. (This, together with the first floor of the rear cottages, was later converted into a flat by the new tenant.)

Date of completion 1975

Cost of works £51,879

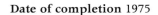

44

OLD SPEECH ROOM, HARROW SCHOOL, MIDDLESEX

New use Gallery for the school's collection of Greek and Roman antiquities and English watercolours. The room is also intended for concerts, reading and general studies.

Architect Alan Irvine, Buzas and Irvine

Client Harrow School

Site The Old Speech Room was originally designed by C. R. Cockerell in 1818 and formed part of a balancing wing he added to the first mid-seventeenth-century school building.

History In the school's quatercentenary year of 1971 the need was expressed for a place to house the school's treasures in a way which would both reflect their beauty and express the school's gratitude for the generosity of the benefactors who bestowed them. The plan was shelved due to the deleterious effects of inflation on the school's disposable funds, but revived again in 1973 when a new appeal was launched. Work began in 1975.

Character The room is of a regular cruciform shape about 70ft in length, 40ft in width and 20ft in height. Elegant plaster mouldings emphasise the form of the room. There are three windows, two large bays with leaded lights and one small window above ground level.

Work done The room's internal height enabled a mezzanine floor to be inserted covering the ends of the room and the central entrance area. The original ceiling was restored, the only change being the new recessed lighting. Four wall showcases and two island showcases were placed beneath the mezzanine. Lighting for these cases was concealed in the depth of the floor above. The lower walls were panelled in brown oak, and two built-in seats of the same material were placed in each of the bay windows. These replaced others which were there previously.

The floor is carpeted throughout, the carpet extending to cover a new dais built into the centre bay.

Accommodation Art gallery

Date of completion May 1976

Cost £52,000

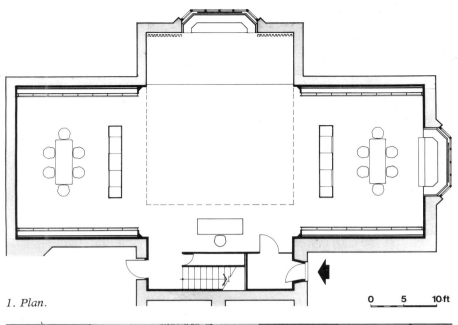

1. Plan.

2. The Old Speech Room before and, 3, after conversion into a museum and art gallery. (PHOTOGRAPHS: EDGAR HYMAN AND PETER CHORLEY).

45

SCHOOL HALL, SEVENOAKS, KENT

New use School library

Architect Keith Bennett

Client Sevenoaks School

Site The School is situated in its own grounds in Sevenoaks, a large prosperous town in Kent. The Hall occupies a central position, and is independent of the other school buildings.

History The library, originally 'Johnson Hall', was the gift of Charles Plumptre Johnson, a governor and benefactor of the school. It was opened in 1934 and for 30 years was used as an assembly hall. The library was housed in a room under the stage and was for the use of sixth formers only. In 1964 the gymnasium was taken over by classrooms and the hall had to double for this use. Changes in teaching methods, with their greater emphasis on library use and private study, led the school to plan a new library which would occupy the whole of Johnson Hall.

Character The one-storey building of double-height space is rectangular in plan, with an apse at one end which contains the stage. The walls are faced with Kentish ragstone and pierced with large, elegant, round-headed metal windows with leaded lights. There are artificial Portland stone cornices and dressings to windows and doors. The walls rise to a cornice and a parapet partially conceals the pitched, slated roof.

Work done The stonework, which saturated rapidly in wet weather, was repaired, cleaned and treated with a silicone water repellent. The worn copper flashing on the cornice was replaced by new leadwork which now continues completely over the parapet. The roof was repaired where necessary, and the slates were treated with a fungicidal spray, to remove a thin layer of growth. The windows were restored with clear glazing to the central panes and those around the stage were unblocked. The old gallery, a fairly recent addition, was replaced by a new one, supported on a structure of pre-cast concrete columns, steel beams and timber joists. This new gallery accommodates 80 study carrels cantilevered from the balustrade, and is open in the centre and around the edges to the floor below. The original stage remains as a general reading area and for exhibitions and displays. The room underneath, with its axial access stairway from the centre of the library, is now used for seminars and has blackout

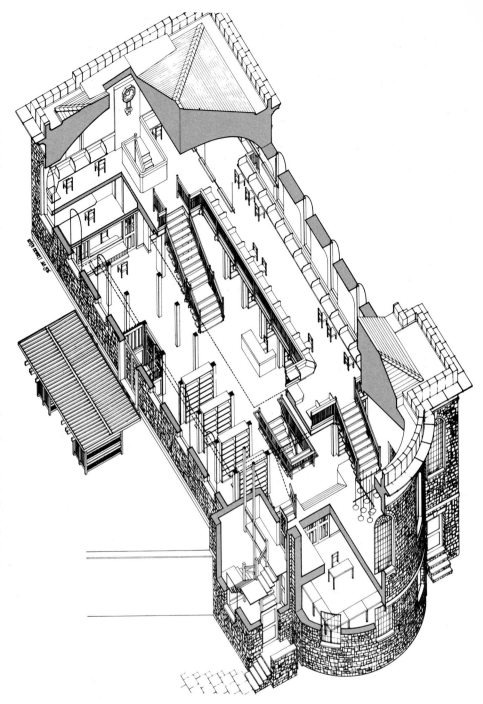

JOHNSON LIBRARY ■ BUILT AS AN ASSEMBLY HALL BY CHARLES PLUMPTRE JOHNSON IN 1934 CONVERTED TO THE SCHOOL LIBRARY IN 1975 THROUGH GENEROUS DONATIONS FROM — THE JOHNSON TRUST & NUMEROUS PARENTS, OLD SENNOCKIANS & OTHER FRIENDS OF THE SCHOOL

facilities so that films can be shown.

To make full use of the available interior space, a free-standing canopy has been built outside the entrance, providing coat-hooks and racks for cases which are not allowed into the building.

Accommodation Lower ground floor (under stage)—seminar room, boiler room, store.
Ground floor—reception, bookstacks, study room, general office, lavatories.

1. Cut-away axonometric drawing showing the three levels. The lettering, designed and carved by the architect, forms a commemorative inscription inside the building.

Intermediate stage level—reading and exhibition area, librarian's office.
Gallery—80 carrels for private study.

Date of completion 1976

46

2. The entrance façade. In converting the 1934 Johnson Hall to a library, one of the fire exits became the main entrance and a free-standing canopy was built in front. (PHOTOGRAPH: ROGER JONES).

3. View from the gallery level down to the main library concourse with, at the far end, the old stage. (PHOTOGRAPH: BILL TOOMEY).

4. The old stage, now a general reading area. (PHOTOGRAPH: BILL TOOMEY).

SOUTHERN ALLEGHENIES COLLEGE GYMNASIUM, PENNSYLVANIA

New use Art museum

Architect Roger C. Ferri (museum design architect; L. Robert Kimball (co-ordinating architects and engineers)

Client Board of Directors, Southern Alleghenies Museum of Art, Michael Struber, Director. (The new art museum is sponsored by a consortium of institutions and is intended to serve the community at large and to be a teaching resource for the art departments of the three member colleges.)

Site The building is situated on the grassy, tree-lined central mall of the campus belonging to St Francis College in rural Loretto, Pennsylvania.

History The gymnasium was built for the college in the 1920s. When it became redundant, it was decided to use the building for a much-needed art museum to house an expanding permanent collection of American art and to provide for temporary exhibitions, both locally organised and borrowed from major museums.

Character The building is of brick and steel, and consists of a single double-height space with a running track on a narrow gallery at first floor level. There is a basement and other ancillary spaces. Large windows above and below the upper level gallery admit plenty of light and give the interior an airy feel.

Work done The gallery on the upper level, with its limited viewing space, was used for the display of smaller works. At ground floor level the space underneath the gallery was filled in, creating a continuous vertical plane up to the parapet formed by the gallery balustrade. The south-facing windows were thus eliminated and the north wall became the only source of natural light. The windows on this side were re-fitted with special glass to filter out damaging ultra-violet rays and to modify the natural light intensity.

Sheets of plasterboard were suspended between the steel trusses overhead. They conceal the ceiling trusses and the mechanical ducts, but at each truss a gap was left to provide for air diffusers and light tracks.

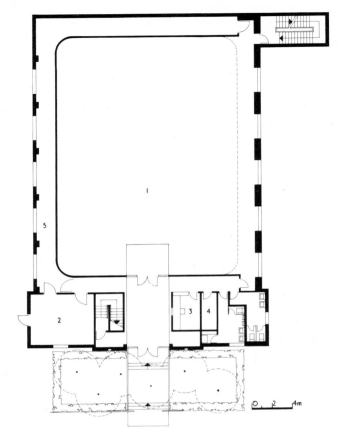

1. Ground floor plan.

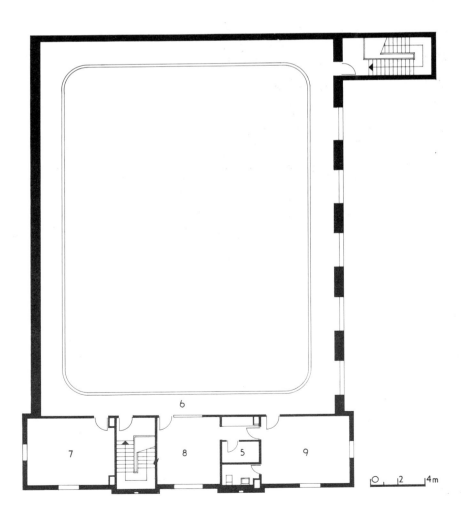

2. First floor plan.

1. EXHIBITION GALLERY	5. STORAGE
2. RECEIVING	6. BALCONY
3. RECEPTION	7. LIBRARY
4. CLOAKROOM	8. SECRETARY
	9. DIRECTOR

The museum was painted in six shades of reddish grey. Outside the architect deliberately made a three-stage transition from the campus mall to the interior of the museum, delineated abstractly by 'drawing' in space with floating black steel lines, a motif echoed in the gates, along the walls and inside the museum itself. The first of these is the garden, made of the surrounding trees and flower beds, which is treated as an outdoor room; the second is the entrance porch which has a 'night sky' vaulted ceiling painted dark blue with stars; the third is a small glassed-in anteroom with a 'morning sky' ceiling.

Accommodation Art museum; basement—art workshops.

Date of completion 1976

Cost $365,000

3. The entrance façade which is reached by passing through a symbolic gate and a formal garden of trees and flower beds. (PHOTOGRAPH: CERVIN ROBINSON).

5. *The art gallery with its first-floor balcony.* (PHOTOGRAPH: CERVIN ROBINSON).

4. *Looking back into the entrance porch with its vaulted ceiling simulating a night sky.* (PHOTOGRAPH: CERVIN ROBINSON).

3 Conversions to commercial use

Introduction

Most of the examples in this chapter are in the inner city and point, however tentatively, to the central urban revival that is so desperately needed. The most spectacular conversions, and those in which evidence of revival is most obvious, are the market halls in Boston and London. Both, of course, are examples of the 'gentrification' of commerce, of a change from the rough-and-tumble of a wholesale market to the genteel retail activities of booths, stalls and small shops. The Central Market Buildings in Covent Garden have just opened, and it is likely that they will have the same catalytic effect on their surroundings as the Faneuil Hall Market has already had on Boston's old harbour area.

The great majority of the examples are redundant buildings, mainly of industrial origin, converted to offices. Four out of the eight are admittedly architects' offices, a rather special breed, as can be seen in the most bizarre of all the examples—Ricardo Bofill's cement factory outside Barcelona. The conversion of Bruce Price's magnificent American Surety Building in New York into offices for the Bank of Tokyo is a case of rehabilitation rather than new use, the old and new use being of the same basic kind.

The tendency nowadays is to make use of what exists—to conserve an area's built fabric and to find uses for its redundant buildings rather than demolish and build new. There are a number of examples in this chapter which are of no architectural distinction whatsoever—the industrial buildings in Camden Town or the laundry in Santa Barbara, for example—and which would certainly have been demolished without a second thought a few years ago. We make no special plea for the preservation of such buildings except to point out that the justification lies in the result. Both buildings have been made to serve their new function with efficiency and imagination.

One other example deserves to be singled out. One of a chain of warehouses along the Nyhavn in Copenhagen has been converted into a delightful small hotel, the kind that many tourists and businessmen would much prefer. Except for the obvious reason that the smaller the hotel the smaller the profit, why has this admirable idea not been emulated elsewhere and why have the planning officers not encouraged it instead of allowing new mammoth hotels to destroy our environment?

LAUNDRY, SANTA BARBARA, CALIFORNIA

New use Restaurant

Designer Donald Hoppen & Associates

Client The Enterprise Fish Company

Site The building is located on the main street, two blocks from the beach, in a run-down area which is just beginning to be revitalised.

History One of the first laundries to be built in the area, the building was

1. BAR
2. RESTAURANT
3. BARBECUE KITCHEN
4. SERVICE KITCHEN
5. REFRIGERATOR
6. FREEZER
7. DRY STORE
8. FUTURE DRY STORE
9. OFFICE

2. Section.

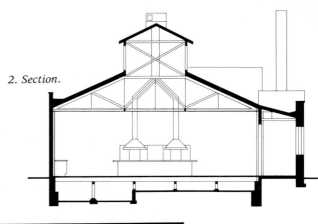

1. Plan.

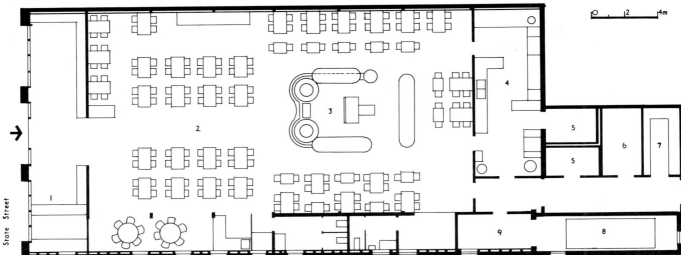

erected about 1905 and served the luxury hotels which existed at that time by the beach. Portions of the brick walls were damaged in the 1925 earthquake and early records show that repairs were carried out which involved re-laying the old bricks with new mortar. The old laundry was acquired by three businessmen who had spent some time looking for a suitable building to house a new restaurant specialising in barbecued fish, and which would include a large central exposed barbecue. The high roof and 'wheelhouse' were perfectly adapted to contain the large flues required and the clerestory provided illumination to the cooking area directly below.

Character The walls fronting on to State Street and the car park are of sand mould brick with structural arches. The rear walls are of concrete. The roof is supported by redwood trusses which span the 50ft width of the building. The clerestory wheelhouse is reminiscent of New England design. The small-paned windows in the clerestory and the double-hung windows are of old blown glass.

Work done The rear part of the building had deteriorated and some portions had to be demolished. The exterior stucco was removed, exposing the three brick arches. Interior brick walls were sandblasted. The vertical grain Douglas Fir floor was repaired, sanded and sealed. The earthquake building regulations required lateral reinforcements, so the brick north wall was bolted to heavy exposed wood posts along its entire length. The street wall of 2ft thick brick was bolted to a steel frame exposed on the interior. This frame serves as the major shear wall and steel tie rods are connected to it by a diagonal grid from truss to truss, forming a horizontal diaphragm.

The nature of a barbecued fish restaurant makes the cooking area the centre of attention. Situated in the middle of the restaurant, it is enclosed by low hand-made Mexican brick walls with glass screens. The giant hoods and flues match the angles of the truss frames and continue up through the centre of the wheelhouse roof.

The atmosphere evoked is of the type of building found near the fish pier. The high boiler was re-painted as a vertical sign.

Accommodation Dining area, central barbecue, main service kitchen, fish market area, refrigerated storage, office, lavatories.

Date of completion August, 1977

Cost $170,000; rate $28 per sq ft including reconstruction, kitchen equipment and furniture.

5. The roof trusses and clerestory wheelhouse. (PHOTOGRAPH: WAYNE MCCALL).

3. *View from State Street with main entrance.* (PHOTOGRAPH: WAYNE MC-CALL).

4. *The barbecue kitchen.*

LAUNDRY, KARLSRUHE-DAMMERSTOCK, GERMANY

New use Architects' offices

Architect Erich Rossman and Partner

Client Erich Rossman and Partner

Site A flat site in the Karlsruhe suburb of Dammerstock. The laundry stands on the Nürnbergerstrasse near a housing estate for whose inhabitants it was originally built.

2. Section.

1. Ground floor plan.
1. SECRETARY AND WAITING
2. INDIVIDUAL OFFICE
3. DRAWING OFFICE
4. INDIVIDUAL OFFICE
5. CONFERENCE ROOM

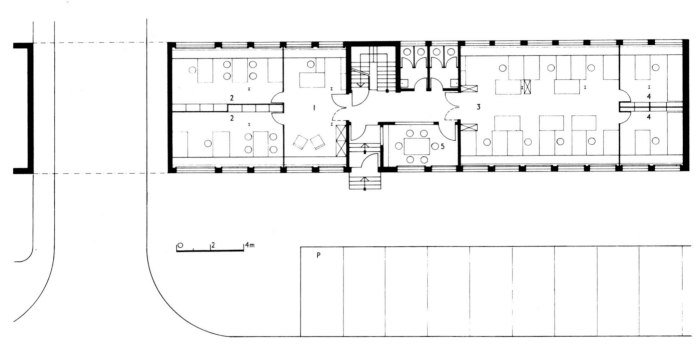

3. The entrance façade from the Nürnbergerstrasse.

54

History The laundry and restaurant, which form one building, were designed by Otto Haesler and built in 1928–9 to serve the community of the adjacent Dammerstock housing estate. After the Second World War the façade of the laundry was faced with tiles and the roof glazing replaced with an asbestos cement covering. As a result of the increasing availability of domestic washing machines, the laundry became redundant and in 1974 the architects acquired it to convert into offices for themselves.

Character The building is typical of the Modern Movement and the functional tradition. It is long and low, and has a continuous, smooth wall plane with metal windows in horizontal strips. This emphatic horizontality is contrasted with a vertical shaft over the through-way which divides the laundry from the restaurant. Inside there is an exposed light steel structure supporting a concrete floor and steel roof trusses.

On the ground floor the windows are very high because of the tall washing machinery that was originally fixed against the walls. The first floor which was a drying room with an inward-sloping, fully glazed roof, lost much of its light, airy character when the roof glazing was replaced by asbestos cement. The windows were divided into centrally-pivoted horizontal panes and were fitted with rough-cast, opaque glass.

Work done The tiles on the façade would not come off without breaking the hollow blocks of which the walls are built. So the tiled area was rendered smooth and painted to restore the plain surface of the original design. On the first floor the old roofing was replaced with a well-insulated sandwich structure which included acoustic tiles, insulation, timber boarding and a metallic roof finish. It incorporates a number of roof lights and sits on top of the steel roof trusses which were allowed to remain exposed by the fire officer provided they were treated with a fire-resisting paint.

To preserve the external appearance of the original design the architects sacrificed outlook. They restored the metal windows and renewed the opaque glass panes. On the first floor, because these windows were not weatherproof, they installed an inner skin of windows in aluminium frames and with clear double-glazing.

Floors were carpeted in a warm grey colour and ceilings were painted to match. The exposed steel structure was painted bright red. New services—

4. Drawing office on the first floor.

heating, ventilation and electricity—were installed.

Accommodation Ground floor—reception and waiting, individual offices, drawing office, conference room, lavatories.
First floor—individual offices, drawing offices, conference room.

Date of completion 1975

CENTRAL MARKET BUILDINGS, COVENT GARDEN

New use Shops, cafés, offices, etc.

Architect The Greater London Council Architects' Department

Client The Greater London Council

Site Covent Garden is situated in the heart of London's West End, roughly bordered by the Strand to the south, Charing Cross Road and Shaftesbury Avenue to the west, High Holborn and Kingsway respectively to the north and east. The area contains numerous restaurants, over fifty pubs and nineteen theatres, including the Royal Opera House which stands beside the Floral Hall. The central market building, the Flower Market, the Jubilee Market and the Royal Opera House, together with the Piazza which links them, are the natural centre of this quarter of London.

History The right to hold a market in the Piazza and to charge tolls was contained in a charter granted in 1670 by Charles II to William, Duke of Bedford. The present central market building, dating from 1830, replaced a large number of removable stands and sheds, and a row of more permanent shops along the south side of the Piazza. At the end of 1974 the whole of Covent Garden Market was removed to Nine Elms, a site away from London's centre. Within 24 hours the colour, humour, noise, congestion and débris of the market vanished and Covent Garden lay open to the ravages of the developer and the road engineer. The danger of turning Covent Garden into an office development area was finally averted with the publication in 1978 of the Covent Garden Action Area Plan, in which the G.L.C.'s Covent Garden Committee showed itself sensitive to the area's unique character and potential contribution to the life of central London. But the change of heart began some years earlier and owed much to the general swing in public opinion away from wholesale redevelopment and towards conservation. In 1973, largely as a result of local pressure, the G.L.C.'s controversial Strand relief road, which would have involved a great deal of destruction, was dropped from the Initial Development Plan for Greater London after a Public Inquiry. The Covent Garden area was designated a Comprehensive Development Area, but at the same time a large number of buildings throughout the C.D.A. were added to the statutory list. As a result, in 1974 the boundaries of the existing Conservation Area were extended, and a new Conservation Area, covering the Seven Dials area, was designated.

The activities in the area include publishing, trades linked to the theatre and catering. Many of these always had their home here, but some moved into space left empty after the departure of the market. Many restaurants and wine bars have started up in the last few years, especially around the Piazza area.

1. Ground floor plan.
1. NORTH COURT
2. SOUTH COURT
3. EAST COLONNADE WITH CONSERVATORIES OVER
4. EXTERIOR COLONNADE
5. CENTRAL PASSAGE
6. SMALL PIAZZA OPPOSITE ST PAUL'S CHURCH
7. NEW SUNK COURT GIVING ACCESS TO BASEMENT

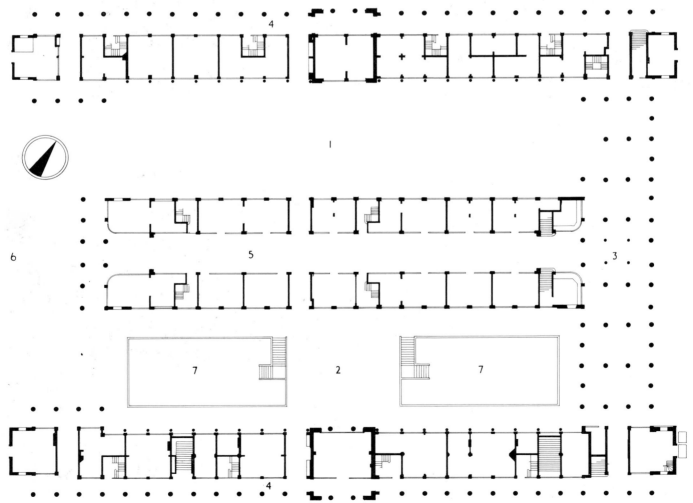

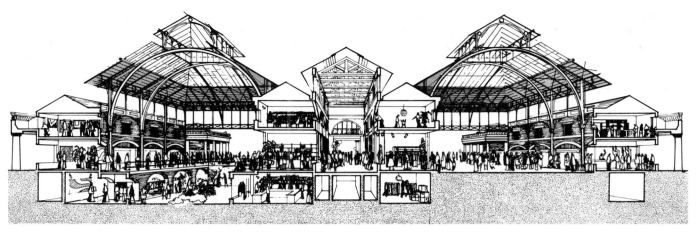

2. Perspectivised section.

3. An engraving of the Piazza and the Central Market Building in the nineteenth century. (PHOTOGRAPH: GREATER LONDON COUNCIL).
4. The west front of the Central Market Building faces St Paul's Church. Continuous paving creates a small pedestrian piazza. (PHOTOGRAPH: GREATER LONDON COUNCIL).

Character The central market building consists of three parallel ranges of buildings joined at the east end by a colonnade of the Tuscan Order. A contemporary account describes how it was arranged. 'Approaching from the east, the chief feature is the quadruple colonnade with the conservatories over. In the central building is a passage 16ft wide, open to the roof, and on each side a range of fruit shops, forced articles, and the more choice culinary vegetables and herbs. Each shop has a cellar under and a room over it, with a trap-door to the former and a small staircase to the latter. There are two exterior colonnades on the north and south sides which serve as

6. *The south court with the two sunken areas which give access to the basement.* (PHOTOGRAPH: GREATER LONDON COUNCIL).

passages in front of the shops. The shops on the north side are for different descriptions of culinary vegetables and the commoner fruits, and those on the south side are exclusively for potatoes and commoner roots. The half of one of the areas is covered with a roof in three parts, open at the sides for ventilation and light; the roof is supported by cast-iron pillars, from which spring circular ribs, instead of horizontal tie-beams; and the result is a very light appearance. Under it is held the wholesale fruit market, and below the surface are fruit cellars. The open space under the quadruple colonnade is occupied at one end as a fruit market, and at the other with stands for fruits and vegetables.'

The principal features of the terrace over the east colonnade were the two conservatories. These occupied about a third of the area of the terrace, the remaining part serving 'as a promenade, and for the display of hardy plants in pots and vases, and other garden ornaments'. In the centre of the terrace was a fountain. The present cast-iron roofs over the courtyards were added in two stages: the roof covering the south court was constructed first during the general improvements of 1875; the roof over the north court was added in 1888 when the

5. *The model seen from the east with the Tuscan colonnade and conservatories over. St Paul's Church stands on the axis and west of the building.* (PHOTOGRAPH: GREATER LONDON COUNCIL).

7. *The central passage before restoration* (PHOTOGRAPH: GREATER LONDON COUNCIL).

8. *The Flower Market immediately east of the Central Market Building which is to be used as the London Transport Museum.* (PHOTOGRAPH: GREATER LONDON COUNCIL).

original roof was dismantled. Both roofs were built by William Cubitt & Co., to the design of William Rogers, who worked in Cubitt's office.

Work done The new use has not involved any major alterations to the building. Its function remains commercial, although selling different kinds of goods from the fruit and vegetables of previous years. Fire regulations had the greatest effect on the conversion. The ends and clerestoreys of the two halls, for example, had to remain open, and their use restricted to activities which do not present fire hazards. The basement, which extends under almost all the building, is a labyrinth of small, brick-vaulted spaces, and its use has been limited. In the south hall it has been opened up to form two lower courtyards, readily accessible from ground level by new concrete staircases. Elsewhere the ground floor and basement of each unit has been linked by a stair replacing the ladder down from the old trap-door, and as a result, some basement space has been lost. The first stage

of the work, carried out in 1975 as part of the G.L.C.'s contribution to European Architectural Heritage Year, was to clear away a number of nineteenth-century additions, together with festoons of electricity cables, gas pipes and other services, and to begin the restoration by examining the structure of the building. The second stage, completed in 1976, was to restore the two main roofs. These proved to be in surprisingly good condition, requiring little in the way of structural repairs. The work consisted mainly of re-glazing and re-decorating, with a certain amount of repair work to slating, and changes in the method of rainwater disposal, which used the columns as rainwater pipes. The original colour scheme of light buff and pale blue was restored. The final stage of the work comprises the restoration of the basement and the three two-storey ranges, and their adaptation as shops and offices. New staircases serve the individual suites of offices on the first floors. Although the fitting out of the shop interiors is left to individual tenants, the restoration of the shop fronts to the original designs remains the responsibility of the Council as does the provision of 'means of escape in case of fire'. The terrace over the eastern colonnades is also being restored, together with the fine paving both inside and outside the building. The Piazza has been closed almost entirely to traffic and the old road paved with granite setts.

Accommodation Out of a total of 35 units, six will be allocated to wine bars, restaurants etc, and the remaining 29 to traders offering a controlled mix and broadly covering artistic and leisure interests, such as arts and crafts, jewellery, fashion, books and specialist foods.

Date of completion June, 1980

Cost £2 million (anticipated)

59

FANEUIL HALL MARKET, BOSTON

New use Market, restaurant, shops and offices.

Architect Stahl/Bennett Inc. (historical work); Benjamin Thompson & Associates, Inc. (Project Architects)

Client The Rouse Company

Site Faneuil Hall and its three market annexes stand at the exact centre of Boston's urban core, on the edge of the harbour. The area, called Dock Square, was the natural place for a market, as it was where ships loaded and unloaded goods. Since then, however, land reclamation has moved the waterfront several blocks away.

History The buildings were designed by Alexander Parris in 1824 as a result of Mayor Josiah Quincy's decision to expand the market which was at that time only a meat market housed in Faneuil Hall. (The hall's upstairs meeting room is famous for being the place where plots were hatched by rebels during the War of Independence.) The buildings were used as a market until 1959, when a new centre was built outside the inner city.

In 1968, a report on the buildings by a group of historians, followed by another for the Boston Redevelopment Authority under the direction of Frederick A. Stahl, among others, persuaded the National Park Service through the Massachusetts Historical Commission to make a grant of $2 million to the City of Boston towards the cost of restoration to a commercial use, which would preserve the character of the area. Stahl's architectural firm was then hired by the B.R.A. to undertake the exterior restoration of the buildings. This done, the B.R.A. invited tenders from developers. In May 1972, Benjamin Thompson, who from the beginning was aware of the possibilities the buildings held, persuaded The Rouse Company to collaborate with him on a development plan. Arrangements were made with the City, their offer was accepted, and work began in 1975.

Character The three buildings are almost identical on plan, being just over 530ft in length and about 52ft wide. The two buildings fronting on to North and South Market Streets are typical five-storey brick and granite warehouses in the functional tradition. Rows of unusually large arched window openings punctuate the façades, and dormers pierce the pitched roofs. The central hall, known as the Quincy Market, is of a more elaborate design. At each end is a

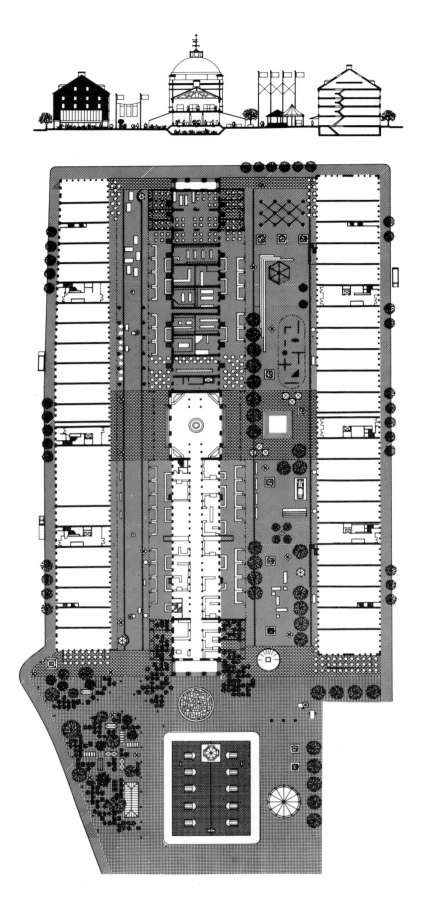

1. *Plan, section and elevations showing conversion to mixed commercial uses.* (DRAWING: CARLOS DINIZ).

2. *Faneuil Hall Markets as seen from Boston Harbour in 1827.* (PHOTOGRAPH: COURTESY OF THE BOSTONIAN SOCIETY).

3. *Aerial view looking towards harbour.* (DRAWING: CARLOS DINIZ).

pedimented portico, and a copper dome bisects the roof line. Inside, a white colonnade runs the full length of the building. The window openings, as large as in the other two buildings, are arched on the basement and ground floors and rectangular on the second floor, except at the high 'rotunda'. In the old days canvas awnings once shaded the displays which spilled out from under the arches on to the pavements. The Stahl report revealed that certain technological innovations were employed in the building's construction, such as the use of cast-iron columns, iron tension rods, laminated wood ribs for the copper-covered dome and the first large-scale use of granite and glass in an unusual post and beam technique.

Work done First, extensive restoration work was undertaken on the Quincy Building, and later on the two flanking buildings. In the Quincy building a false ceiling under the dome was removed, (revealing it to view for the first time for many years) and an eliptical hole was cut in the original floor to create a gallery at first floor level. 'Canopies,' a glass version of the awnings of the past, are now attached to the sides of the building and extend over part of North and South Market Streets, now closed to traffic. Glass garage-style doors can be raised or lowered as required, yellow shades can be drawn across the glass ceilings, and heating has been provided. In order to facilitate a free exchange between the central aisle and the canopies, glass has been removed from the window openings at the first floor level. Air-conditioning on the street floor relies entirely on the breezes blowing in from the ocean and passing through the building.

The tenants are carefully selected food vendors. There is a conspicuous absence of the poster and candle sellers found in other similar markets. Vendors' displays and signs are controlled, but don't call for uniformity. To preserve the perspective of the colonnade, displays must not extend into the central aisle; only the signs are allowed to do so. For those who do not want the complication and expense of renting a stall, there are a number of specially-designed hand-carts which can be parked under the canopies.

In the North and South Markets wares for sale are more upmarket—antiques, expensive clothes, etc, and are divided into 'zones', grouping the different kinds of shops. Commercial activities are confined to the cellar, ground, and first floors; the upper ones are leased as office space.

4. The central building, known as the Quincy Market with South Market Street now closed to vehicular traffic. (PHOTO-GRAPH: FRANCO ROMAGNOLI).

5. The central colonnade in the Quincy Market. (PHOTOGRAPH: FRANCO RO-MAGNOLI).

North and South Market Streets have been provided with benches and planted with trees. Proposals include the closing of another street, and the inclusion of other buildings to spread the revitalising influence of this restoration.

Accommodation Quincy building—food market for retail food, cafés; restaurants in gallery at first floor level; restaurants and Banquet Hall on second floor.

North and South Markets—cellar; first and second floor; shops, third and fourth floors; offices.

Date of completion Quincy building—August, 1976
South Market building—August, 1978
North Market building—August, 1979

Cost $16 million construction cost, including site and exterior improvements.

CEMENT FACTORY, BARCELONA

New use Architects' offices

Architect Taller de Arquitectura of Ricardo Bofill

Client Taller de Arquitectura of Ricardo Bofill

Site The cement factory lies on the main road from Barcelona to Madrid near the village of San Justo just outside Barcelona.

History In the early 1970s the team of young architects who made up the *taller* took over a 20-acre site on the outskirts of Barcelona with a view to creating a new community—to include Walden 7, the block of flats nearby, also designed by the *taller*. The first project for the cement factory was for a community centre, to include a place to design and make clothes, a vegetarian restaurant, a students' hostel, two or three small concert halls, and a trip up a lift to the top of the chimney. But lack of resources made this idea impractical, and the *taller* decided to use part of the complex as their office, swathing the rest in a blanket of vegetation, with a view to further conversion, as circumstances permitted, to cultural, commercial or civic use.

Character The complex is an extraordinary group of gigantic cylindrical silos and a chimney built in 1921 of in-situ concrete, the first of its kind in Europe, rising magnificently to 100ft. As Peter Hodgkinson, a member of the *taller*, says, 'The very function of their architecture, mixed with the excess of "brutalist" concrete produced images of all the world's temples'.

Work done First, all the scrap iron was removed by gypsy scrap metal dealers, a task which took six months. After having detailed measured drawings made of the buildings, the unwanted sections were demolished. Here again Peter Hodgkinson's description is worth quoting: '. . . our demolishers, experts in all tricks with explosives, prepared us cocktails of explosion waves. At times gigantic buildings fell like an ox at the slaughter house, or through some failure in the chain of dynamite, only one charge blew and a tile, dislodging itself from a far-off roof, would fall with a tinkle into the factory yard . . . This activity also played havoc with our nerves as we were warned before each explosion by a very small dark-skinned man who used to rush through our drawing offices waving a piece of red plastic tied to a stick shouting, '*!Pronto, pronto, Que no salga nadie!*' (Hold it! Hold it! Nobody leave!) leaving the entire team in a suspended state of shock awaiting the violent bang. As his timing was, to put it mildly, erratic, we could be seen, fingers blocking ear holes, pencils hastily discarded and faces white for periods of fifteen to twenty minutes awaiting the blast of release'.

Once demolition was complete, the underlying soil was exposed, prepared earth was brought in and planted with a creeping, purple-flowered plant and trees—mainly cypresses, but also four very old olive trees, imported from the Pyrenean foothills, were planted in strategically placed groups. The planted earth was provided with a dense network of black plastic irrigation tube, attached to frequent watergun turrets. The roof tops of the silos and accompanying buildings were made into small intimate gardens; and a walkway of cypresses were created across the top of the eight silos.

The area to be converted was limited to a group of six and four silos, and a vast rectangular building divided into many levels, including two enormous spaces and a great court surrounded by façades without windows, which abutted another group of eight silos. The silos which were to form the office accommodation presented problems which were ingeniously solved. Drains were passed along old tunnels and pipes were sent up elevator shafts. Floor beams were suspended from grouts chiselled out of the insides of the walls. Interior walls were cut away to join the silos by breaking through the curved walls and bridging the space between one round element and another. Windows were drawn with chalk on the outside, and men working with pneumatic drills suspended from ropes, would chisel through the concrete, exposing the reinforcement bars which were then cut through with blow lamps. After that the entire piece could be pushed out leaving a perfect opening.

Final touches were made with a sense of fantasy typical of the *taller*. The door is Palladian, the windows ogival and the semi-circular parking area is a classical ruin, complete with broken creeper-covered columns. These details have the virtue of softening the hard forms of the concrete, and of changing the character of the cement works to such an extent that it is now dubbed *el convento* by the local inhabitants. One of the happiest days of the *taller* was when an old nun came to the studio door and asked the time of the next mass.

Accommodation Architectural offices

Date of completion 1977

1. General view of the cement works. Only the large rectangular block and a group of six and four silos on the right have been converted.

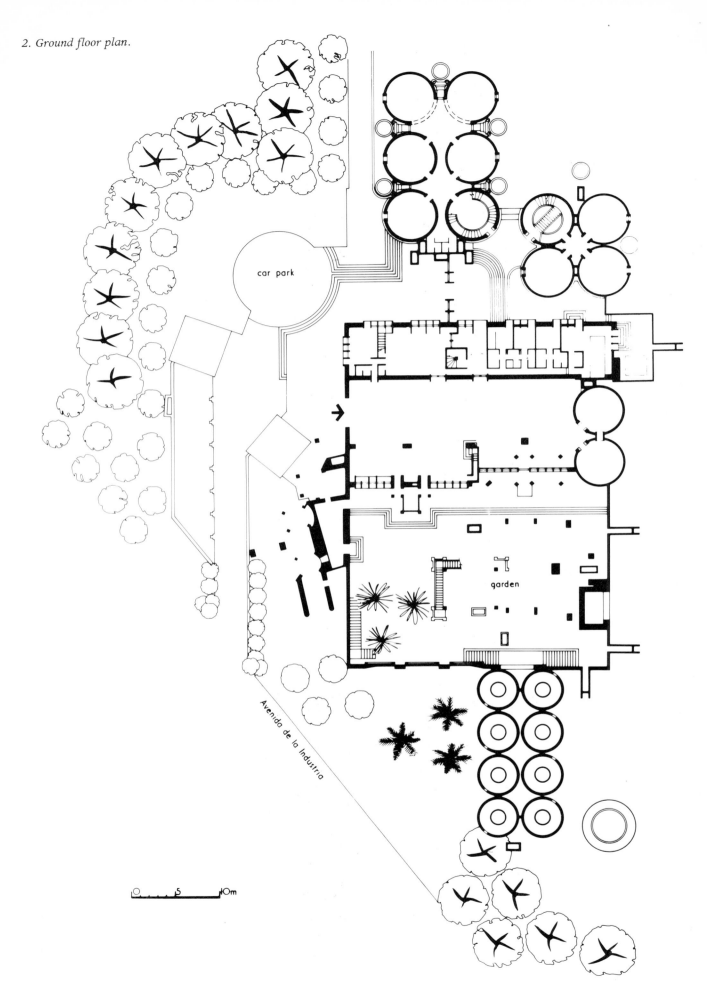

2. Ground floor plan.

car park

Avenida de la Industria

garden

0 ... 5 _____ 10m

3. A pair of silos connected to offices.

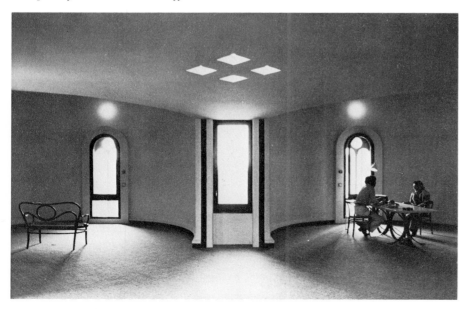

4. A pair of silos open up to form a larger space.

WAREHOUSE, TORONTO

New use Offices and restaurant

Architect A. J. Diamond & Barton Myers

Client A. J. Diamond & Barton Myers (A. J. Diamond, partner in charge)

Site The building stands on the corner of King Street and John Street just north of the CN Tower in downtown Toronto, quite near the expensive new office developments of the financial district.

History 322 King Street West was one of the many substantial industrial buildings built for manufacturing and warehousing in the decade after the fire of 1904. Rising land values have pushed these activities further out of town, and the architects acquired the building in 1971 with a view to converting it into offices, using one floor for themselves and letting the rest.

Character A handsome structure of brick and timber, the building has five storeys. The main door is flanked by columns and surmounted by a rounded pediment. The name of the building's first owners, 'The Eclipse Whitewear Company' is still inscribed on the entablature which crowns the first floor. Above this, and on the other three façades, are large, regularly-spaced window openings which originally held windows with small, wooden panes.

Inside, the timber structure is exposed—the ceilings of cedar, the columns of pine and the floors of maple.

Work done The interiors were sandblasted and the wood and brick surfaces left natural. The old panes were replaced by fixed plate glass in concealed wooden frames. Hot-water convectors with steel cover plates replaced the old steam pipes. The building was re-wired, with an exposed metal conduit pipe on the ceiling to serve the light fixtures. A new air-conditioning system was installed. The building is served by two existing lifts, one for freight and the other for passengers.

A kitchen was installed to serve the restaurant on the ground floor.

Accommodation Basement—offices.
Ground floor—restaurant, lounge, kitchen, lavatories.
First, second and third floors—offices.
Fourth floor—outdoor courtyard and offices.

Date of completion 1973

Cost Approx. $500,000

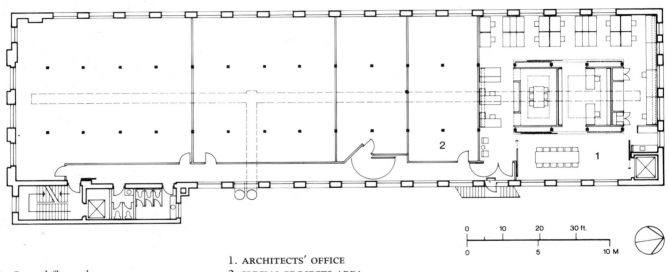

1. ARCHITECTS' OFFICE
2. SPECIAL PROJECTS AREA

1. Second floor plan.

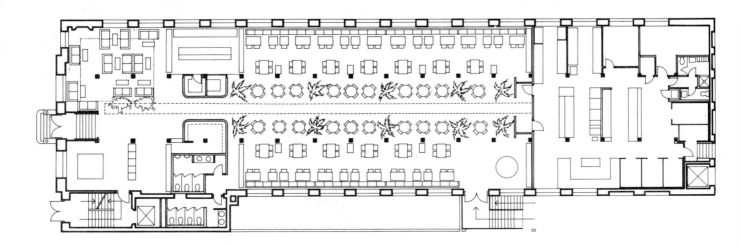

2. Plan of ground floor restaurant.

3. *The entrance façade on King Street.*
(PHOTOGRAPH : IAN SAMSON).

4. *The restaurant on the ground floor.*
(PHOTOGRAPH : IAN SAMSON).

5. *The architects' office on the second floor.*
(PHOTOGRAPH : IAN SAMSON).

WAREHOUSE, COPENHAGEN

New use Hotel

Architects Flemming Hertz & Ole Ramsgaard Thomsen

Client A. Arp Hansen

Site The building occupies a prominent corner position on the north side of the Nyhavn at the end of a row of mainly residential buildings.

History The building was erected as a warehouse in 1805.

Character The construction is of brick with exposed timber joists, posts and beams. It has seven storeys, two of which are in the roof. A fine example of its kind, the warehouse is now 'listed' as a Grade 2 building. A spine wall on each floor divides the space longitudinally. Small openings, each with its own shutter, pierce the façades at regular intervals. At the front on each floor there are two loading openings, rising up to a pair of gables with projecting supports for lifting tackle. The tiled roof is steeply pitched.

Work done No changes were made to the existing structure, only fireproofing and insulation of the floors, and replastering of the ceilings. The exposed timber was sandblasted. The original window openings were preserved, but the old windows were replaced by new, the small windows being set flush with the façade. In the large openings french windows were inserted, recessed to form a balcony with a metal railing.

The spine wall is used to advantage to divide the spaces, but additional partitions were formed in timber stud and covered with plasterboard. All new

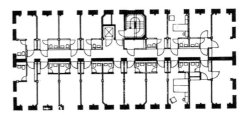

1. Plan at lower ground floor level with reception and restaurant.

2. Plan of typical bedroom floor.

3. View from the harbour with the converted warehouse on the right.

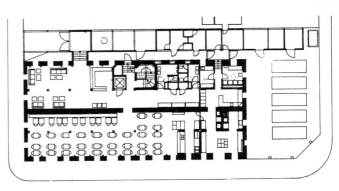

elements are unashamedly contemporary, so that the old structure maintains its integrity. Fortunately the flat ceilings made for easy subdivision.

Accommodation Lower ground floor—reception/waiting area, restaurant, kitchen, stores, lavatories.
Six upper floors—80 bedrooms providing 140 beds.

Date of completion 1971

Cost 5·5 million Danish Kroner.

4. The restaurant on the lower ground floor.
5. A typical bedroom.

ST. PAUL'S HOUSE, LEEDS

New use Offices

Architect Booth, Shaw and Partners

Client English Property Corporation Limited

Site An urban site in the industrial city of Leeds in Yorkshire. The north elevation of the building takes up part of the south side of Park Square, which is surrounded on its other three sides by Georgian terraced houses. The square is the only one of its kind left in Leeds town centre and is itself a Conservation Area. Its centre is planted, and a pedestrianised walkway now runs by the side of St. Paul's House, making an attractive environment for the office workers who now inhabit the building.

History The building was designed in 1878 as a clothing factory and warehouse by the Bradford architect, Thomas Ambler. He was commissioned by John Barron, the rag trade magnate. It is listed under the Town and Country Planning Acts as being of special architectural merit. Over the years it suffered badly from neglect and became so dangerous that its minarets and parapet had to be taken down and stored until a decision on its future could be taken. In 1971 the English Property Corporation bought the freehold with a view to turning it into office space and maintaining and restoring the exterior.

Character The building is arguably the most distinguished example in the country of the use of the Moorish style in commercial architecture. According to Pevsner it is 'emphatically Moorish, at least round the top. Ground floor and mezzanine windows tied together by a giant segment-headed arch, first- and second-floor windows tied together by a trabeated frame. Then a small third floor with Moorish arches and a truly Mohammedan cresting with four corner minarets' [actually five].*

The original structure was of brick and cast iron and the decorative details were executed in Doulton's terra cotta, tiles and brick. A superb pair of wrought iron gates adorned the main entrance.

Work done The interior was completely gutted and a new reinforced concrete structure inserted, linked to

*Buildings of England: Yorkshire—West Riding, 2nd edition revised by Enid Radcliffe, Penguin Books, Harmondsworth, 1967

3. The new entrance in Park Square with its bronze-faced canopy.

1. Plan of typical open office floor.   2. View across Park Square.

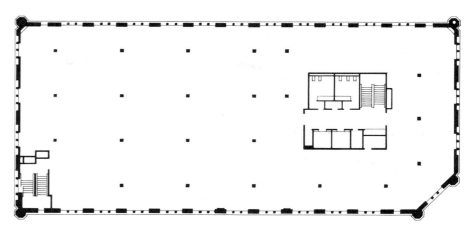

69

4. *Detail of original entrance.*
5. *Second floor window.*

the shell by limited-movement metal cleats. A new penthouse floor was built as a glazed mansard, partially hidden behind the parapet. The main entrance was moved from the south-east corner of the building to the north side, opening on to Park Square. The new doors are of armour-plated glass and sheltered by a bronze-faced canopy. The wrought iron gates were transferred from the old entrance. All existing windows were replaced by aluminium windows with an acrylic bronze finish. The old light-well to the basement has been filled in and a gradual ramp to sill level formed and covered with brick paviours to match the original brick. The parapet and minarets have been refashioned for cost reasons in fibreglass, which is indistinguishable from the original. The whole façade has been cleaned to reveal its original salmon pink, and some details have been picked out in gold and crimson.

The building now provides 68,500 sq ft of office space.

Accommodation Basement—services, offices, lavatories.

Ground floor—reception area, offices, lavatories.

First to fifth floors—offices, lavatories.

Date of completion 1976

Cost Approximately £1·5 million

INDUSTRIAL BUILDING, CAMDEN TOWN

New use Architects' offices

Architect Richard Sheppard Robson & Partners

Client Richard Sheppard Robson & Partners

Site Camden Town in north-west London is a lively area and one which probably contains one of the highest concentrations of architects in the country. The building stands on back-land, surrounded by a triangular city block containing a rich mix of uses—housing, shops, offices and light industry. The approach to the building is through a gap in a row of modest terrace houses and shops in Parkway.

History The building was originally a warehouse and later housed a plating works. During the century of its existence it had gradually been surrounded by single-storey shacks, covered in filth and random plumbing runs. It came on the market in 1972 and was bought by the architectural partnership, whose Bloomsbury offices were becoming too expensive.

Character It is an undistinguished nineteenth-century industrial building of a sort often found in London. It has three storeys and is built in the form of a triangle with an opening in the north end and a courtyard in the centre.

Work done The surrounding sheds were pulled down, revealing the warehouse's hollow triangular form. The stock brickwork of the walls, which were quite sound, was sandblasted inside and out, and the same treatment was applied to the timber roof trusses. The old metal windows, some of which had corroded beyond repair, were replaced by centre-pivoted softwood windows. A linking bridge was built between the two separated wings of the building at the north corner. A new glazed entrance was formed, clad, like the windows of the bridge, in lead. The interior spaces have been painted white and carpeted in a buff haircord. Lighting is by spotlights fixed to aluminium track. Timber is pine left natural. The courtyard was finished with hard paving bricks and the spaces left by the demolition of the sheds were planted.

Accommodation Ground floor— reception and administration offices, conference rooms, telephone room, print room, library and archive storage, lavatories.

First and second floors—two flats, both occupied by partners, three drawing offices, tea/coffee area.

Date of completion 1974

Cost £220,000

1. Ground floor plan.

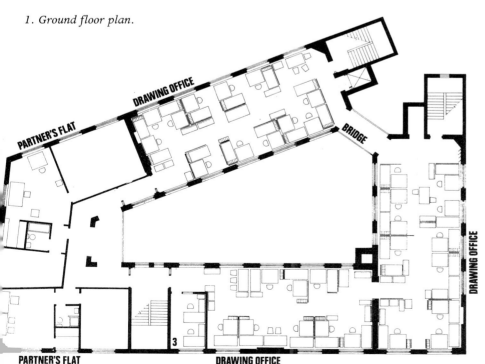

1. RECEPTION
2. WAITING
3. SECRETARY
4. ACCOUNTS
5. POST ROOM
6. PRINT ROOM
7. MAINTENANCE
8. PLANT
9. GAS METER
10. DEAD STORAGE
11. TELEPHONE SWITCHBOARD
12. KITCHEN

2. First floor plan.

3. *The bridge before and, 4, after conversion.* (PHOTOGRAPH: BRECHT-EINZIG).

5. *The entrance in the courtyard.* (PHOTO-
GRAPH: BRECHT-EINZIG).

6. *A drawing office on the first floor.*
(PHOTOGRAPH: BRECHT-EINZIG).

STUDENTS' UNION,
COPENHAGEN

New use Showrooms and offices

Architect Jørgen Raaschou-Nielsen

Client Paul Cadovius

Site An urban site in the centre of Copenhagen on Hans Christian Andersen Boulevard and overlooking the Town Hall Square.

History The house was built as a students' union in 1910 and designed by Ulrik Plesner, one of the best-known architects of the national romantic movement. It was used by the students until 1972 when Paul Cadovius, a furniture manufacturer, bought it on impulse as a head office for his firm, Cado.

Character The house is built of red, hand-made bricks, with decorations of limestone. The foundations are mostly of granite. The main entrance has a triple-arched portico, the windows vary from very large to small, and the whole house gives an impression of romantic irregularity. From one side the building appears to have three main floors and an attic, but in fact it is built on a slope, and has two further floors below street level on the other side. There are also changes of level within the building, making in all eleven different levels. The rooms are of varying sizes, but the lecture hall is very large, with panelled walls and an elaborately stuccoed ceiling. The steeply pitched roof is tiled and has decorated gable ends above a cornice.

Work done The heavily polluted façade was cleaned by an especially gentle process, involving a chemical paste, and the limestone decorations were simply brushed clean. Finally a treatment to prevent further damage from pollution was applied.

The impressive main staircase was in such bad repair that it could not be saved. It was replaced by a staircase of steel construction with several landings which could also be used for accommodating displays. The loft was cleared of the accumulated junk of over half a century, and the old partitions were removed and new ones inserted, providing an exhibition space and a canteen. In the former lecture hall a three-level steel structure was erected which takes advantage of the height of the room by providing a large amount of display space. The levels are linked by a spiral staircase similar in proportion to the old one which led up to the gallery.

The old decrepit windows were replaced with new windows incorporating

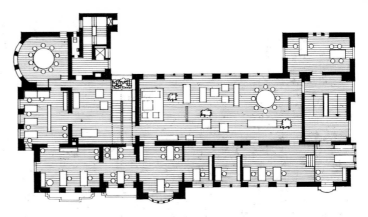

1. Plan of one of the office levels.

2. View from Town Hall Square circa 1910 when the building had just been completed.

large panes. The building was re-wired
and the plumbing renewed. The stucco
was repaired and the oak wall panelling
painted white to provide a neutral
background for the furniture on display.
The paint is of a special kind which can
easily be removed if future generations
should want to strip the panelling. The
building was carpeted throughout and
furnished with Cado furniture, some of
it designed and made in limited quan-
tities especially for the building.

Accommodation   Basement—show-
room and offices
Ground floor—reception area and of-
fices.
First floor—offices.
Second floor—showroom and offices.
Third floor—showroom and offices.
Fourth floor—canteen and offices.

Date of completion May 1974

Cost Approximately 20 million kroner.

*3. The former lecture hall converted to
exhibition space by the insection of two
intermediate levels.* (PHOTOGRAPH: FINN
CHRISTOFFERSEN).

*4. The loft with its partitions removed to
provide additional office space. Part of it
is used as a canteen.* (PHOTOGRAPH: FINN
CHRISTOFFERSEN).

AMERICAN SURETY BUILDING, NEW YORK

New use Offices for the Bank of Tokyo

Architect Kajima International Inc. and Fred Safran (architect to the owner).

Client The Bank of Tokyo and Sylvan Lawrence Company Inc. (owner).

Site No better address than this—100 Broadway—could be found in New York. The building stands just above Wall Street, facing Trinity Church and its historic churchyard.

History The building is an outstandingly fine early skyscraper designed by Bruce Price, and completed in 1896 as the American Surety Building. The Bank of Tokyo has occupied offices in the building as a tenant since 1952, first as an agency of the parent bank in Japan, and later as the Bank of Tokyo Trust Company chartered in New York.

During the building boom of the 1960s there was a plan to erect a new building further along Broadway. But when the lease at 100 Broadway came up for renewal in 1973, the bank decided on a new long-term lease based on renovation, with costs to be shared by owner and tenant. The owner improved all basic services and the bank embarked on the restoration of the exterior and on an almost total remodelling of the interior.

Character Price called his Beaux Arts design a 'rusticated pillar' and it is a design typical of its time. The steel-framed building was treated as a classical column on a vastly enlarged scale, its height divided into the equivalent of base, shaft and capital. The richly ornamented, white marble façade starts at ground level with a 'base' of giant Ionic columns rising through two storeys, their backs originally flush with the front wall. Caryatids stand between the windows of the second floor, supporting the 'shaft' of twelve rusticated storeys. The 'capital' consists of the last seven storeys which are decorated with pediments, more caryatids and cornices that become increasingly ornate at the top. Inside, the upper floors were unremarkable in contrast to the ground floor with its gilded coffered ceiling and 32ft high marble Corinthian columns.

Work done In order to minimise the disturbance to the users of the building and to the neighbourhood the work was completed in as short a time as possible and phased, so that the tenants never left the building while the work was in progress. The conversion involved thir-

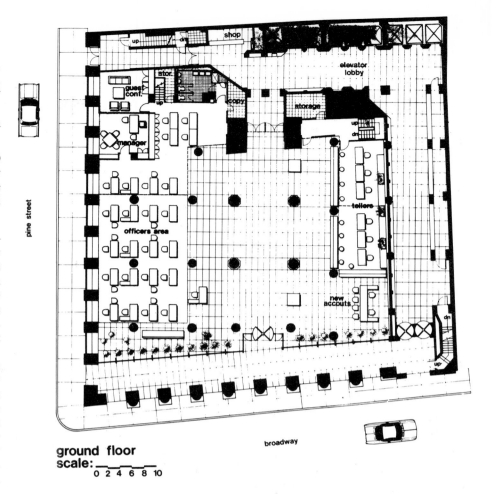

1. Ground floor plan.
2. Mezzanine floor plan.

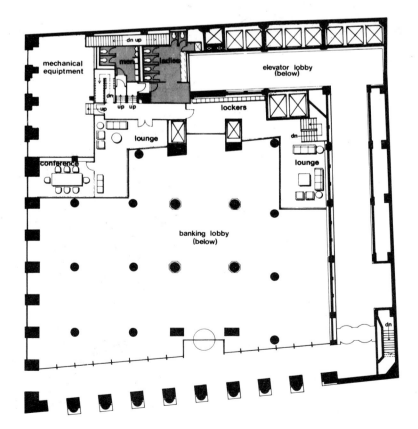

3. The white marble façade on Broadway. (PHOTOGRAPH: EZRA STOLLER).
4. Behind the façade there is a new ground-floor arcade. Through its glass screen can be glimpsed the original decorated ceiling of the great banking hall. (PHOTOGRAPH: EZRA STOLLER).

5. The original central bay of the banking hall has been surrounded by new construction—a mezzanine with facilities for small conferences and a first floor of offices. (PHOTOGRAPH: EZRA STOLLER).
6. The lift lobby on the ground floor is a white marble 'funnel' in sharp contrast to

the original decoration which remains exposed at high level. (PHOTOGRAPH: EZRA STOLLER).

teen of the building's 21 floors. Each of the office floors is entered via a spacious lobby. The new bronze-glass and metal window units make good use of the 2ft exterior wall thickness by being set in splayed recesses to reflect the natural light. One of the areas which the architects have left intact is the central banking room, where the elaborately coffered bronze-gold ceiling and its supporting structure of monumental columns with gilded Corinthian capitals have been carefully restored. In sharp contrast is the design of the new multi-level arrangement which surrounds and

opens on to this space. Also startling is the brushed aluminium sculpture by Isamu Noguchi which hangs in the middle of the richly decorated banking hall. The office entrance and lift lobby at the south-west corner of the building retains its black and gold ornamental ceiling and frieze, but below this is a new white marble screen with lift openings, once again in complete contrast. Outside, the wall behind the pillars has been removed and a new wall of clear glass erected several feet back. The resulting arcade makes for a pleasant view over the road to Trinity Church for those

inside and an invitation to those outside. The floors above are simple, and standardised, with the new lighting specially designed to conserve energy.

Accommodation Ground and first floor—banking facilities, entrance lobby.
Upper floors—offices, restaurant and auditorium.

Date of completion 1975

Cost $11 million

SWEET FACTORY, NEW YORK

New use Artists' apartments and studios

Architect Pomeroy, Lebduska & Associates

Client Frederick Richmond Foundation

Site On Henry Street at the edge of the Brooklyn Heights, near Brooklyn Bridge.

History The building, dating from 1870, was originally the home of Peaks Mason Mints. It fell into disuse and in the early

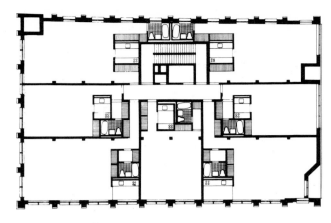

2. Typical upper floor plan with seven apartments.

1. Ground floor plan.

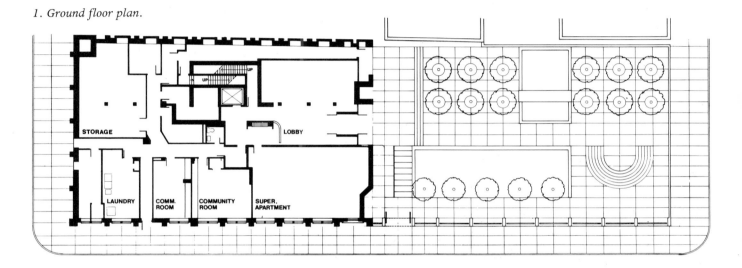

1960s was scheduled for demolition as part of the Cadman Plaza Urban Renewal Programme, to be replaced by a car park. The building came to the attention of the architects at this time and they made an application for conversion which was accepted by the city authorities. But it was not until 1970 that financing was made available and work could begin.

Character The building is a seven-storey, rectangular structure. It has masonry walls on a timber frame, with concrete plank floors and steel framing at the core. Slightly arched window openings are placed in bays 8ft 6in wide, which are separated by pilasters studded at each level with the ends of the metal ties supporting the floors. Originally there were windows on only three sides, and another building adjoined the north-east wall. Now the sweet factory stands free with a garden where its neighbour once stood.

Work done Under a preservation order, the exterior was restored and preserved intact except for the north-east elevation, where large windows were inserted between the steel channels reinforcing the wall, thereby neatly incorporating them into the design. On the other façades new steel windows were inserted. A new entrance was created on the north-east side, opening into the sculpture garden, which was also designed by the architects. The interior was divided into seven apartments per floor, each of which was equipped with a kitchen and bathroom only. The rest of the space was left for the residents to adapt to their own needs. New wooden plank flooring was laid over the old concrete, the old timbers were sandblasted and the brick walls were left exposed.

Accommodation Ground floor—lobby, which also serves as an art gallery, superintendent's apartment, community room, laundry, storage space for art works, workshop space and darkroom.

Upper floors—artists' apartments.

Date of completion 1975

Cost $1,100,000

3. The short south-west elevation and the two long elevations were preserved intact and restored.

4. *The north-east elevation is new. Another building abutted the sweet factory on this side. Its removal made way for the garden and entrance court.* (PHOTOGRAPH: DAVID HIRSCH).

5. *An apartment with interior design by Jeff Gilbert.* (PHOTOGRAPH: DAVID HIRSCH).

POLICE STATION, ST. LOUIS, MISSOURI

New use Design studio and offices

Architect Anselevicius/Rupe/Associates

Client Team Four, Inc.

Site 14 North Newstead Avenue, in the centre of St. Louis, is two blocks south of Lindell Boulevard, a former high-class residential street, and three blocks east of the world famous Forest Park.

1. Section AA.

2. Ground floor plan.

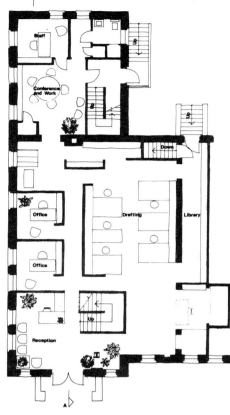

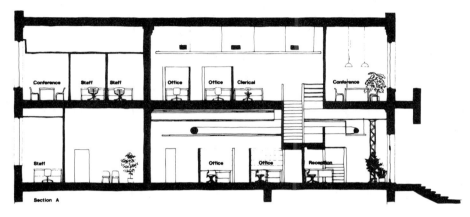

3. Elevation to North Newstead Avenue.

History Built as the Newstead Avenue Police Station in 1905, the building served this purpose until 1960 when it was sold to Charles Guggenheim, who remodelled part of the building for use as a documentary film studio. The studio occupied portions of both the first and second floors and the remaining portion of the second floor was leased to two artists who created a spacious apartment in the south wing and a studio in the adjoining drill hall. The stable on the first floor housed the trucks of a sports network television station, and their operators worked in the remodelled cell block.

In 1967 the building was sold to a firm of planning and landscape consultants and in 1973 the design firm Team Four acquired the building for their offices.

Character As a police station the building was sturdily constructed of masonry with very high ceilings and a steeply pitched slate roof. The main framing is steel, but the floor construction is wood. The roof structure is of four gigantic timber trusses. The major portion of the interior finishes are plaster walls and ceilings, but the ceiling of what was once the front desk area is wood panelling.

Work done Because of the nature of Team Four's organisation most of the work from the earlier alterations had to

be removed. This resulted in a large open space for the drafting and design studio, which is separated from the reception and other areas by low walls. The wood panelled ceiling is now exposed and the tall windows on the north provide natural light to the drafting areas.

A new open staircase connects the lower floor drafting room and offices with the large conference room and offices on the second floor. Views from the multiple landings overlook the drafting and reception areas and enhance the openness of the design.

In order to preserve and emphasise this feeling of openness, the heating and air conditioning ducts and light fixtures were suspended within the space. The walls are painted white with accents of bright colour, and the entire area is carpeted.

Accommodation First floor—reception area, drafting room, offices and work/conference area.
Second floor—work area, offices and main conference room.

Date of completion 1973

Cost $45,000; rate $10.00 sq ft.

4. *The reception area with the new staircase to the first floor.* (PHOTOGRAPH: ROBERT PETTUS).

5. *The drafting room on the ground floor with the library behind. New work includes the suspended ductwork and light fittings below the preserved and restored wood panelled ceiling.* (PHOTOGRAPH: ROBERT PETTUS).

HOSPITAL BUILDINGS, ST. LOUIS, MISSOURI

New use Offices and studio

Client CEMREL, Inc.

Architect Anselevicius/Rupe/ Associates

Site The site at 59th and Arsenal Streets is near the centre of St. Louis and is approximately one mile south of Forest Park and the major east/west express highway. These buildings, formerly used as hospital buildings, are adjacent to the remaining hospital buildings on the east and surrounded by modest but well-maintained houses on the other sides.

History Long before the Civil War the city, growing more concerned about the plight of her old and indigent citizens, had acquired property from Kemper College to be used as a 'poor farm'. The buildings were constructed around the turn of the century and were known as the City Infirmary and later as the St. Louis Chronic Hospital.

By 1968 the buildings were no longer adequate for the improved quality of care St. Louis wanted for her old people. Patients were moved to other facilities throughout the area, and their former home was abandoned.

The buildings, though well built and innovative for their time, were in a sorry state when CEMREL took them over.

Character Building 'A' on 59th Street is the older of the two main structures and is built of patterned masonry. The exterior walls are load-bearing, as are the walls that form the main corridor. Walls at right-angles to the corridor are also masonry and served to divide the space into patients' rooms and at the same time provide lateral support.

The floor structure consists of steel I-beams spanning between bearing walls and a concrete slab spanning between the beams. Formwork for the slab was sprung between the beams resulting in a series of small vaults.

Building 'B' on Arsenal Street is a four-storey masonry building. The floors are reinforced concrete slabs and are supported by a gridwork of beams and columns and on the exterior walls. The linking structure between the building was demolished because of its structural condition and the fact that it did not provide an adequate connection.

Work done An analysis of pedestrian and vehicular traffic indicated the need for a new entrance from 59th Street, with parking at that level and a sloping drive up to the level of the ground floor. By developing a courtyard in the area between the buildings, an entrance at the intersection of the buildings was logical. A new link was built at the intersection to accommodate the new entrance, lift and fire escape, and to provide for the distribution of mechanical and electrical services. A loading dock at the 59th Street level makes use of the lift for distribution of materials. The existing slate roof and masonry walls were cleaned, repaired and water-proofed. The existing wood windows were replaced with new aluminium windows. The bars on the windows and balconies were replaced by new railings, making the balconies usable work areas in good weather.

In 'A' building the rooms along the exterior walls are sub-divided with low screens to preserve the existing spaces. The wide corridors provide space for

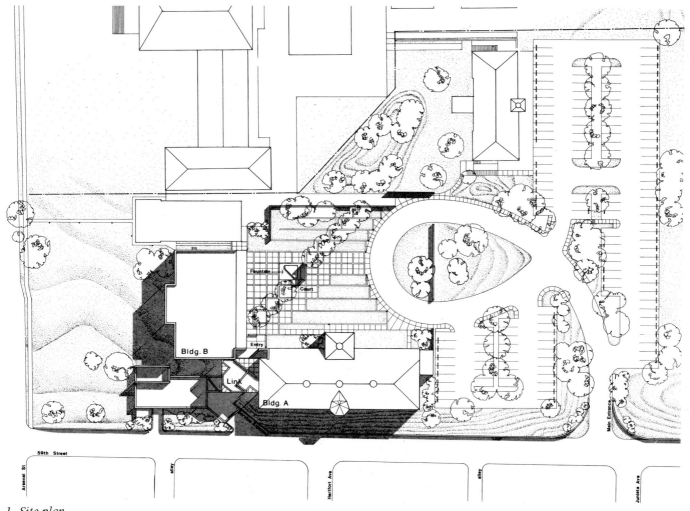

1. Site plan.

secretaries, filing and storage. Lavatories, conference rooms, and common facilities are located centrally.

'B' building, essentially a loft space, was designed with a dropped acoustical ceiling in which fluorescent light fixtures incorporate heating and air conditioning. A core area, composed of mechanical equipment, lavatories and permanent work areas has been included on each floor. Demountable dry-wall partitions were built where privacy was required. In other areas the principles of office landscape have been applied. Large meeting rooms, a graphic studio and a computer room are among the accommodation included in this building.

Brickwork was exposed on some interior walls by removing the plaster, and the remaining plaster walls were surfaced with dry-wall partitions.

Accommodation 'A' building—offices and work areas.

'B' building—First floor: reception area and gallery for displaying art and office space.

Second floor: ancillary office areas.

Third floor: offices and work areas.

Fourth floor: graphics studio and work area.

Date of completion 1973
Cost $2 million; rate $29 per sq ft.

3. West elevation of 'A' building on 59th Street. (PHOTOGRAPH: ROBERT PETTUS).

2. Ground floor plan.

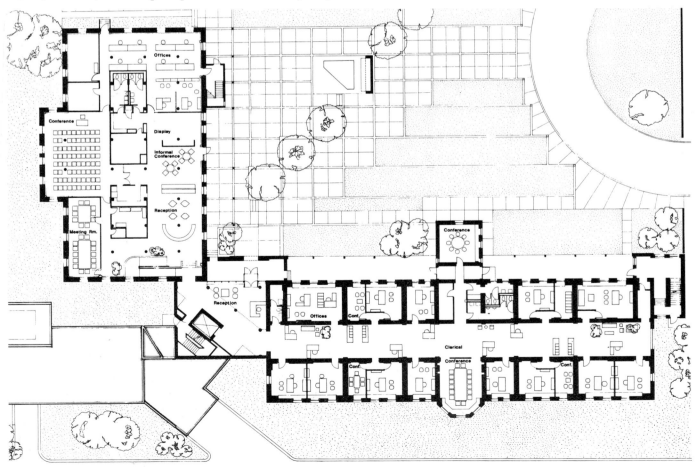

4. The new court at the rear. 'A' building is on the left and 'B' building on the right. The entrance to both buildings is through the new link block in the angle. (PHOTOGRAPH: ROBERT PETTUS).

5. The reception area in the link block. A tower of light draws attention to the receptionist. (PHOTOGRAPH: ROBERT PETTUS).

6. The main corridor in 'A' building, wide enough to provide space for secretaries. The old plaster was removed to expose the brickwork. (PHOTOGRAPH: ROBERT PETTUS).

7. The reception and informal conference area on the ground floor of 'B' building. It also serves as an art gallery. (PHOTO-GRAPH: ROBERT PETTUS).

4 Conversions to housing

Introduction

Most of the cities in the world still contain enough cultural, commercial and business activities to make people want to live in them. If a large number of families have in fact moved out it is for other reasons, of which the most usual are the lower property values of suburbia or the countryside, combined with greater mobility through the unrestricted use of the private motor car. The task of all those concerned with the regeneration of the inner city is to find ways of keeping the existing population and encouraging others to come back. A thriving population is the surest way of supporting all those other activities which make for a lively town.

In the introduction to the first chapter we showed how official planning policy in Bologna has been responsible for rehabilitating housing so that the existing population can stay there and the more usual processes of a middle-class take-over and consequent 'gentrification' are avoided. With its elaborate planning machinery Britain could do the same, and indeed should do so without further delay in London's docklands, where there is a wealth of warehousing crying out for conversion and much derelict land waiting to be built on. The way has already been pointed by a number of excellent warehouse conversions, carried out by private developers, at St. Katharine's Dock, Wapping and beyond.

Old warehouses are usually found in or near the town centre, especially when associated with a port or central market area like Covent Garden. But ports have either died or moved downstream, and markets and industry have gone to the suburbs where land is cheaper and more plentiful. Many strongly built central warehouses, therefore, lie empty, waiting to be converted into offices, flats, hotels, art galleries and other kinds of commercial or cultural centres. In some of the other chapters we have shown examples of warehouses put to cultural and commercial use—an art gallery in Bristol, offices in Leeds, an hotel in Copenhagen and a restaurant in Toronto. In this chapter we limit ourselves to eight examples, of which five are in the United States, one is in Britain, one in Holland and one in Denmark. All are urban examples and five out of the seven—in New York (two), Boston (two), Amsterdam and Copenhagen—are in the inner city. Three examples (two in New York and one in Boston), all of which incorporate studios, recall the plight of that predominantly urban creature, the artist, and his need for special accommodation with good light and high ceilings which old warehouses and other redundant industrial buildings are so often able to provide.

'FAITH', 'HOPE' AND 'LOVE'—THREE WAREHOUSES IN AMSTERDAM, HOLLAND

New use Housing and a shop

Architect E. J. Jelles

Client 'Faith'—Private client
'Hope'—Private client
'Love'—A wine and cheese retail business

Site These three canal-side warehouses are situated in the Prinsengracht in the Jordaan district of Amsterdam.

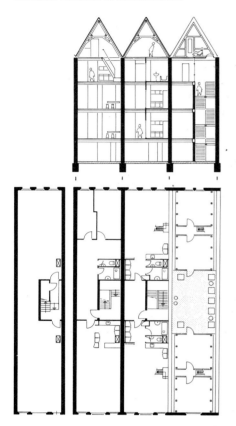

1. From left to right: ground floor plan; first and second floor plan; third floor plan; attic. Above: section through the three warehouses.
2. Elevation of the three warehouses and front-to-back section through one warehouse.

3. The warehouses before conversion seen from the Prinsengracht.

History Built around 1700 they were used as warehouses until 1970 when they were bought by Jesuits whose House was being dissolved and who wanted somewhere to house their lib-rary, which was being donated to the Ministry of Education. But the Ministry refused the gift of the warehouses because of the expense of upkeep, and they were sold again to three different clients. Work started on their con-version in 1972.

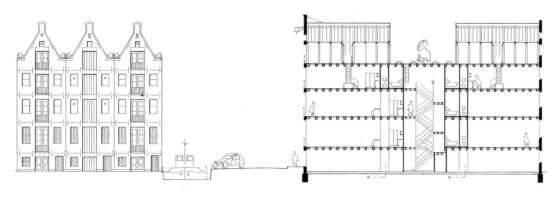

4. Two of the warehouses in the process of conversion.

Character These five-storey warehouses are solidly built of brick with fine ornamental gable ends typical of Amsterdam. There is a large central opening for loading on each floor. The steeply pitched roofs are constructed of oak trusses which are exposed internally and covered in tiles externally.

Work done The brickwork, which was in good condition, was cleaned and re-pointed, and left exposed inside. A staircase (lit by a sky-light) was inserted up the centre of each building. Some apartments are small bed-sitting rooms with a kitchen and bathroom, and some are more spacious. The apartments on the top floor have bedrooms and a protected roof terrace where some of the roof structure has been removed. At the back of the buildings there is a quiet enclosed garden as well as storage sheds for each apartment. There is a small shop on the ground floor. Tubes carrying wiring and pipes for each apartment are fitted to the walls of the stairwell. The wiring for the apartments is carried along narrow plastic tracks fixed to the walls. This has the double advantage of minimising damage to the brickwork and increasing the freedom of the occupant, who can 'plug in' anywhere he likes on the track.

Accommodation Ground floor 'Love'—shop.
First, second, third and fourth floors: apartments.

Date of completion 1974

Cost 350,000 Dutch Guilders

5. One of the living rooms on the Prinsengracht side.

6. The roof terrace which divides the front from the back rooms on the top floor.

THE BLUE WAREHOUSE, COPENHAGEN

New use Flats

Architect Flemming Hertz and Ole Ramsgaard Thomsen

Client The Blue Warehouse

Site The Blue Warehouse is situated between the waterfront and Toldbodgaden, one of three warehouses situated on the waterfront adjacent to the royal residence, the Amalienborg Palace. The others are also being converted, one also into flats and the other into storage space for costumes and properties belonging to the Royal Theatre.

History There were originally four warehouses in this complex, one of which was demolished in 1953. They were built around 1780 and designed by C. F. Harsdorff. This explains their common character, although their different sizes make them quite different in appearance.

Character The Blue Warehouse is rectangular on plan and has seven storeys, two of which are in the roof. Small window openings punctuate the façades. At the front and back a central bay rises to a gable with a wide loading opening on each floor. The structure is of brick and heavy timber.

Work done Two lifts were installed and adjacent staircases constructed in reinforced concrete. Each floor was partitioned into six different sized flats. French windows were inserted into the loading openings, set back to make space for a small balcony with a railing. The original interior surfaces were cleaned, sandblasted and left natural, except for the spaces between the beams which were plastered.

Accommodation Ground floor—two entrances, services, four studio flats. Upper floors—36 flats.

Date of completion 1979

Cost Approximately 30 million Danish kroner.

1. Section and ground floor plan.

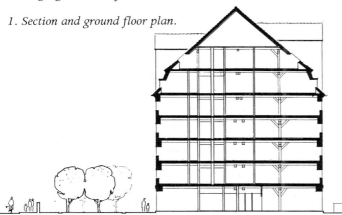

1. CAR PARKING UNDER TREES
2. PEDESTRIAN PARK
3. QUAYSIDE PROMENADE
4. PLAYGROUND
5. GARDEN
6. ENTRANCE
7. LANDING
8. CORRIDOR
9. CARETAKER'S FLAT
10. SERVICES AREA
11. HALL
12. KITCHEN
13. BATHROOM
14. DINING ROOM
15. LIVING ROOM
16. BEDROOM
A, STUDIO FLAT (110m²)
B, FLAT OF 115m²
C, FLAT OF 160m²
D, FLAT OF 195m²

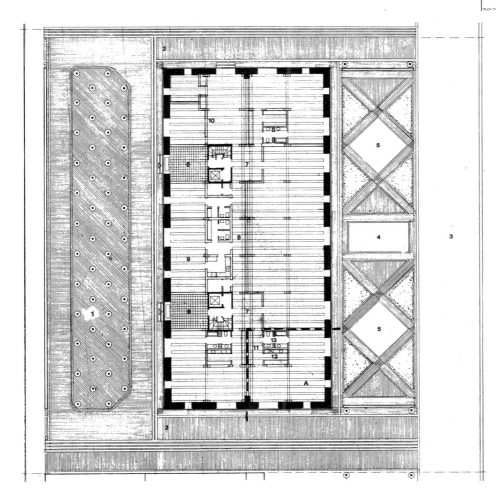

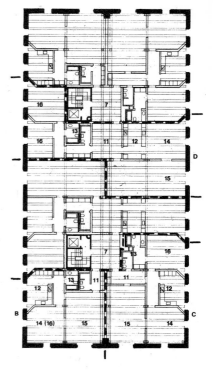

2. Typical upper floor plan.

3. Elevation of warehouse.

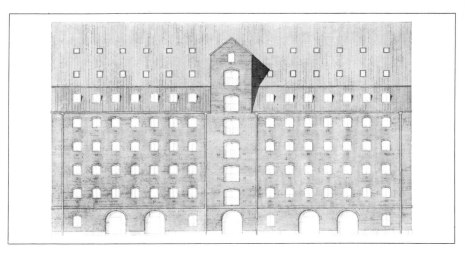

4. Living room. (PHOTOGRAPH: ERIK BREDAHL).

5. Kitchen. (PHOTOGRAPH: ERIK BRED-AHL).

TANNERY COMPLEX, PEABODY, MASSACHUSETTS

New use Residential complex, with park and pond

Architect Anderson Notter Finegold Inc.

Client Crowninshield Corporation

Site An 8·7 acre riverside plot only three blocks away from the town's business centre. The original plot contained five tannery buildings of varying sizes, a power plant, the owner's mansion, several minor structures and a large mill pond.

History The oldest building on the site is the mansion, formerly the residence of the Crowninshield family, whose members figured prominently in American maritime history. The estate was gradually taken over by the A. C. Lawrence Leather Company and in the nineteenth century Peabody boasted that it was the 'leather capital of the world'. Since the Second World War, escalating costs forced most of the mill operations to relocate in the south, leaving behind abandoned buildings. This complex was vacated in 1970. Efforts to attract new industries to the largely out-dated facilities failed and the buildings fell prey to decay and vandalism. As an eye-sore and a crime-pocket the site also contributed to the decline of adjoining neighbourhoods. In 1972 the complex was chosen as an investment for the Massachusetts Housing Finance Agency. A plan was drawn up to make three of the factory buildings into apartment blocks, the mansion into community facilities (marked 'commons' on the plan) and the site into a pleasant environment for the residents.

Character The mansion is a fine three-storey, early nineteenth-century brick house with a hipped roof. The three remaining factory buildings are rectangular on plan. Two of them are of brick and timber construction, six storeys high and with many regularly spaced window openings. One of these is buttressed with cast-iron struts. The third building, of only three storeys, is of reinforced concrete.

Work done Several sheds were demolished, but some walls were retained to screen car parks and the brick and tile floors were transformed into terraces. The pond was dredged and cleaned and the surrounds were planted. Some of the old tannery vats and drying wheels were installed in the gardens as plant pots and, wherever possible, remnants of the old industrial use were retained as a reminder of the past. Community facilities were located in the mansion and the three remaining buildings were converted into apartments. The original timber structure of the roof was retained, cleaned and exposed. Two existing lifts were refurbished and three additional ones installed. Industrial walkways at second floor level were

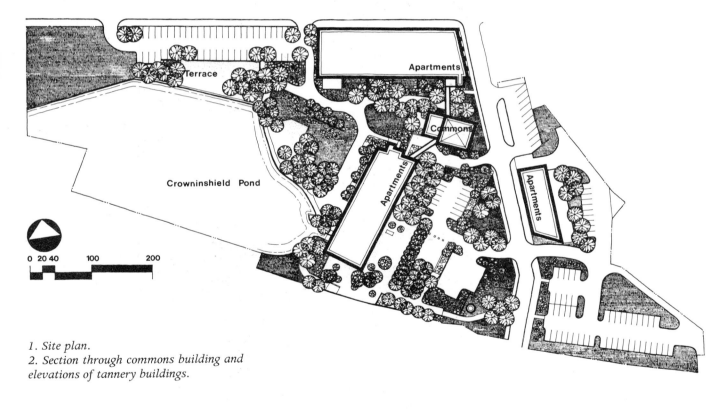

1. Site plan.
2. Section through commons building and elevations of tannery buildings.

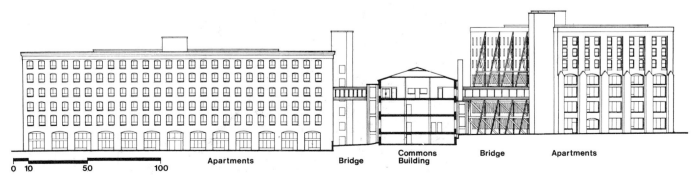

3. The tannery buildings after conversion
with the dredged pond in the foreground.
(PHOTOGRAPH: PHOKION KARAS).

retained and converted to glass sky-
walks to connect the two largest apartment blocks with the mansion. A second
renovation phase is now under construction and includes the conversion of
a seven-storey reinforced concrete factory into a further 173 units of housing
for the elderly.

Accommodation Mansion—offices,
laundry, playrooms and other community areas.
Tannery buildings—284 apartments of
varying types, 10 per cent of which are
specially designed for the elderly and
disabled.

Date of completion 1975

Cost $6 million.

4. One of the tannery buildings with the
old mansion converted to community
facilities in the background. (PHOTO-
GRAPH: PHOKION KARAS).

90

BELL TELEPHONE LABORATORIES, NEW YORK

New use Housing and studio for artists

Architect Richard Meier & Associates Architects

Client The Westbeth Corporation Housing Development Fund Company Inc.

Site An urban site on West Street, a few blocks below Fourth Street. The outlook commands views of the Hudson River and upper and lower Manhattan.

History The Bell Telephone Company erected the buildings between 1898 and 1920, and used them until 1966. A year or so later, they were bought by a co-operative effort between the National Council on the Arts and the J. M. Kaplan Fund with a view to providing much needed apartments and studios for working artists in New York City.

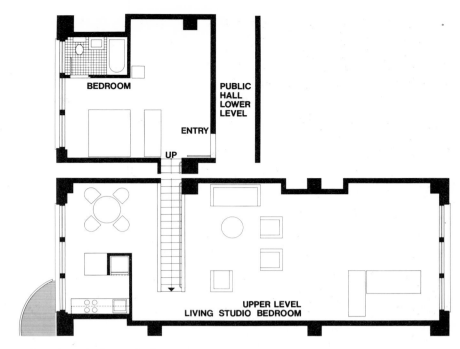

1. Ninth floor plan.　　　　　*2. Plan of two-bedroom duplex apartment.*

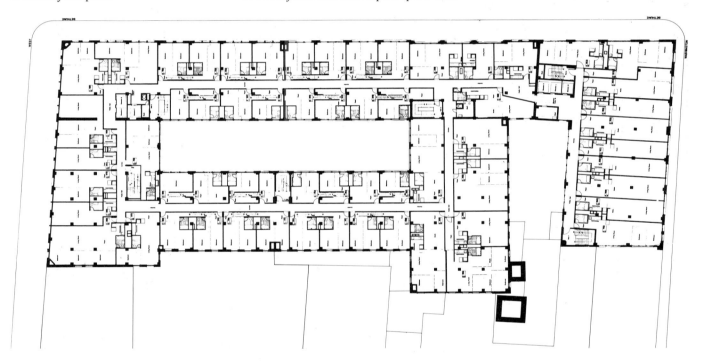

Character The buildings are 13 storeys high, and surround a courtyard which was formerly covered by two storeys and a roof, and was used as a loading area for trucks. The interior spaces have high ceilings, large windows, thick masonry walls and fireproof constructions.

Work done The most significant alteration to these buildings was the removal of the superstructure over the loading bay, making an internal courtyard open to the sky, which is now the focus of access to the apartments and to the shops and galleries at ground and mezzanine level. The existing vehicle entrance from West Street, with its handsome wrought iron gates, still remains, but two pedestrian arcades were created to link the yard to Bethune Street on the north side and Westbeth Park on the south, which was made by demolishing two buildings, and is now a pleasant community area with a central fountain.

Balconies were built over the internal courtyard, and inside the spaces were enlarged by the elimination of through corridors on all but the third, sixth and ninth floors of the central building.

Inside the apartments, only the bathrooms and kitchens are enclosed. Movable cupboards are provided to serve as room dividers as well as storage space. The tenants can build their own walls if they wish and, as the lowest ceiling height is over 10ft, almost every apartment has room for a large open loft space. This is the first time the Federal Housing Administration and New York City have allowed such flexible interior plans.

Accommodation Ground floor and mezzanine—shops and galleries.
12 upper floors—384 studio apartments.

Date of completion 1970

3. The courtyard, which is now open to the sky and the main access to the apartments. (PHOTOGRAPH : EZRA STOLLER).

4. On the south side the community area with its central fountain was made by demolishing two buildings.

5. The West Street façade with vehicular entrance. (PHOTOGRAPH EZRA STOLLER).
6. A living room.

MERCANTILE WHARF BUILDING, BOSTON

New use Commercial and housing

Architect John Sharratt Associates

Client James F. Sullivan, Edward C. Fish, Mercantile Associates.

Site This old warehouse is situated on the waterfront in the North End area of Boston, very near the Faneuil Hall market area.

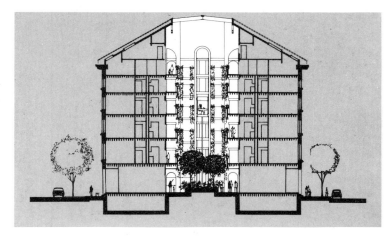

2. Section showing the top-lit central atrium.

1. Typical upper floor plan (1st–4th floors).

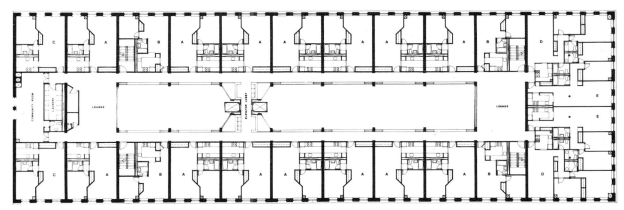

3. View from the public park on Atlantic Avenue. The building was half as long again before being truncated by an expressway in the '50s. (PHOTOGRAPH: STEVE ROSENTHAL).

History Gridley James Fox Bryant was the architect of this French Second Empire style structure, which was completed in 1857. It was used for many years as a ship chandlers' and sailmakers' warehouse, supplying the vessels docked within a few yards with supplies for their voyages. In this century it was used by several food processing warehouse operations which continued until the 1960s. In 1972 the Boston Redevelopment Authority sponsored a competition from architects and developers for the renovation of the building. It was won by John Sharratt Associates in collaboration with the Peabody Construction Company.

Character Although the building looks from the outside to be a single unit with 12 bays, it was originally formed of 18 separate units with a common façade. Six of these were demolished in the 1950s to make way for an elevated expressway, and the remaining building measures 300ft by 100ft. The façade is covered with rusticated granite blocks, the structure is of granite, brick and timber and the pitched roof is slated. On the ground floor are large regular openings, each crowned with a keystone. From the first to the fourth floor the regularly-spaced window openings decrease progressively in size. The height of the interior spaces is graduated correspondingly, and originally housed shops, storage areas and workshops.

Work done The façade has retained its

93

4, 5. The top-lit central atrium rises through the full height of the building and is surrounded by apartment corridors that are reached by two glass lifts. (PHOTOGRAPHS: STEVE ROSENTHAL).

6. One of the apartments on the top floor, formerly occupied by sailmakers, where the extra height has enabled the architects to insert mezzanines. (PHOTOGRAPH: STEVE ROSENTHAL).

original character. The stonework was cleaned and windows were replaced by new triple-paned windows in metal frames. The problems of the interior, due to the unusual width of the building, were solved by completely gutting the inside and creating a long top-lit central atrium. Corridors run around this atrium on each floor, giving access to 122 apartments on the upper floors. On the ground floor are shops and restaurants around a central pool and garden. Two glass lifts take residents from the garden up to their apartments. These are of 17 different designs from single-bedroom flats to large flats with several bedrooms and lofts. Rents vary from 'low' to 'market', subsidised by the Massachusetts Housing Finance Agency. Each floor from the first to the fifth has two lounges, a community room and a laundry.

Accommodation Ground floor—shops, restaurant, interior garden with pool. Upper floors—apartments.

Date of completion July 1976

Cost $5,594,000

RIVERHEAD GRANARIES, DRIFFIELD, HUMBERSIDE

New use Flats

Architect MacCormac and Jamieson

Client Riverton Properties

Site At the head of the eighteenth-century canal connecting Driffield to the city of Hull. The two granaries, which have been converted, are part of a larger group of eighteenth- and nineteenth-century granaries and houses. The west elevation faces a cobbled forecourt and the east directly on to the canal.

History The buildings are about 200 years old and were used continuously as granaries until 1965 when they fell into disuse and suffered some decay. They are listed as Grade I buildings of historic interest.

Character The buildings lie at the edge of a town, both enclosing urban space and framing a surprising vista down the canal into open country to the south. They are constructed of brick external walls with an internal structure of oak posts, primary beams and joists supporting the floors. The roofs consist of trusses supporting purlins and rafters. The external character is largely a consequence of the size and distribution of the openings. These are small and widely spaced, and their shallow brick arches give the building its distinctly eighteenth-century quality in contrast to the harsher and more robust appearance of neighbouring nineteenth-century buildings.

Work done The buildings lent themselves readily to conversion into small flats, consisting of structural cross walls at 5 to 6m centres which have become party walls. The open top floors have been subdivided with proprietary steel-framed partitions, clad in plasterboard, to achieve party-wall acoustic standard, and 'floating' floors have been formed over existing floors. The whole interior has been grit-blasted to remove lime-wash, to expose decay and to reveal the texture of the old materials.

Externally, care has been taken to maintain the scale of existing openings in which pivoted casements have taken the place of the old shutters. Only at ground level, on the canal elevation, have the small windows been replaced with french windows, which give access to balconies constructed with propped cantilevers and balustrades. On the street side the two new stair enclosures are constructed like the original cantilevered hoist housing, with weatherboarding and canopies to protect the entrance areas. The new dormer windows are weatherboarded to match and the existing loading doors in the elevations have been reconstructed with vertical boarding. The front doors to the ground floor flats are recessed to conceal the dustbins within external lobbies protected from outside by half doors.

Accommodation 22 one- or two-person dwellings, basically of two kinds. Twelve flats with living rooms and bedrooms divided by folding doors. There are some double-height units with bed spaces on mezzanines and seven units take up the first and second floor of the larger building, with bedroom and bathroom at entry level and living space under the roof.

Date of completion 1979

1. *Ground floor plan.*
   1. LIVING ROOM
   2. DINING ROOM
   3. BEDROOM
   4. KITCHEN

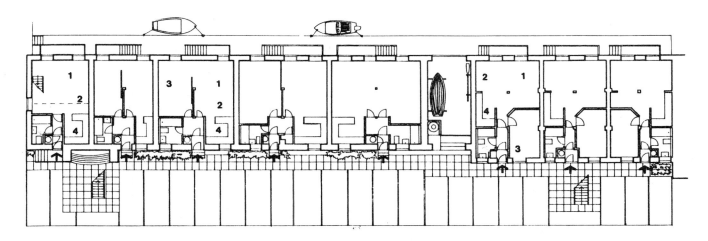

2. *Long section.*

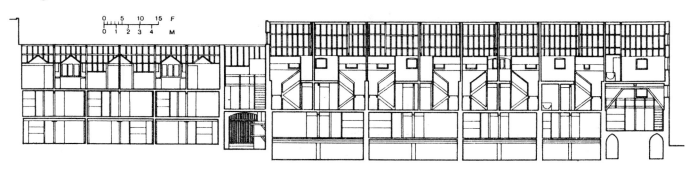

3. *View from the cobbled forecourt with one of the new stair enclosures which imitate the original hoist housing.* (PHOTO-GRAPH: KEITH GIBSON).

4. *View from the canal. The French windows and balconies are new.* (PHOTO-GRAPH: KEITH GIBSON).

5. *A living room on the ground floor with French windows giving on to a balcony overlooking the canal.* (PHOTOGRAPHER: KEITH GIBSON).

WAREHOUSE LOFT, NEW YORK CITY

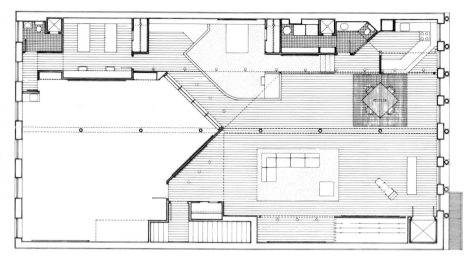

New use Apartment and artist's studio

Client Miss Sophia Sosnoff

Site Within the designated historic Soho Cast-Iron District, Lower Manhattan, New York City.

History Designed by the architect Robert Mook and built in 1872 as a store and warehouse for Amos Eno. This is one of many distinctive commercial cast-iron buildings built in lower Manhattan, which until recently has variously housed printing presses, light manufacturing of welding equipment, stationery and wine bottling.

The search by artists for large, low-rent spaces led to the phenomenal transformation of the Soho 'manufacturing' district into the artists' enclave it is today. This space was one of the first of this trend.

1. Plan and section.

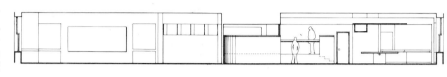

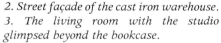

2. Street façade of the cast iron warehouse.
3. The living room with the studio glimpsed beyond the bookcase.

Character The building is rectangular on plan (84 by 47ft) and has five storeys. It has masonry flanking walls and a central cast-iron spine structure comprising seven 12ft bays, with floors of heavy timber beams.

Work done The client was an artist who required a minimum-budget conversion of the open space on the third floor of the building into a working/living 'loft'. The space was divided roughly into three, with the working area at the back, the living area at the front, and sleeping areas, bathrooms and kitchen along one side. The main living area was designed as a vehicle in which to display art, and one of the features of this space is the specially designed exhibit and storage space. In response to the client's informal living needs is a large, permanently fixed dining table which is located beneath an industrial subway grating intended for hanging plants. An open kitchen is tucked into the front corner, near to the dining table. Elevated up four steps for light, air and privacy is the main sleeping area, a vantage point from which one can look through a high glass window above library shelves into the working studio. A more private bedroom with its own bathroom is contained in the rear corner of the space, built for the teenage son.

The entire space is lit by exposed bulbs which at night provide reflected light on paintings and throw into relief the white geometric interior forms.

Accommodation Work area, living/exhibition area, kitchen, sleeping area, bathroom, enclosed bedroom with its own bathroom.

Date of completion 1973

PIANO FACTORY, BOSTON

New use Artists' housing

Architect Gelardin Bruner Cott, Inc.

Client Gelardin Bruner Cott, Inc.

Site The building fronts on to Tremont Street in Boston, and is only ten minutes walk from the Back Bay business district.

History The piano factory was built in the last century for the firm of Chickering and Sons. When Bruner and Gelardin first saw it with a view to conversion, it had deteriorated into a warren of shabby cubicles and bays occupied by about 70 small manufacturers, artists and small businesses.

The architects, taking on the role of developers, bought the building, although not without a great deal of opposition from the tenants. A grant from the Boston Redevelopment Authority provided funds to re-house most of them, and another from the Massachusetts Housing Finance Agency helped towards building costs.

Character The building is roughly rectangular and surrounds a central courtyard. A large number of windows pierce the façades, and this factor, together with the limited depth (49ft) of the building, makes it especially suitable for housing. There are five floors and a basement to each wing except at the back, where the building is only two storeys high. On the front façade is a three-sided apsidal bay containing the main entrance, and rising the full height of the building to a hexagonal turret crowned by a dome above roof level. The structure is of brick with a heavy timber post and beam internal framework. There are no load-bearing internal walls.

Originally there was a boiler house with a 100ft high chimney at the back.

Work done The architects tried to create the apartments as large, open areas with kitchen and bathroom cores placed back to back in each pair of flats, which could be serviced by a single set of plumbing ducts. The roof space was used to provide mezzanines for the upper loft apartments, with new dormer windows.

New dividing walls were limited to those enclosing each flat, bathrooms and some bedrooms. The walls and timbers (except for the ceiling joists) were sandblasted and left exposed. New partitions were painted with a flat white paint. The doorways were made especially wide for easy transport of large sculptures, and

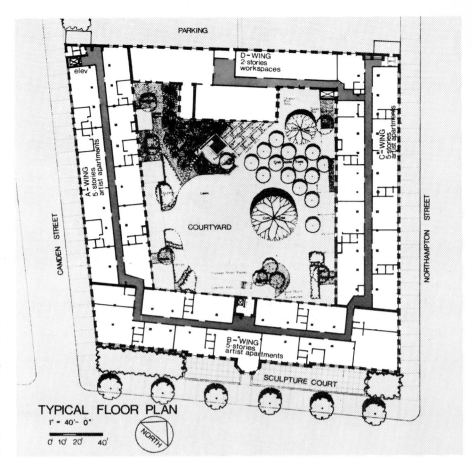

1. Typical floor plan.

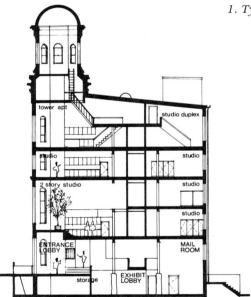

2. Section through B-wing.

special freight lifts can carry heavy artist's materials to the upper flats. Two sliding fire doors were placed at the angle of the wings on each floor. The whole building was re-wired, re-plumbed, and new heating services were installed.

The central courtyard was landscaped and planted, and a sculpture court created at the front.

The units were let to bona-fide artists at three scales of rent, depending on their means.

Accommodation 116 studio and one-bedroom units ranging in area from 500 to 1500 sq ft, 52 two-bedroom units (925–1500 sq ft), 6 three-bedroom units (1,525–1,740 sq ft). Workspaces in D-wing.

Date of completion 1974

Cost $3·4 million for building costs only.

3. *Looking across Tremont Street to B-wing.* (PHOTOGRAPH: GREG HEINS).

4. *View from the courtyard with A-wing on the left and the lower D-wing containing workspaces on the right.* (PHOTOGRAPH: GREG HEINS).

5. *The apartment in the tower of B-wing.* (PHOTOGRAPH: GREG HEINS).

5 Churches

Introduction

This chapter examines the workings of the government legislation of 1968 known as 'The Pastoral Measure' where it concerns the problem of redundant churches. Britain is the first country to tackle the problem of church redundancy in an organised manner, even though this is a problem found in all industrialised countries. However, the Pastoral Measure only covers the Church of England, which still leaves many Roman Catholic and non-conformist churches at risk.

Out of about 18,000 Anglican churches in Britain, by 1980 probably 1000 will have been declared redundant. Because of shifts in population from the country to industrial centres, some parishes may be joined to others, or dissolved entirely, and others may be created nearer to the heart of a new community. City centres have become depopulated, which means that there is no resident community around a church. Clergymen, each of whom has only a small number of parishioners, may join together in a group ministry, needing only one church between them. Some churches, though conveniently situated, may be too large, or too expensive to maintain, and are replaced by new, smaller buildings.

The problem with churches is that even though 11,500 of them are buildings listed as being of architectural merit, they are exempt from the 1913 Ancient Monuments Act providing for demolition control, listing and grants for repair and maintenance.* Until very recently, churches received no state help whatsoever towards their upkeep, which, since about 8,500 are basically medieval, is clearly very expensive.

The Pastoral Measure

In 1960, the problem of unused churches, many of great architectural and historical merit, at the mercy of decay and vandalism, was examined by a committee, chaired by Lord Bridges, known as 'The

*In the earliest legislation concerning ancient monuments in the U.K.—two Ancient Monuments Protection Acts dated 1882 and 1900—no distinction was drawn between ecclesiastical and secular monuments, although all ecclesiastical buildings are the property of the Church of England. In 1913, the Ancient Monuments Bill was amended in the Lords by Archbishop Davidson to exclude ecclesiastical buildings. Although the Commons were mainly against this exemption, parliamentary business was pressing, so they allowed it to become law.

Bridges Commission'. Following this, legislation entitled 'The Pastoral Measure 1968' provided primarily for people's religious needs, but secondarily 'for the use, preservation and disposal of redundant churches'. Under the Pastoral Measure, the Advisory Board for Redundant Churches and the Redundant Churches Fund were set up to help the Church Commissioners (the administrative body for The Church of England) with this task.

Before The Pastoral Measure, an Act of Parliament was needed to dissolve the legal status of consecration, so that each redundant church had to have its own Act before it could be disposed of. The Measure overcomes this problem. It also sets out the process to be followed for a redundant church, which is as follows.

1. A parish wishing to declare its church redundant makes a proposal to a committee of the Diocese known as the Pastoral Committee which then submits it to the bishop together with the views of locally interested parties, information on the architectural and historical qualities of the church and other neighbouring churches, and draft proposals for the future of the church. If the bishop approves, he forwards the proposals to the Church Commissioners in London.

2. The Church Commissioners seek the preliminary advice of the Advisory Board for Redundant Churches, and then draft and publish a Pastoral Scheme which gives effect to the diocesan proposals. Representations can be made for 28 days after this, and if they are allowed, the Scheme is modified or dropped and a new Scheme published, with a further 28 days for representations. Over-ruled objectors may appeal to the Privy Council.

3. The Church Commissioners submit the draft Pastoral Scheme for confirmation to Her Majesty the Queen in Council and publish it in *The London Gazette*. The church is then legally declared redundant and is taken out of the charge of the incumbent and parish, and becomes the responsibility of The Diocesan Board of Finance, which must see to its upkeep during a waiting period of between one and three years while the Redundant Churches Uses Committee of the Diocese tries to find a new use for it.

4. The next step is for the Church Commissioners to prepare and publish a Redundancy Scheme of which there are three kinds, depending on the advice of the Advisory Board; one to propose demolition, one to sanction a proposed new use, and one to recommend the preservation of the church as a national monument in the care of the Redundant Churches Fund. In the first case, the Redundancy Scheme supercedes the Pastoral Scheme and the Advisory Board issues a certificate stating that the church is not of sufficient architectural or historical interest to save. The Redundancy Scheme is then advertised, and 28 days are allowed for representations. If these do not appear, or are over-ruled, it is submitted to the Privy Council. The Church Commissioners, who now automatically own the building, proceed with the Redundancy Scheme, either demolish it, hand it over to the Redundant Churches Fund, give it or sell it for a new use, or lease it, in which case the Diocesan Board of Finance keeps the freehold.

The Advisory Board for Redundant Churches

Set up under the Pastoral Measure in 1968, this is a statutory body consisting of a chairman and between six and ten other members appointed by the Archbishops of York and Canterbury jointly after consultation with the Prime Minister. Its expenses are met by the Church Commissioners out of their general fund. It is solely concerned

1. *These diagrams show that from 1969 to 1977 (the first 8½ years of the Pastoral Measure) nearly £2½ million or 80 per cent of the sale proceeds of redundant churches went to the living church. Over the same period the Redundant Churches Fund received nearly £350,000 from the balance of sale proceeds and nearly £700,000 each from the Church and the State. During this period 185 churches were demolished and the future of all or part of 577 was decided. Diagram A represents the first quinquennium (1969–74), diagram B the first 3½ years of the second quinquennium.*
a. 67 per cent (£1,150,000)
b. 6 per cent (£100,000)
c. 27 per cent (£490,000)
d. 67 per cent (£851,000)
e. 19 per cent (£245,000)
f. 14 per cent (£181,000)

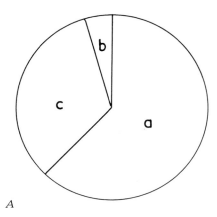

A

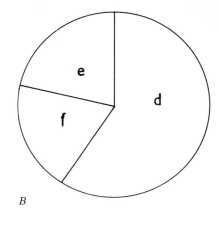

B

a. and d. (a fixed two thirds) went to the living church for new churches, clergy houses and stipends.
b. and e. went to the Redundant Churches

Fund, the amount being determined by the Synod for each quinquennium.
c. and f. (the surplus) went to the living church.

2. *Under present arrangements contributions from the Church and the State provide the Redundant Churches Funds' income. These diagrams show how the fund is financed and the proportion of the Church Commissioners' income which was made available to it in 1976–77. Diagram C represents the fate of the 577 churches.*
g. Preservation by the Redundant Churches Fund (21 per cent)
h. Preservation by the Department of the Environment (1 per cent)
i. Demolition (32 per cent)
j. Alternative use (46 per cent)

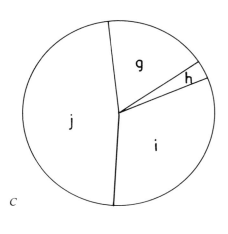

C

Diagram D shows the sum made available to the Redundant Churches Fund in relation to the Church Commissioners' income.
k. Reinvestment (3·1 per cent)
l. Administration, commissioners and ancillary bodies (6·7 per cent)
m. New church buildings (4·3 per cent)
n. Clergy housing (12 per cent)
o. Clergy and widows' pensions (14·6 per cent)
p. Clergy stipends (59 per cent)
q. Redundant Churches Fund (0·36 per cent)
Diagram E shows how the sum in q is made up
r. Grant from the Church Commissioners
s. Share of sale proceeds
t. Grant from the State

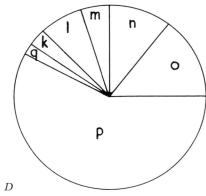

D

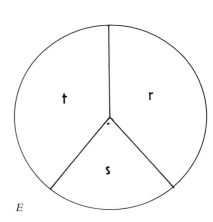

E

with the architectural and historical problems of redundant churches, and although its views are the primary consideration when the Church Commissioners are deciding what to do with a redundant church, its function is purely advisory, and its advice can be over-ruled if the Church Commissioners feel they have strong reasons for doing so.

The Board usually sees a church twice, once before the declaration of redundancy, when it gives preliminary advice to the Church Commissioners. If a building is badly vandalised, or alternative plans come up, it can change its advice. It sees the church a second time to approve the plans submitted to the Church Commissioners by the Diocesan Redundant Churches Uses Committee, if a new use has been found, or if no new use has been found, at the end of the waiting

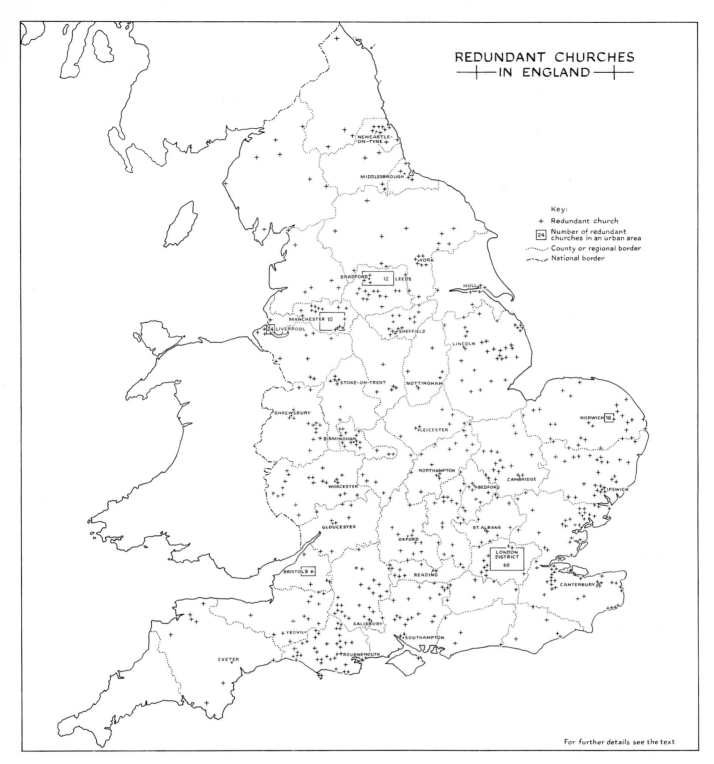

REDUNDANT CHURCHES
IN ENGLAND

Key:
+ Redundant church
24 Number of redundant churches in an urban area
.... County or regional border
-·-·-· National border

For further details see the text

3. Map of England showing the size of the problem. The categories of redundant churches include alternative use, preservation by the Redundant Churches Fund, preservation by the Department of the Environment, demolition, use still sought and the disposal of sites of churches demolished other than under the Pastoral Measure.

period, to recommend its preservation by the Redundant Churches Fund, or to agree to demolition.

In order to get as full a picture as possible of a redundant church, the Board prepares full documentation of the architectural, historical and structural aspects of the building, as well as photographs, plans and maps and specialist reports on fittings such as bells. These remain in the archives as a permanent record for the future. It can also ensure the preservation of certain fine features of an otherwise unremarkable church by requiring that they be incorporated into a new church, or removed and stored with a view to reinstatement elsewhere.

In certain cases, when churches are considered by the Board to be of sufficient national importance, it can suggest their placement in the

103

4. *St George's, Portland, Dorset, taken on by the Redundant Churches Fund and restored for £11,000* (PHOTOGRAPH: NATIONAL MONUMENTS RECORD).

care of the Department of the Environment according to section 66 of the Pastoral Measure, which allows them to return to ecclesiastical use, should the Church of England require them. The first two churches handed over in 1972 were the magnificent church of St. Peter, Barton-on-Humber, which has a Saxon tower and noble medieval nave and chancel, and the neo-Gothic church of St. Mary, Studley Royal in the Diocese of Ripon.

In 1969, the first year of the Pastoral Measure's operation, only 7 churches were declared redundant. The number peaked in 1973 to 170, but has decreased slightly ever since.

The Redundant Churches Fund
Set up at the same time as the Advisory Board, the purpose of the Fund is to preserve a number of churches as national monuments 'in the interest of the Nation and the Church of England'. It consists of a chairman and between four and six members appointed by the Queen, having taken the advice of the Archbishops of Canterbury and York through the Prime Minister.

The Fund must take on any church the Church Commissioners

5. St Mary's, Old Ditton, Wiltshire, taken on by the Redundant Churches Fund and restored for £18,800. (PHOTOGRAPH: NATIONAL MONUMENTS RECORD).

6. St Mary's, Kempley, Gloucestershire, taken on by the Department of the Environment. (PHOTOGRAPH: NATIONAL MONUMENTS RECORD).

choose to allocate to it, provided it has funds, and must repair and maintain it. A church in the care of the Fund remains consecrated and can be used for occasional services, a maximum of two per year plus an occasional baptism or wedding. (It cannot be used more frequently in case impoverished parishes should try to hive off their financial responsibilities on to the Fund by pretending their church is redundant.) The Fund is allowed to charge entrance fees, and can raise money by appeals, and is allowed to accept gifts and bequests. It can also contribute to the cost of maintaining a church during its waiting period.

In the first five years, 1969–1974, the Church Commissioners and the Department of the Environment each provided £200,000, four-fifths of the total spent, and the remaining fifth came from a third share of the proceeds of sales of redundant churches and sites. In the second quinquennium the DOE's and the Church Commissioners' shares were £750,000 each, with £350,000 from the sale of churches and sites. In the third, 1979–1984, it is proposed to split a total of £2,900,000—half to be provided by the DOE, two-sixths by the Church Commissioners and one-sixth from sales.

The Department of the Environment

The DOE, in spite of the ecclesiastical exemption mentioned above, is taking an increasing interest in the preservation of churches. Apart from taking over certain churches of great historical importance, also mentioned above, it has earmarked £2 million a year for a system of state aid for churches in use, which began in September 1977 with the church at Long Melford, and has been followed by grants to 132 others in the nine months to May 1978. Each grant from the DOE must be matched by an equivalent one from the parish.

Finding New Uses

There are problems in finding a new use for a once-consecrated and public building. Often the reason for its redundancy militates against finding a new use for it; for example if it is away from the centre of a community, badly served by public transport, too large or too difficult to heat. A new use must respect as far as possible the form and spirit of a church. So any use which maintains the interior space is better than one that breaks it up. And it is better used by a community than a private owner. But there is the problem that community centres often hold bingo drives and are licensed. Some small churches make good houses, especially if the owner is prepared to live in a high space with open galleries, but this kind of use closes a church to the community. There is now a code of practice linked to the Pastoral Measure which requires that access to the church and the graveyard must be allowed by the new user. Bodies may be removed from the churchyard, and the new owner may be required to contribute towards the cost of removal and re-interment elsewhere, but they often stay. To avoid disturbance of graves, pipes and wires can be laid under the path, where no burials have taken place. The code of practice also protects the buildings by requiring the new owner to undertake repairs, to erect a notice declaring the nature of the new use, not to undertake any alterations other than those approved by the Advisory Board and not to demolish the church.

In general, the Advisory Board considers that it is better to find any new use for a church rather than sterilize it as a monument, but there is a lot of controversy about this, not only among the members of the Board, but elsewhere. There is continual debate as to whether or not churches of special architectural merit should be allowed to go into private ownership if no suitable public use can be found.

The Operation of the Pastoral Measure

There are disadvantages to the Pastoral Measure in practice. For example, it all takes an enormously long time, and the longer a church stands empty during its 'waiting period', the more vulnerable it is to vandalism and decay. The Diocesan Board of Finance is responsible for its upkeep during this period, but is understandably reluctant to invest large sums of money in a building which is soon to be taken off its hands. A potential new user might be put off by the expense of necessary repairs although he could expect to see this reflected in the sale price. It would be better to make the Church Commissioners or the Redundant Churches Fund responsible for churches at this stage, and in fact quite often the Redundant Churches Fund will pay for repairs, especially if the church is likely to come to them in the end. In the case of churches of outstanding interest, where a new use would not be suitable, they should be entrusted to the Fund or the Department of the Environment without delay.

Dioceses are not always the best people to be responsible for finding

7. *Holy Trinity, Tunbridge Wells, now demolished.* (PHOTOGRAPH: NATIONAL MONUMENTS RECORD).

new users, although they can play a useful role in an advisory capacity. In the past they were hampered by inexperience, or had an interest in getting a church demolished, so deliberately didn't try to find a new use. Too often they resented offers of help and advice from local voluntary organisations. The classic example of gross mis-management by a diocese is that of Holy Trinity, Tunbridge Wells, now demolished. However, many dioceses have been very sensitive to local opinion and have energetically sought new uses.

The Advisory Board for Redundant Churches has continually pressed for revision of the Pastoral Measure, both within and without its terms of reference. For example, the Pastoral Measure takes no account of the fittings of churches. As a result of pressure by the Board and others, a stained glass museum and repository were established in 1972 in Ely to store fine glass from churches due for demolition. But there is still no central repository for other fittings, although in 1974 the Church Commissioners issued a circular urging every diocese to appoint a Redundant Churches Furnishing Officer, responsible for making an inventory of furnishings, and seeing that they are allocated to other churches or suitably disposed of. As a result of this, several dioceses (but by no means all) have established repositories in redundant churches. There is still no provision for the preservation of gravestones and other external monuments, nor any source of funds to pay for their removal and storage, in cases where this is necessary.

There are other anomalies in the Advisory Board's terms of reference. For example they do not allow for the Board to take structural condition into account when offering advice, and it has on occasion refered to recommend demolition even though the decayed structure has made this inevitable in a church which was otherwise worth preserving.

A code of practice was drawn up by the Church Commissioners which helps to clarify the Pastoral Measure, which is incomprehensible to many as it stands. Since 1973 a working party has been drawing up a proposed revised Measure, and this may come before Parliament in 1980. It is probable that the revised Measure will propose the amalgamation of the Redundant Churches Fund and the Advisory Board, because in these times of economic stringency, priorities will have to be carefully assessed, which can better be done if both bodies operate by one set of terms of reference.

Our churches perform a vitally important role in our architectural and social heritage. Whatever the Pastoral Measure's faults, it does at least recognise this. In 1913, the Church of England undertook to look after its buildings, but it has failed in this, understandably, with financial stringencies making maintenance increasingly hard. But nevertheless, its very poverty militates against the demolition of fine old churches. Anti-conservationists within the dioceses should perhaps reflect that in an increasingly secular society, they will never again be able to afford to build churches which in their number and in their splendour silently preach more than a thousand sermons.

The continuing use of churches forms an integral part of urban and rural renewal. To keep these two problems separate we have included only urban examples in this chapter and have kept the three country churches for the second part of the book, The Countryside. The word 'urban' is used in the widest sense to include both inner city examples like All Saints at Oxford and London suburban examples like the churches at Streatham and Richmond. We would have preferred to take as examples the churches of a city like Norwich or York but found that such homogeneous groups were either too well known, their problems having been recognised well over a decade ago, or, by the ambitious nature of the programme, lacked individual examples of sufficient quality and significance. The churches at Streatham and Richmond, on the other hand, seem to us to be of particular relevance for the future. They are both examples of extended use whereby part of the space remains a church alternating with other uses, and part is converted to house new activities. In so far as the original use is preserved and the new activities are all for the benefit of the local community these conversions resemble the proposals, made in Chapter 7, The Changing Village, of making the church the focal point of parish life again, as it used to be in the late Middle Ages.

Although no longer in use as a church, the example at Manchester also fits the category of community centre. Of the other four examples two remain available to the general public and two have been put to private uses. Holy Trinity at Colchester joins the growing list of churches converted into museums and the Synagogue at Houston in Texas now makes an excellent theatre and base for a well-known company of actors. The Synagogue has the clear span necessary to accommodate an activity which requires width and good visibility, whereas the structural division into a narrow nave and two aisles, as is the case with Holy Trinity, restricts the choice of a new use. In this sense Classical churches like the other Holy Trinity at Southwark and All Saints at Oxford, both now lost to public use, have an advantage over Gothic and Neo-Gothic churches. The single wide-span structure of Holy Trinity can accommodate a full orchestra and was chosen in preference to a number of Victorian Gothic churches. Classical churches, moreover, are almost invariably raised on podia over crypts which can absorb ancillary accommodation that might otherwise encroach on the church proper. This is clearly illustrated in both Holy Trinity and All Saints where the crypts not only provide space for essential utilities but form an indispensable extension to the main activity on the floor above.

ST LEONARD'S CHURCH, STREATHAM

New use An example of extended use. The church continues to play an important part in the religious life of the parish, but is also used for concerts, plays and conferences.

Architect Douglas Feast and David Roberts of the Douglas Feast Partnership

Client Streatham Parochial Church Council

Site In the London residential suburb of Streatham.

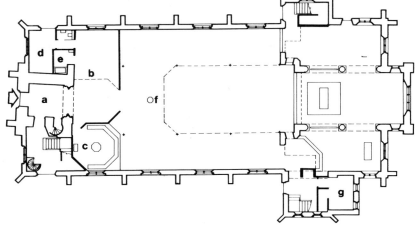

1. Plan at ground floor level.

2. Long section looking north. The side galleries have been joined at the west end to provide an organ loft. 1 mm = 1 ft.

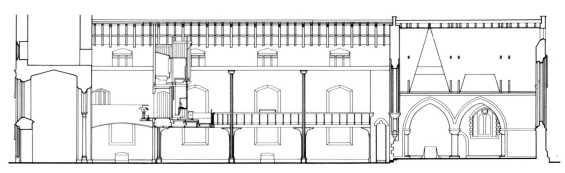

History The church is a mixture of fifteenth century (tower), 1830 (nave) and late Victorian (chancel). It was gutted by fire in May 1975—with only the tower and spire, the external walls, stone arches and cast-iron columns left standing. The Parochial Church Council sensibly decided to re-build the church so that it could be used not only for religious services but also for conferences, plays and concerts.

Character The tower is built of flint and rubble, the nave of Roman cement rendered in imitation of Bath stone and the chancel is faced with Kentish ragstone. Before the fire, the original roof was vaulted, there was high choir and clergy seating on either side of the chancel, blocking it off from the aisles, in one of which was the vestry. A Victorian rood screen stood in the main chancel arch.

Work done The fabric of the building was restored. The window traceries were faithfully renewed in Bath stone and the stonework, badly spalled by the fire, was cleaned but otherwise left alone. A new trussed roof was erected, flat over the aisles and pitched over the nave, with triangular dormer windows passing light through a false clerestory over the altar in the chancel. The

exposed Douglas fir contrasts attractively with the whitewashed walls, turned very pale brown by the use of boiled linseed oil as a binder. The chancel aisles were opened up, and the choir and organ moved to a new gallery at the west end of the nave. The side galleries were reconstructed to a steeper rake and have been carpeted for sitting on until funds make the installation of proper seating possible. The most westerly bay of the nave was divided off to form a narthex (partly double-height) and small chapel (with vestries at gallery level). The screen which makes this separation is solid except where the small hexagonal chapel for weekday services required a view of the church. Here the plateglass window enables the chapel to form a visual part of the nave space while remaining acoustically and thermally separate. York stone, which before only paved part of the original nave, now extends throughout the public areas.

Accommodation Space for services, concerts, plays, conferences.
Small space for evening services, narthex, office, kitchen, bookshop.

Date of completion May 1977

Cost Approximately £260,000

3. Externally the church remains unchanged, though the new dormers and clerestory can be glimpsed from further away. The spire was spared by the fire and has been strengthened to take a new peal of eight bells. (PHOTOGRAPH: IRENE BOOTH).

4. *View from the chancel into the nave, showing the two side galleries joining at the west end. The new chancel roof incorporates triangular dormer windows to throw light on the altar.* (PHOTOGRAPH: BILL TOOMEY).

5. *View from the new Chapel of Unity, a small hexagonal space for weekday services, divided from the nave by a plate glass screen.* (PHOTOGRAPH: BILL TOOMEY).

ST. MATTHIAS CHURCH, RICHMOND, SURREY

New use An example of extended use. The church is still used for worship, but the conversion has also made space for a community centre.

Architect Hutchison, Locke and Monk

Client Richmond Parochial Church Council

Site The church occupies a dominant site at the conjunction of several roads on the top of Richmond Hill. The surrounding neighbourhood is mainly middle-class residential, but large houses are increasingly being converted into flats and bedsitters. A new estate has recently been built nearby.

History The church was designed as a chapel of ease for the Richmond Hill residents by George Gilbert Scott, and consecrated in 1858. The spire was completed in 1862, and later additions are the south porch, the chapel (built as a memorial of World War I), the clergy vestry, the organ blower room and, more recently, the timber-framed meeting rooms at the west end of the nave. The church is one of three in the parish, and has a lively congregation, so there is no question of its becoming redundant. But it was felt that this area of Richmond lacked community facilities especially with the recent influx of residents who needed a local centre in which to meet their neighbours. The architects were engaged in 1975 to examine 'whether the building could be adapted to provide a range of welfare, social and recreational

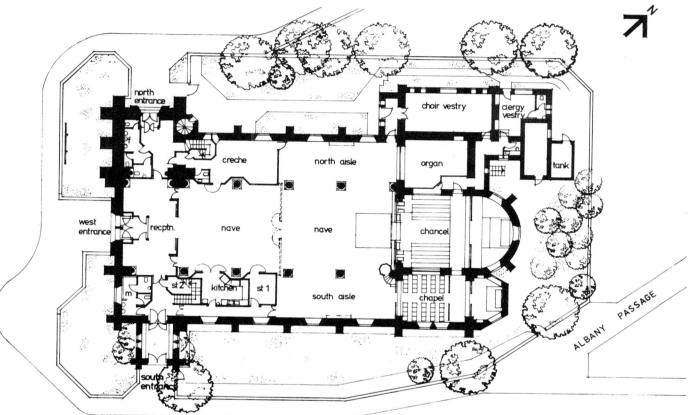

1. Ground floor plan.

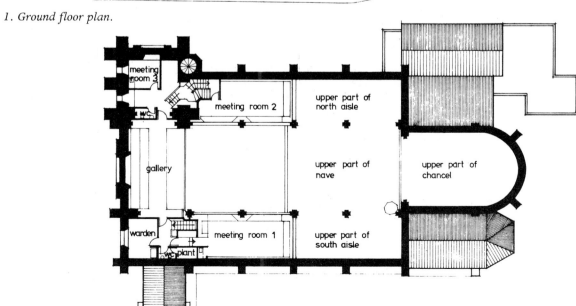

2. First floor plan.

3. View from the south-west from Friars Stile Road. The boundary wall has been reduced in height to make the west entrance doors more inviting. (PHOTO-GRAPH: RICHARD BRYANT).

4. The nave looking east. Stacking chairs have replaced the old pews which have been used in the wall panelling. The beam across the nave supports the track for the sliding screens which divide the nave.

5. The south aisle meeting room on the first floor. (PHOTOGRAPH: RICHARD BRYANT).

(PHOTOGRAPH: RICHARD BRYANT).

facilities, and thereby be used by a wider section of the community than at present, whilst still maintaining its primary function as a place for Christian worship'. The architects submitted a scheme, which was accepted, and work began in the summer of 1977.

Character The church is described by Pevsner as 'Richmond's grandest church'. A tall, bare, Gothic building, it is roughly rectangular with an apsidal chancel, off which are a number of small rooms for the organ, vestries etc. The interior is divided into a nave and two aisles by arcades of lancet arches above which is a clerestory. The pitched roof is of timber, exposed on the inside, and covered with slates. There is a delicately carved wood screen enclosing the chancel. The west or main door is surmounted by a large rose window, and to the left of this rises the tall spire.

Work done A two-storey construction of concrete and glass was erected in the west end of the nave, and extended around part of the north and south aisles. Divisions have been kept clear of the main features to emphasise the original design. As little change as possible has been inflicted on the fabric, especially the carving, so that if a future generation wanted to return it to its original form, they could do so simply by dismantling and making good. The arches were glazed above the springing line and filled below with screens made from the old pews. Inside the west door, a glass lobby was formed, so that passers-by can see the activity inside. The nave can be divided into two separate spaces by large sliding screen doors, again made from the old pews; and a curtain can screen the chancel during secular activities. Movable seating can be arranged to seat from 250 to 520 people (including the gallery at the west end). Work externally was limited to re-arranging the boundary walls and paving and repairing the stonework around the west entrance. Some of the stained-glass windows were altered for ventilation purposes and ventilation hoods were made in the roof. The church was re-wired and plumbed, with two lavatories installed on either side of the west entrance. A new gas-fired boiler was installed at first-floor level to heat the new rooms. The old boiler was retained for the main body of the church.

Accommodation Ground floor level— entrance lobby, reception/coffee bar area, nave which can be used as one or two spaces, kitchen, lavatories, crèche. First floor level—three meeting rooms, gallery, warden's office, boiler room, lavatory, void over east end of church.

Date of completion November 1978

Cost £150,000 (not including furniture, fees, VAT, etc).

FIRST CHURCH OF CHRIST SCIENTIST, DAISY BANK, MANCHESTER

New use Arts centre for the Elizabeth Gaskell College of Education

Architect City of Manchester Architects' Department

Client City of Manchester

Site The church is situated in a residential street in a mainly middle-class area of Manchester not far from Victoria Park.

History Construction of the First Church of Christ Scientist began in 1930 and the building is Edgar Wood's only major work in Manchester. Until 1971 the church was maintained in immaculate condition with the help of a bequest, but in December of that year, the church closed and became a target for vandals, who caused some serious damage over the ensuing years.

1. *Ground floor plan.*
2. *The high gable entrance with turret and chimney* (PHOTOGRAPH: TONY COTTRELL).
3. *The right-hand leg of the Y seen through a chiselled stone arch.* (PHOTOGRAPH: TONY COTTRELL).

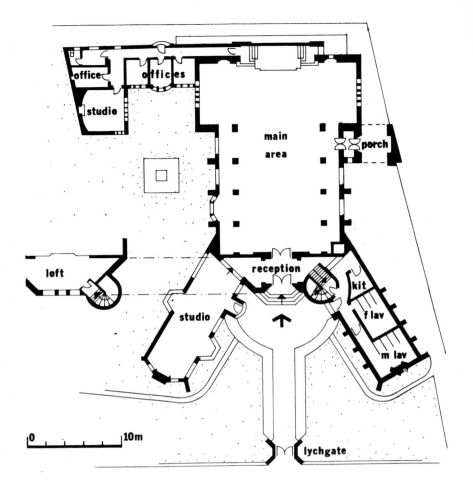

114

4. The main area being used for rehearsal by a local drama group. (PHOTOGRAPH: TONY COTTRELL).

Some important pieces of furniture designed by Wood are now to be found in the Whitworth Art Gallery, Manchester, and much of the rest was removed to other Christian Scientist churches. Some three years later the City of Manchester had the foresight to save this important building. The Elizabeth Gaskell College of Education (now merged with two other colleges to form the City of Manchester College of Higher Education) persuaded the City to allocate the church to the College's use as an arts centre.

Character Sir Nikolaus Pevsner described this church as 'one of the most original buildings of 1930 in England or indeed anywhere . . . indispensable in a survey of the development of the twentieth century church design in all England'.

The church was planned as an inverted letter Y. The wings spring from a steep gabled end with a round arched doorway surmounted by a very unusual round-headed window shaped like a cross. To the right is a short fat round tower, housing the stairs which lead to the organ loft. The spaces inside rise the full height of the building, and the roof trusses are left exposed.

The huge rounded arches of the aisles are important for their early use of reinforced concrete. The screen is unusual with its ornate detail in wood picked out in cream and green paint and gold leaf. Wood, it is said, found his inspiration for this in the Near East.

Work done The fabric of the building was restored, and the original green Swedish marble on the panels fronting the dais and at the base of the columns has been repaired with matching Verde Viana marble from Portugal. Additional accommodation has been added to the east of the buildings by the architects, to harmonise as far as possible with the original structure. The extension houses administrative offices, a technician's office and a small studio. In the organ loft, the old organ, which was badly vandalised, was replaced with a new smaller one.

Accommodation East wing—studio. West wing—kitchen and lavatories. Chapel—adaptable space for performances of dance and acting classes.

Date of completion July 1976

HOLY TRINITY CHURCH, COLCHESTER

New use Agricultural museum

Architect Peter Masters, Colchester Borough Architect

Client Colchester Cultural Activities Committee

Site On the south side of Culver Street, a non-residential area in the East Anglian town of Colchester.

History Being sited in an area already well served by three large Anglican churches, the church became redundant in the 1950s, and for many years was the victim of damage caused by weather and vandals. The church stood empty until 1964–5 when it was proposed as the University Church. Re-roofing and heating work proceeded for this purpose, but the university decided that it did not want a church. The suggestion that the Council take it over as a museum came in 1967 but first another idea, that the local Technical College use it as a rehearsal and lunchtime concert hall, was actively pursued. These plans, however, were also dropped, the Borough Council once again considered its use for a museum and finally the church was conveyed to the Council on 14 July, 1972, for the sum of £100. The building is subject to a covenant under Section 62 of the Pastoral Measure 1968 in that it is to be used as a museum for community purposes.

Character The exceptionally fine west tower and west wall of the nave date from the eleventh century, but the rest of the church dates from the fourteenth and fifteenth centuries. The east vestry, north chapel and north aisle were added in the nineteenth century, a mixture which is reflected in the asymmetry of

2. The west tower.

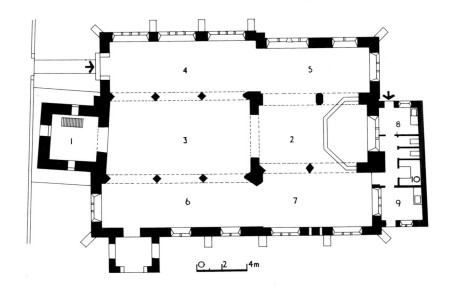

1. Ground floor plan.

1. TOWER	6. SOUTH AISLE
2. CHANCEL	7. SOUTH CHAPEL
3. NAVE	8. ATTENDANT
4. NORTH AISLE	9. OFFICE
5. NORTH CHAPEL	10. STORE

this interesting church. The plan is of a nave and two aisles separated by Gothic arcades resting on shafted columns. The tower ($11\frac{1}{2}$ft square) is built in three stages, each with an offset plinth. It has small, round-headed windows and traces of a round-headed wall arcade occur on the third stage.

The walls of the chancel, chapel and aisle are of flint-rubble and septaria with

courses of Roman brick and dressings of Reigate stone. The tower incorporates even more Roman brick and Roman dressings. The pitched roofs are tiled.

Work done The work required was mostly of a restorative kind. The walls were cleaned and repaired where necessary. A large hole in the roof was mended and stonework was restored. The windows were mostly too damaged for restoration and were replaced with clear glass leaded lights incorporating some opening ventilators at high level. The internal porch door was replaced by a fully glazed one, and a pair of new external doors were fitted. The electrical installation, though existing, was extended to light the exhibits and operate the working models.

Accommodation Exhibition space, office, store, two lavatories, attendant's room.

Date of completion 1972

Cost £23,000

3. View looking towards the west end. (PHOTOGRAPHS: COURTESY OF THE COLCHESTER ESSEX MUSEUM).

SYNAGOGUE, HOUSTON, TEXAS

New use Denney Theatre

Architect Harvin Moore-Barry Moore

Client Houston Independent School District

Site Near downtown Houston, fronting on Austin Street at the corner of Holman Street. Since 1971 the High School for Performing and Visual Arts has been located here.

History The building was erected in 1924 by the Congregation of Temple Beth Israel, designed by the architect Joseph Finger. In 1949 Irving Klein remodelled the original synagogue: air conditioning was installed, large windows were bricked in, the interior was panelled, the lighting modernized and an educational wing constructed. The property was bought by the school district in 1965 shortly after the congregation moved to a new suburban synagogue. From 1965 to 1971 the buildings were used to house various adult education programmes; and in 1971, when HSPVA was founded, it established itself temporarily in the building. In 1976 the synagogue was remodelled to house a teaching theatre.

Character The brown brick building with cast concrete portico columns presents a classical façade to the street, typical of religious structures of the period. The interior is distinguished by a large stained skylight featuring a Star of David and four Menorahs, a heavily ornamented plaster ceiling, stained glass windows over the existing balcony, and a carved stone archway which formerly framed the Ark. All such special architectural features of the building's religious past were repaired and carefully restored.

Work done All component parts of a professional theatre are included in this teaching theatre—a 'floating' stage, overhead stage grid, orchestra pit, backstage areas, scene shop, prop shop, box office, storage, lobby, technical booth for light and sound control, public lavatories, dressing rooms and classrooms. A laboratory theatre is being built by student design classes in the basement.

All component parts were fitted into the virtually empty but sound shell of the building. Much new space was gained under the new tiered seating.

The client's requirements made priorities of the stage, orchestra pit and auditorium. These took up the greater

1. Ground floor plan.

2. Plan of upper level.

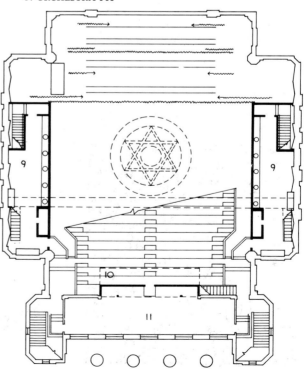

1. FOYER	7. STAGE
2. BOX OFFICE	8. MECHANICAL
3. STORAGE	9. DRESSING ROOM
4. SCENE SHOP	10. TECHNICAL BOOTH ABOVE
5. PROP SHOP	11. DRAMA CLASSROOM
6. ORCHESTRA PIT	

3. The colonnaded entrance façade on Austin Street.

part of the building and the backstage and dressing room facilities were placed, for spatial economy, one on top of the other by means of a new mezzanine floor.

The stage can be enlarged when necessary with a temporary platform over the pit which is supported on a grid of thirteen battens. All the draperies can be removed if required. The lighting can be controlled from five different positions at the front of the house. There is an elaborate sound system including an intercom connecting eleven stations.

The chairs in the auditorium can be removed, exposing the carpeted steps, which provide seating for a larger number of people.

Accommodation Basement—laboratory theatre and public lavatories.
Ground floor—foyer, main theatre, stage, backstage workshops and storage, orchestra pit.
Upper level 1—dressing rooms, drama classroom.
Upper level 2—technical booth, lighting bridge.

Date of completion October, 1976

Cost $475,000; $29.70 per sq ft, including lighting and dimming equipment and all furnishings.

4. The auditorium looking towards the technical booth at the back. (PHOTOGRAPH: RICK GARDNER).
5. The auditorium looking towards the stage. (PHOTOGRAPH: RICK GARDNER).

ALL SAINTS' CHURCH, OXFORD

New use Library for Lincoln College, Oxford

Architect Robert Potter of the Brandt, Potter, Hare Partnership

Client Lincoln College

Site The church stands in the High Street on the corner of Turl Street and forms one of the monumental 'incidents' in that famous street. Its tower and spire provides one of the two major punctuations in the otherwise low façades from Magdalen Tower to Carfax Tower. Seen down the narrow Turl they dramatically close the view which starts at the open end by Trinity gates. The small churchyard makes informal gaps for small trees to break through the stone frontages of these central streets.

History The present building was erected in 1699 by public subscription, immediately after the collapse of the medieval church on the same site, to the designs of the brilliant amateur Henry Aldrich, Dean of Christ Church, an early and devout Palladian who left behind several notable works in Oxford and a book on architecture. The tower is not entirely his and may owe something to the collaboration of Hawksmoor. The church, which had been the collegiate church of the adjacent Lincoln College since the latter's foundation in 1427, was declared redundant by the diocese in 1972 and assigned to the college for use as a library.

Character Aldrich's church is an oblong box of three by five 15ft bays, divided by Corinthian pilasters internally and externally, and surmounted by an attic, giving a total interior height of 45ft. The massive belfry tower abuts on to the west wall, and the west bay also has columned and pedimented doorways facing the High Street and Turl Street. Internally this west bay was fitted in the nineteenth century with a gallery cutting across the heads of the doorways. Outside, the giant order stands on a pedestal zone with blank segmental arches in each bay; inside, this zone was masked by the high oak box pews on whose backs the main pilasters rested without any base mouldings, giving a very odd effect after the removal of the pews in the 1880s.

Work done The essence of the conversion scheme was to provide sufficient space for a library accommodating approximately 5000ft of shelving and, if practicable, to house the original

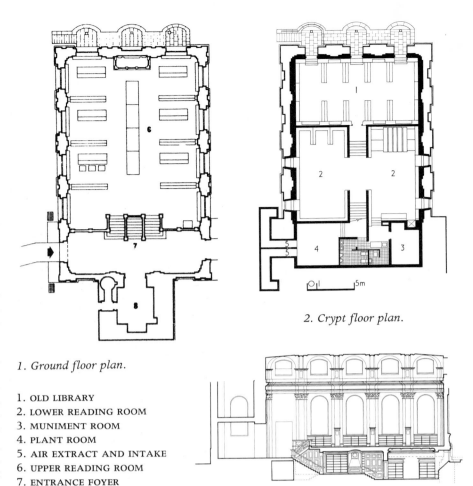

1. Ground floor plan.

1. OLD LIBRARY
2. LOWER READING ROOM
3. MUNIMENT ROOM
4. PLANT ROOM
5. AIR EXTRACT AND INTAKE
6. UPPER READING ROOM
7. ENTRANCE FOYER
8. LOWER ROOM

2. Crypt floor plan.

3. Section.

seventeenth-century library and its fittings, together with convenient space for up to 100 readers. The solution adopted was to double the available floor area by sinking a basement within the depth of Aldrich's foundations and raising the floor level over the four eastern bays to the tops of the lost pews so that the main order again rests on ground some 4½ft higher than the old floor. This changes the interior proportion, though visually it is perhaps nearer to the original effect than after the removal of the pews. The result conforms to what Aldrich's book prescribed for a 'Corinthian Oecus'—a hall of three by five bays whose pilasters may stand either on pedestals or on the floor, and which exploits the proportion of three by five in its elevations as well.

It was discovered that the sixteenth-century senior library which had been re-sited in 1906, could be adapted with very minor modifications and accommodated in the eastern part of the basement. The rest of the college library consists of a rare books room and a general working library of modern books used daily by undergraduates, both as a place of reference and as a congenial work space free from noise

and interruption. All these spaces have been accommodated on the lower floor of the church, lit by windows made in the blank segmental arches mentioned above.

The entrance is by the west bay, cleared of its Victorian gallery but left at the original floor level. A central flight of steps leads to the lower level with a double flight to each side for the approach to the upper level of the remaining four bays, which now constitute the main reading room. This has been furnished with eighteenth-century type bookpresses jutting out from each of the great pilasters on either side, forming 12ft square working bays between them. In these, desks with further shelves have been formed out of contemporary woodwork. The best of the carved panels have been incorporated in a balustrade dividing the raised floor from the lower level entrance bay.

The contemporary carved stone altarpiece has been retained but raised to the new level; and the several good monuments massed on the blank west walls, the ledger stones being incorporated in the pavement of the entrance bay. The windows, filled with indifferent Victorian grisaille and figures, were re-

4. View from split-level entrance up to the main reading room and down to the lower floor. (PHOTOGRAPH: J. W. THOMAS).
5. The interior before conversion showing the floor at the lower level and the pilasters sitting on a dado. (PHOTOGRAPH: J. W. THOMAS).

glazed to the old five by three module (known from a surviving fragment) in plain glazing of Neo-Georgian type. Double glazing has been provided for sound insulation from the busy High Street.

The interior has now regained its former beauty, the honey-coloured stone responding well to careful cleaning, and the elaborate plaster ceiling to redecoration. Some original colour was discovered in the heraldic charges on the ceiling but most of the shields had been overpainted at some time. Both were cleaned and refreshed but not repainted.

The exterior stonework, long neglected and sometimes clumsily repaired, has been thoroughly renovated, partly through a grant from the Historic Buildings Council. The cost of the rest of the work was met by the College and its old members as well as a number of individual benefactors. For three months before the start of the contract, excavation of the interior was carried out by the Oxford Archaeological Society who recorded all traces found of the medieval church and earlier structures on the site.

Accommodation Lower ground floor—senior library, rare books room, working library.
Upper ground floor—reading room.

Date of completion October 1975

Cost £392,000

6. All Saints from the High Street. (PHOTOGRAPH: J. W. THOMAS).

HOLY TRINITY, SOUTHWARK, LONDON

New use Rehearsal hall for the London Symphony Orchestra and the Royal Philharmonic Orchestra

Architect Arup Associates (Architects, Engineers and Quantity Surveyors)

Client The Trustees of Henry Wood Hall

Site In south-east London, well situated in relation to the two important music centres, the Festival Hall and the Barbican, the church is in the centre of an early nineteenth-century square, of which it is an integral part. Trinity Church Square and the adjoining Merrick Square were declared a conservation area in 1968.

History The church, designed by Francis Bedford and built in 1824, was the first part of Trinity Church Square to be completed. It has not been used as a church since 1960, and was the first church in the diocese to be declared redundant under the Pastoral Measure of 1968. Several proposals were put before the Redundant Churches Committee, including flats with a swimming pool as well as a petrol station. Finally in 1971 the plan for using it as a rehearsal hall was accepted. Work was scheduled to begin on October 1st, 1973, but the preceding night the building was gutted by fire, started by a smouldering pile of leaves abandoned by children. A survey revealed that the only heavy damage had been sustained by the roof and the galleries, so the client resolved to continue with the conversion.

Character The Greek Revival Holy Trinity has two distinctive external features: an entrance portico in the form of an Ionic temple front and a tall steeple carried apparently by the portico but, in fact, supported on the walls of the vestibule. When it comes to the interior, the structural division into nave and aisles of Gothic churches, whether medieval or Victorian, is a restricting factor in accommodating a full orchestra, and in their search, Arup Associates rejected three Victorian churches for this reason. The interior dimensions are 100ft in length by 60ft in width by 35ft in height. It also had the advantage of a single-span roof structure and a 60 by 40ft clear space at the choir end (where the galleries were at one time cut back), ideally suited to the accommodation of even the largest orchestras.

Work done The ground under the crypt was excavated and a new floor constructed 1ft 6in below the old level to provide sufficient head-room. The foun-

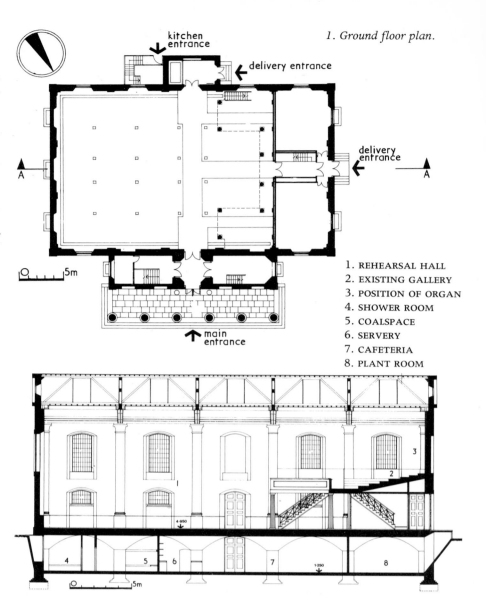

1. Ground floor plan.

1. REHEARSAL HALL
2. EXISTING GALLERY
3. POSITION OF ORGAN
4. SHOWER ROOM
5. COALSPACE
6. SERVERY
7. CAFETERIA
8. PLANT ROOM

Long Section A·A

2. Section AA.

dations were underpinned, a job which was interrupted by the discovery and removal of five or six hundred coffins bricked up beneath the portico. New steel roof trusses replaced the old timber ones which were destroyed in the fire, and this provided more space for the installation and maintenance of mechanical and electrical services. The original lead roof had already been replaced with copper, which was used for the new roof. The floor of the choir was brought down to the level of the nave floor, providing a 60ft by 60ft space for the orchestra. The gallery at the west end, destroyed by the fire, was rebuilt with one bay only on the south and north sides. The new gallery now accommodates a choir of up to 200 and a fine new organ given to the building in memory of the late Angus Menzies by a trust formed for the purpose by his friends. Beneath the gallery are two recording rooms. The windows have

been double-glazed for sound insulation, and the fifteen ceiling panels contain an elaborate lighting and ventilation system to modern specifications. The crypt, its floor 18in lower than before, houses libraries, a restaurant, storage space and services. The old piers and brick arches were sandblasted and the floor tiled to provide a cosy, intimate atmosphere. The old church pews have been restored and now furnish the bar and restaurant.

Accommodation Crypt—two orchestral libraries, bar, restaurant, instrument store, services, lavatories, showers and cloakroom facilities.
Nave—rehearsal hall for full orchestra, recording rooms under the gallery.
Gallery—accommodation for choir and organ.

Date of completion June 1975

Cost £557,000

4. The cafeteria in the crypt with the old pews adapted as seating.

3. The entrance portico and steeple.

5. The rehearsal hall seen from the gallery. The rehearsal area has a new timber floor. Elsewhere the old stone floor has been preserved.

6 Railway stations

Introduction

A great deal has been written about the railway age and its miracles of engineering. This chapter deals with only a handful of small stations which have been converted to new uses. These include a garden centre (part of a larger recreation complex which includes a new swimming pool), a sports hall, a restaurant and offices, and two transport museums. Two of the examples, at Darlington and New London, Connecticut, still operate as railway stations, with part of the building converted to other uses. At Darlington the extended use is a railway museum and the old track aptly displays old locomotives. One station, at Tintern in the Wye Valley, is included in the following chapter, 'The Changing Village'. It belongs more properly to the countryside and is of a type with which England is particularly well endowed.

In Britain 3,539 stations have been closed and over 100 demolished, the majority of them small ones. In the United States only some 20,000 out of the original 40,000 stations survive and many of these are no longer in use. The plight of Britain's unique railway heritage was well demonstrated in the recent exhibition 'Off the Rails'.* Successive British governments were castigated for neglecting the railways in an age of increasing energy shortage, in favour of heavy investment in road building. The reduction in services, cut-back in staff and automation have left many railway buildings redundant. In trying to find new owners for these, British Rail have generally asked too much and have often failed to sell them. British Rail have also failed to maintain many old stations that are still in use. The most vulnerable part are the canopies of ironwork and timber, 'the feature' as Gillian Darley describes it in the catalogue of the exhibition, 'that distinguishes the small station from all other structures of the era'. There are many examples of canopies being allowed to fall into disrepair until they become dangerous. At that point they are hastily taken down for the sake of public safety, to be replaced by crude modern substitutes. Because of the effort and expense involved in exercising their legal powers, local authorities have so far seemed reluctant to secure the proper maintenance of a structure by British Rail.

*'Off the Rails—saving railway architecture', held at the RIBA Heinz Gallery, 19 January to 11 March, 1977. Catalogue edited by David Pearce and Marcus Binney.

Much of the delight and interest of small stations lies in minor parts and fixtures such as footbridges, signal boxes, platform seats and notice boards, most of which are well represented in this chapter. An attractive footbridge is preserved at Monkwearmouth. Tintern, now a visitors' centre (see 'The Changing Village', p. 167), has converted its charming signal box into a warden's office and tool shed, while the high-level platform of the restored water-tower provides good views of the valley for the visitors who come to learn about the area before exploring it.

In the United States most of the stations still standing are owned by the railroad companies, who have little need for them. According to a recent report, 'they are given only token maintenance while the basic building fabric is eaten away; or they are used on a limited basis with no attempt at maintenance; or they are abandoned altogether'.† Amtrak, established by Congress in 1971 to ensure that passenger services did not disappear altogether, only operates over the road-beds of the different companies and pays them for the operation of its trains. It does not own rights-of-way, stations, fixed equipment or air rights and so has no interest in preserving old stations, a responsibility which still falls on the railroad companies. The task of preservation, the same report goes on to say, 'demands action by the federal government, by state and local government and by the private sector'.

Yet America appears to have been more successful in converting railway stations, especially the larger ones, to new uses. While St. Pancras in London continues to languish, Washington's Union Station has been active as a government visitors' centre for some years. The vast and impressive Terminal Station at Chattanooga in Tennessee was rescued by a group of local businessmen and converted into a restaurant and commercial centre. At Savannah the early Central Georgia Station (1860) now serves as a tourist reception centre and at Yuma in Arizona the more modest Southern Pacific Railroad Depot has become the Yuma Fine Arts Association. Perhaps the most ambitious schemes of all have been the conversions of the Pittsburgh and Lake Erie Railroad Station into a shopping centre, hotel and office building, and of the Union Station at Indianapolis into a commercial complex combined with a mass-transit station still used by Amtrak.

In Europe the station at Strasbourg has been successfully converted into a market hall and the Gare d'Orsay in Paris, briefly included for its temporary uses in the chapter entitled 'Found Space', will become a museum of the nineteenth century, filling the cultural gap between the Louvre and the Centre Pompidou. In England the destruction of Euston and New Street, Birmingham, and the recent threat to Liverpool Street and Broad Street stations are a reminder that only the strength of public opinion can prevent an official and so-called rational attempt at demolition and redevelopment. 'Save', the organisation which organised the exhibition 'Off the Rails', has proposed the formation of a Trust. It points out that there is already a Transport Trust for engines and other railway and transport relics; that there is already a National Trust for historic places, a Redundant Churches Fund for unwanted churches. So why not a Trust to take responsibility, and where necessary raise money, for interesting railway buildings?

†*Reusing Railroad Stations*—a report from Educational Facilities Laboratories 1974. Available from EFL, 477th Madison Avenue, New York, N.Y. 10022.

POCKLINGTON RAILWAY STATION, YORKSHIRE

New use Sports centre

Architect Arthur Quarmby Associates

Client Pocklington School

Site The station is situated on the edge of the small market town of Pocklington and was at one time a significant feature in the life of the town and of the neighbouring school.

History The station was built in about 1847 by Thomas Hudson, the 'railway king' of York, to the designs of the architect G. T. Andrews. It was closed down in 1965 as part of the Beeching economies. In 1966, a new headmaster, Guy Willatt, proposed to his Governors that the school should acquire the station from the then owners, Pocklington Rural District Council, with a view to turning it into a covered play area. The negotiations progressed satisfactorily and the advice of the Sports Council was sought on conversion. It was decided that it should also be made available to sporting associations from the town and surrounding district. A more ambitious programme was therefore devised to meet the requirements of the Sports Council who were able to award a substantial grant towards the cost of the work.

Character A small single-storey building, linked to the station master's house by ancillary rooms. The elevation to the road has a shallow porch recessed behind five arches. The construction is of a soft, locally produced brick with ashlar sandstone quoins, cornices and other facings. The raised platforms and the large roof were added some 30 years later. More recently, part of the main façade was destroyed to admit a boarded and glazed extension to the ticket office.

Work done The station is 'listed' as a Grade II building of architectural merit and alterations were planned with great discretion. The large openings at the east and west ends of the main building were built up with a matching brick, the walls being set back to preserve the impact of the heavy quoins. A clerestory window allows the trusses at either end to express themselves. Internally the platforms were removed and a new floor of composition wood was laid. The walls, which had been painted, were sandblasted and treated with a silicone solution to eliminate dusting and to bring out the colour of the bricks. The extension to the ticket office was removed and the original design restored, using local bricks recovered from the demolished

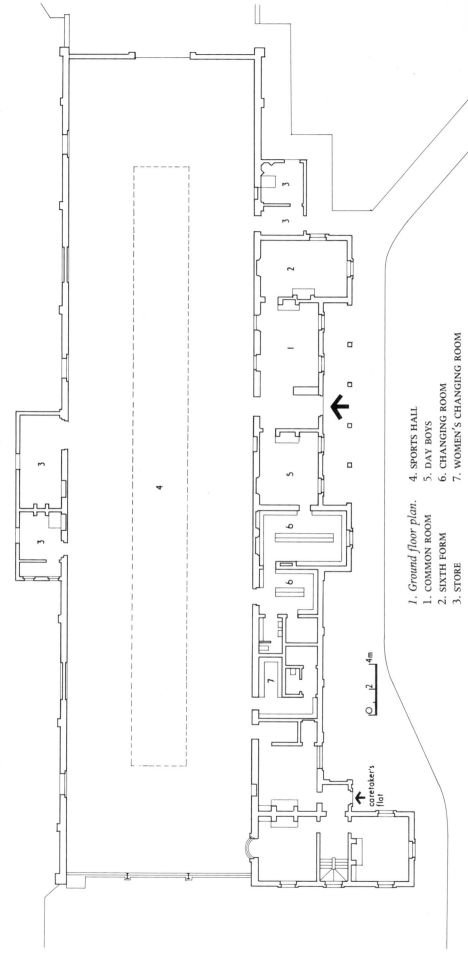

1. Ground floor plan.

1. COMMON ROOM
2. SIXTH FORM
3. STORE
4. SPORTS HALL
5. DAY BOYS
6. CHANGING ROOM
7. WOMEN'S CHANGING ROOM

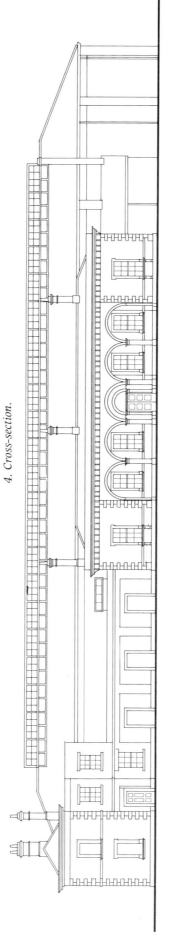

2. The station shed in a derelict condition and, 3, after conversion to a sports hall.

4. Cross-section.

0 2 4m

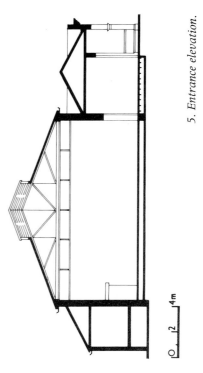

5. Entrance elevation.

0 2 4m

platforms and sandstone matched exactly with that of the adjacent window facing. The missing window frames were replaced to match those existing.

The hall provides facilities and accommodation for badminton, tennis, volley ball, cricket nets, fencing, indoor football, table tennis and basketball, as well as ancillary facilities. The stationmaster's house had an attractive bay window overlooking the platforms and track. This has been preserved and protected with a single, virtually invisible curve of clear polycarbonate. The window almost fulfills its original supervisory purpose in that the house has been modernised under a separate contract and is now the home of the school's sports master who will become custodian of the hall when he retires. It is a matter of regret that the budget was not sufficient either to allow for the façade to be delicately cleaned and the corroded stonework restored, or to permit the outdoor playing areas to be completed as planned. But it is hoped that these will form part of a subsequent operation.

Accommodation Sports hall, men's and women's changing rooms, lavatories, showers, refreshment room and recreation rooms.

Date of completion February 1974

Cost £50,000

DARLINGTON NORTH ROAD RAILWAY STATION, YORKSHIRE

New use An example of extended use with part of the station converted into a railway museum and part retained as a station.

Architect Hayton, Lee and Braddock, in collaboration with G. Lowes, Darlington Borough Architect.

Client Darlington North Road Station Museum Trust

Site The station stands on the west side of North Road, Darlington, to the south of the railway line which now runs to Darlington Bank Top Station. The area to the south side of the station once accommodated coal depôts, an old lime depôt (now used as a car repair workshop), carriage works, and a locomotive scrap yard.

History The Stockton and Darlington railway, the world's first public steam railway, first operated in 1825 with a single track. Although at the beginning passengers travelled on the train, it was primarily intended to carry coal from the pits in north-west Durham to the River Tees at Stockton. In 1842 the present station was built to accommodate the passengers who before had waited in the goods warehouse on the other side of North Road. The railway shed behind the building originally consisted of two sections divided by a wall, but later the station was enlarged by replacing the wall with a row of cast-iron columns. In 1894 a second track was at last installed, making the platform into an island reached by a wooden footbridge.

From 1939 the passenger services gradually decreased. Since 1972 only one track has been in use, making half the station redundant. Even before this, discussions regarding the use of the station as a museum had taken place, leading to the formation of the North Road Station Museum Trust. Work began in 1974 with the help of Darlington Borough Council and other interested bodies. The museum was opened in September 1975 by the Duke of Edinburgh. It won commendations in the 1975 British Tourist Authority 'Come to Britain' trophy and the 1976 R.I.C.S./*The Times* Conservation Award Scheme.

Character The station is a long, low building with a first storey only over the central section. In this section is the main entrance approached via a long shallow porch supported on slender cast-iron columns. Large sash windows pierce the walls at regular intervals, giving the façade a light, graceful appearance. The two spaces which make up the station are regular rectangles, with the rafters and cast-iron beams and columns exposed to view. The back section, still used by British Rail passengers, is open at either end, containing a platform and the single remaining track. The front section contains the now redundant track and platform, as well as the station building. A spiral staircase of cast-iron leads to the upper rooms, and the old wooden stairs and footbridge span the track. The platforms are lit by a small clerestory and by roof glazing.

Work done This consisted of restoration work to the building as a whole and the conversion of one part into a railway museum. The row of cast-iron columns, which ran the length of the old 'island' platform, were once again walled in, although around each pillar the wall was stepped back and glazed to maintain some link between the two halves of the station. The ends of the museum building were enclosed with a small extension at either end, obviating the need to cloak the existing cast-iron columns. Glass walls and pitched roof glazing let in light and echo the original appearance of the station.

The track is used to display old locomotives and at one platform edge a viewing area has been formed to give close-up views of their wheels. The platform level now continues around either end of the track—at the west end by a renewable structure, so that the engines on show can be taken in or out if necessary through a large glazed door.

The old wiring was adequate and new spot-lighting was installed. Lavatories were improved and now include provision for the disabled. The architect went to great trouble to find old materials and fittings to match those in the gentleman's lavatory and other parts. The roof over the platform was stripped, defective timbers were replaced and the roof was re-covered with felt roofing tiles. Over the rest of the roof area, some making good with second-hand tiles was necessary. Other general repairs were undertaken and the existing booking office furnishings were restored as faithfully as possible. The whole building was redecorated.

Accommodation Exhibition areas— including wall-hung displays, old locomotives etc, model club, old booking office, lecture theatre, store, workshop, office, lavatories. A cafeteria and caretaker's flat are proposed.

Date of completion 1975

Cost £165,000

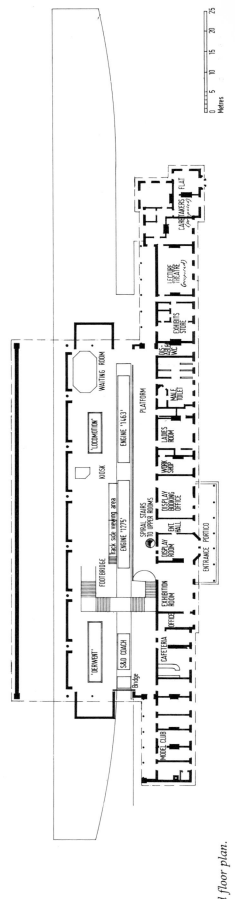

1. Ground floor plan.

128

2. The main façade with the entrance portico.

3. The restored spiral stair next to the old passenger entrance, and Engine 1275 in the foreground. (PHOTOGRAPH: K. PATISON).

4. The east end extension to the museum and the platform at the back which is still in use.

MONKWEARMOUTH STATION, TYNE AND WEAR

New use Transport museum

Architect Borough of Sunderland Architects' Department

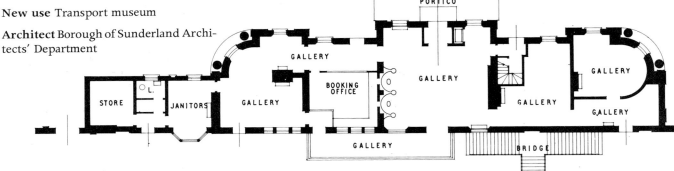

1. Ground floor plan.

Client Tyne & Wear County Council Museums Service

Site The station is situated on the still busy Middlesborough/Newcastle railway line in the middle of Monkwearmouth, a northern suburb of the industrial town of Sunderland. To the north of the station there is a large siding area and to the west of the tracks is the goods station, now disused.

History The station was designed by Thomas Moore, a local architect, and was commissioned by George Hudson, 'the railway king', who was anxious to mark his election as MP for Sunderland in 1845 by building a more impressive station than would be normal for a place like Monkwearmouth. The station was opened as the Sunderland terminus for the line to Gateshead and Newcastle, but in 1879 the railway was extended across the River Wear to a new station at Sunderland Central, and Monkwearmouth lost much of its importance. By the 1950s there were less than 100 passengers a day using the station, and by 1970 all railway use ceased. Its future was in jeopardy until it was bought by the Borough Council for conversion to a transport museum.

Character The station has an imposing Neo-Classical façade, with a pedimented Ionic portico of monumental proportions. This temple form is flanked by two wings decorated with Doric columns and pilasters. The building is of one storey except for the portico, behind which an extra floor is inserted over what was the booking hall. The platform at the back is overlooked by a bay window from the station master's office, and a footbridge crosses the track.

Work done The restoration of the exterior consisted of the repair and cleaning of all the stonework; the re-slating of the roof; the repair of the decorative ironwork; and the provision of new steel railings. The forecourt was

2. The imposing Neo-classical façade.
3. The station from the platform side showing the new glazed gallery extension.

also newly landscaped and floodlighting installed.

On adapting the interior to the needs of a museum, it was found necessary to build a new draught lobby at the entrance; to make alterations to internal walls and form new openings for improved circulation; to build a new glazed gallery on the platform for exhibits associated with that side of the station and to allow public viewing of the existing busy Newcastle to Middlesborough railway tracks.

Internally, repair work was carried out to all the existing joinery (doors, windows, skirtings, etc) and plastered surfaces. The floors were overhauled and a new carpet was laid. A new electrical installation and the provision of gas-fired convector heaters completed the rehabilitation programme.

Accommodation Ground floor—galleries for exhibits, booking office restored as an exhibit in its own right, two storerooms.
First floor—picture stores, office, workshop and reception area.

Date of completion 1972

Cost Approximately £50,000

4. The gallery or old booking hall with a glimpse of the gallery extension through the window. (PHOTOGRAPHS: TURNERS PHOTOGRAPHS LTD).

UNION RAILWAY STATION, NEW LONDON, CONNECTICUT

New use An example of extended use, with the building still partly used as a railway station, but with offices and a restaurant added.

Architect Anderson Notter Finegold Inc.

Client Union Station Associates of New London (a development entity of Anderson Notter Finegold Inc.).

Site In the centre of the town, overlooking the Thames river which flows through the business district towards Long Island Sound.

History Designed by the Boston architect Henry Hobson Richardson and completed after his death in 1887, the station has always had its detractors. It was built originally against the wishes of local inhabitants and as recently as 1973, when it had fallen into disrepair, it was criticised for blocking one of the few open views of the river from the town centre. In 1971 the New London Redevelopment Agency bought the station from its former joint owners, the Penn Central and the Central Vermont Railroad. A plan at this time to demolish the station as part of an urban renewal programme was successfully challenged by a group of private citizens, who set up the Union Railroad Station Trust to rescue and restore it. They invited the architects to produce a feasibility study which was undertaken from the point of view of a developer wanting a sufficient return on his money to make the job worthwhile. So convincing was this study that the architects were persuaded to form a new company, Union Station Associates of New London, with the purpose of undertaking the actual conversion work. They were encouraged by Amtrak, the National Railroad Passenger Corporation established by Congress in 1971 to ensure that passenger services did not disappear altogether. Having at first promoted the erection of plastic prefabs for new stations, Amtrak were turning to the idea of supporting the survival of existing stations. Their commitment to a 20-year lease of part of Union Station proved a decisive factor in enabling Union Station Associates to obtain the necessary finance, part of which came from government sources ($4 million for improving the area around the building) and part from private individuals.

Character The building, which foreshadows the Arts and Crafts style of a

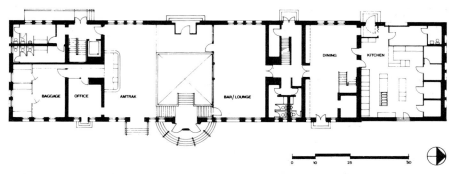

1. Ground floor plan.

2. North-south section looking east.

3. The station from the forecourt soon after it was built and 4, the same view today

(PHOTOGRAPH: RANDOLPH LANGENBACH).

decade later, is a handsome two-storey structure of intricate brickwork, with the upper storey slightly overhanging. The large window openings are divided into smaller units by brick mullions. The slated roof is hipped, its eaves line broken by a large central gable which is flanked by two heavily hooded dormer windows. The booking hall on the ground floor was a spacious room with a high ceiling of exposed oak beams and a timber-boarded floor. Most of the interior spaces on both floors were enriched by fittings and features, mainly in oak, such as fireplace surrounds and wainscoting.

Work done The whole of the exterior was restored: the slate roof was made good; the brickwork cleaned and pointed; the windows, doors and trim repaired and painted. Inside, a modern Amtrak station was designed within the historic structure. A large opening was made in the floor of the old booking hall and a grand staircase built to connect this with an additional airport-style waiting space and several small offices in the basement. Provision has been made at this lower level for a newsstand and florist. All the woodwork was stripped of later coats of paint and refinished to become the main design theme. Original oak wainscot was used in the new oak ticket counter, the walls around the well and beside the stairs.

Amtrak's staff and passengers needed about a third of the ground floor. The remaining space, together with a new mezzanine, have been made into a two-level restaurant with bar and kitchen. A new hydraulic lift provides access to all the levels, especially the professional offices on the first floor. The new office

area, which will eventually include the attic floor, retains most of the old features like fireplaces, mantels and wainscoting. The whole building except the restaurant mezzanine has been made accessible to the handicapped.

Accommodation Basement—waiting area, shops, storage, services.
Ground floor—ticket offices, baggage office, waiting areas, restaurant, bar,

5. *The Amtrak booking hall with the new grand staircase.* (PHOTOGRAPH: RANDOLPH LANGENBACH).

lounge, kitchen, lavatories.
Mezzanine—restaurant.
First floor—offices.
Attic—future offices.

Date of completion August 1978

Cost $835,000

RICHMOND STATION, YORKSHIRE

New use Garden centre, part of re-creation centre

Architect Napper, Errington, Collerton Partnership

Client Richmondshire District Council

Site The station is situated near the centre of Richmond, a pleasant market town in the North Riding of Yorkshire, which it served when the railway line was in use.

History The station was built in 1848 to the design of George T. Andrews, under the direction of George Hudson, nicknamed 'the railway king'. It used to be the terminus for the Darlington/Richmond connection of the London & North-Eastern Railway Line until 1969 when the line was closed. The building was rapidly deteriorating when the local authority bought it from British Rail in 1972 with a view to restoring the station as part of a new recreation centre on the site.

Character This station is one of the best examples of Gothic Revival railway architecture in England, and is listed as a Grade II building of special architectural and historic interest. It is a single-storey structure of stone, with a slate roof and an internal platform to one side and end only. Of particular interest externally is its open porte-cochère of four-centred arches with substantial buttresses between.

Work done The repair and restoration was confined initially to the external shell of the building. On the roof much of the patent glazing was renewed and the roof was re-slated with new lead flashings and gutters. The masonry walls were re-pointed and the windows and external doors were removed, repaired and replaced. The elaborate carved woodwork of the timber gable was also repaired. The main new work was the provision of a glazed wall to close in the open end of the station. Sympathetic modern materials were thought preferable to imitative period detailing, so a simple steel and glass structure was fitted directly to the steel tee-sections by the use of neoprene gaskets.

Date of completion 1974

Cost £39,000

1. Layout plan of the new recreation centre.
1. SWIMMING POOL
2. ENTRANCE
3. TERRACE
4. PROPOSED CONVERSION OF ENGINE SHED TO PUBLIC HALL
5. RICHMOND STATION

2. The station seen from the terrace at the side of the new swimming pool structure (PHOTOGRAPH: HENK SNOEK).

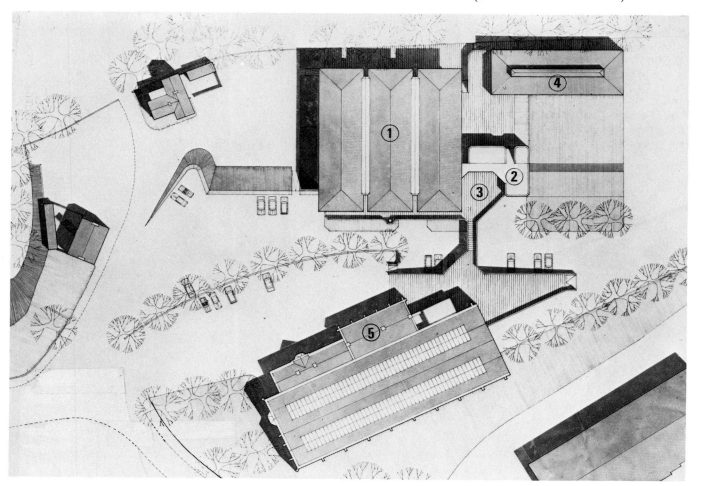

3. The pedestrian bridge which links the station (left) with the new swimming pool structure. (PHOTOGRAPH: HENK SNOEK).

4. The new glazed end to the station seen from the pedestrian bridge. (PHOTOGRAPH: HENK SNOEK).

5. Inside, the station has been converted into a garden centre. (PHOTOGRAPH: HENK SNOEK).

PART II
THE COUNTRYSIDE

7 Case study: the changing village

The problem of the village today is complementary to that of the inner city as described in the first chapter on Bologna. The decline of the inner city accelerated after the First World War and was the result of suburbanisation and dependence on motorised transport. Railways created one-class dormitory settlements around stations intended to serve rural areas, while car and bus services caused ribbon development along major roads. The villages lying beyond this commuter belt have tended to decline 'as agriculture has become less labour-intensive, as rural industry has declined and as government has withdrawn investment'.[1] Just as the depopulation of the inner city was caused by urban industries moving out, so the village community has altered its balance as a result of changes in farming. Today in Britain the money which the government is giving the inner city is depriving the village of essential funds.

Once upon a time the English village represented a fair cross-section of the population. It was a self-sufficient community with its squire, parson, doctor and school-teacher, its farm workers, its small tradesmen and artisans. It had a church and a school, a village hall, a shop and a pub. Today the absence of these services has forced people to move to towns and has discouraged newcomers from replacing them. It has given planners an excuse to reinforce the decline by refusing to allow new housing where there is no school or bus and concentrating instead on 'key settlements' in the county development plans. It is these that attract new housing, industry and government investment and it is these that are becoming towns while the rest are dying.

Of Britain's 13,000 villages half may disappear unless far more positive action is taken both at government and at local level. Every year, for example, between 40,000 and 60,000 acres of good quality land are lost to agriculture, despite one of the most highly developed planning systems in the world. While changes in farming, more than anything else, have caused the decline of the village, it is the diminishing numbers of farm workers, less than 20 per cent of the population, that still produce half the nation's food. When five men were once needed for one machine, one man can now operate five machines and, as Reg Brice, a senior education officer in Somerset has said, 'machines don't sire children to send to school'.[2]

[1]Graham Moss, *The Architects' Journal*, 18 January 1978
[2] *The Times*, 7 November 1978

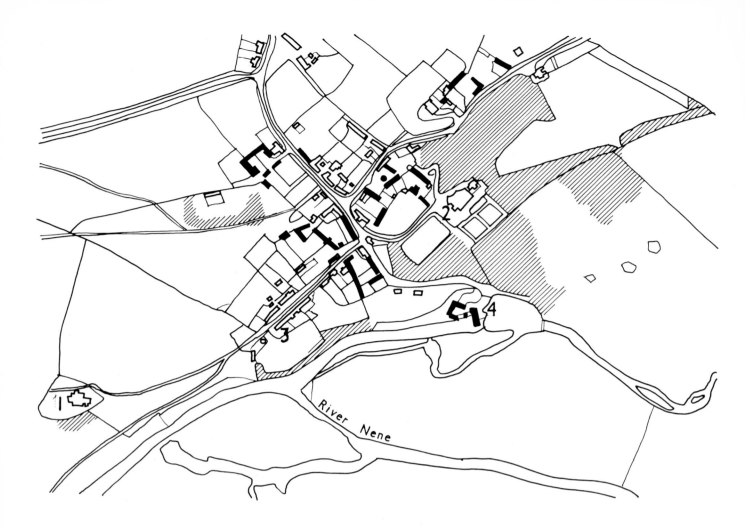

1. *Wadenhoe Village, Northamptonshire. Buildings shown in black are stone barns, stables, etc, which could be converted to housing.*
1. ST MICHAEL'S CHURCH
2. WADENHOE HOUSE
3. KING'S HEAD
4. CONVERTED WATERMILL, STABLE AND COTTAGE

There is also a reluctance to farm among a younger generation which often prefers to find better-paid work in the towns. The Forestry Commission in Mid-Wales, for example, used to employ farmers on a part-time basis, but found they were not willing to go back to milking cows and feeding pigs after a hard day's work in the woods. They also showed a preference for living in council houses, selling their cottages to commuters who have restored them and disposed of the unwanted land to anyone able to use it productively.[3]

The story of North Cheriton in Somerset, with its population of 186, is fairly typical. Its school, with a roll call of 11, was the last to close in the county (July 1977). Pub and pastor had already gone and, as a result of the school closing, the village stood to lose its hall which had been used by the children and for the upkeep of which the county council had been paying £140 p.a. The school closed because the young families which moved out were replaced by retired people and because the impossibility of obtaining planning permission to build new houses prevented other young families from coming to the village.[4]

Wadenhoe in Northamptonshire, with some 35 families, is somewhat better off, though the village school closed many years ago and there is virtually no public transport. The church is well maintained and draws its regular congregation also from the other villages nearby. It has a village hall, a shop with a post office and a

[3]*The Decline of Rural Services*, a report by the Standing Conference of Rural Community Councils, August 1978
[4]*The Decline of Rural Services*, op. cit.

popular pub with mooring facilities on the River Nene. Most of the land and buildings belong to the Squire who employs a number of agricultural workers and runs a small riding school and stud for ponies. His house, which is too large for today, is well maintained and used as a training centre by institutions, giving some local employment. The conversion of the seventeenth-century water mill, stable and cottage—the first example illustrated in this chapter— shows how these buildings can be preserved and used again. In an earlier survey of the village[5] Kit Martin, one of the architects of the mill, had demonstrated that nearly 50 per cent of the floor area was in the form of stone farm buildings, which made an important contribution to the village scene. These buildings have been redundant for some years because they are too expensive to maintain for farm use, the wrong shape for present-day equipment and badly related to the fields they serve. Their conversion, he argued, could double the population (though one would hope not all would be commuters) at the same time preserving the character of the village.

Lacock, in Wiltshire, owned by the National Trust, with a magnificent barn converted into a museum of photography which is also illustrated in this chapter, still has a post-office, two village stores, a village school, four inns, a village hall, a playground and a doctor's surgery.

If the private motor car has contributed to the decline of the English village, if it has made almost every village a suburb, it must also be said that many villages have been given new life by commuting residents. In any case the trend for villages to become dormitory suburbs is irreversible and the important thing is to make sure that those people without a motor car do not suffer. This means arresting the decline of and improving rural public transport.

This decline is, of course, the direct result of the increase in private transport. In Suffolk, for example, a report showed that 80 per cent of parishes found there was an 'inadequate service which failed to meet the basic requirements of travel for shopping, visiting doctors and dentists, hospital visiting and failed lamentably with evening facilities for social and cultural activities outside the village'. The answer lies in informal solutions such as community minibuses, social car-schemes, the use of school buses or post buses and car sharing. The report *The Decline of Rural Services*[3] recommended that 'rural communities are given every encouragement to devise their own solutions to local transport needs if conventional public provision is not possible or appropriate', though it also warns that improved transport can threaten the viability of the village shop or post office. The report by the National Council of Social Service, *Rural Transport I*, gives a description county by county of all the known examples, among them Michael Taylor's successful private bus service in a remote part of the West Highlands. Having bought a small, ailing bus company that also carried mail, Taylor increased the delivery service by including newspapers, milk, and railway parcels.

The motor car when combined with tourism may either harm or enhance a village. Graham Moss[7] warns against an over-conservationist, over-protective attitude to planning. 'Conservation', he writes 'tends to place inflated rarity value upon an area or a village. Afriston in Sussex has acquired such tourist, land and building value

[5] *The Changing Village*, unpublished dissertation by Kit Martin
[6] *Some Aspects of Rural Bus Transport in Suffolk* by the Community Council for Suffolk, 1975
[7] 'The Village: a matter of life or death,' *Architects' Journal*, 18 January, 1978

139

2. Dove nest, Windermere: the conversion of an apple store, dairy and farmworkers' cottages to provide self-catering accommodation.

3. A small barn in Derbyshire, the subject of a pilot project to convert the building into a 'tent' for hikers.

4. Plan showing the minimum conversion proposed to the barn.

1. LIVING AREA
2. COOKING
3. DRESSING
4. SLEEPING PLATFORM
5. LATRINE SITUATED TO NORTH OF BARN
6. CLOTHES HOOKS
7. RUCKSACK HOOKS
8. BENCH
9. CLOTHES LINE
10. DOOR TO BE BOLTED INTERNALLY

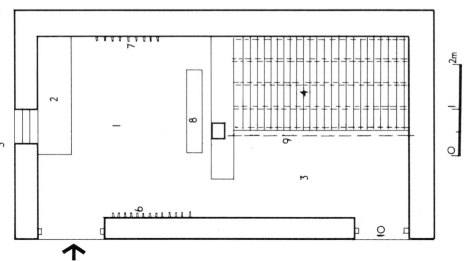

as to exclude all but the wealthy or more committed landowners. In this situation conservation villages can tend towards an unbalanced population dominated by physical appearance rather than community spirit'. And in a letter to *The Times*[8] Mrs Joan Yeo Marsh reckons that the current concern for conservation is turning her village of Waltham St. Lawrence with Sherlock Row into a commuter's roost. She cites three planning requests, all appropriate to the needs of a village, which were among those rejected—a carpenter's workshop, a potter's workshop and trading in antiques from a house.

If Lacock is an example of a beautiful village which has successfully come to terms with its tourists, Wadenhoe has not yet found any need to. Despite the attractions of the surrounding area of the river and of the village itself, Wadenhoe continues to keep a low profile. Although there is not yet an organised tourist base—no bed and breakfast or short-term letting—a large number of people come fishing and use the river for boating. Three or four 'permanent' caravans used by week-enders are allowed near the river and the squire occasionally lets one of his fields be used for camping by one of the local Boy Scout groups.

Farmers have discovered that there is money in tourism. Farm tourism means working farms where catering for leisure is a subsidiary activity. In 1977 more than 3,000 farmers were involved in the business and more than 15,000 farmers in England and Wales (over 6 per cent of the total) catered for leisure.[9] With the growth in tourism more and more people are likely to be attracted by a holiday on a farm, with its healthy outdoor activities, its good simple food and its moderate prices.

Farm tourism may lead to a loss in food production, but this is probably offset by helping to keep the farming community going and by the good use to which the surplus buildings and the poor land are put. The numerous possibilities, many of which imply the re-habilitation or new use of an old building, include accommodation in the farm house, on a self-catering basis or on a camping site; activities based on the farm's resources such as riding, fishing, game shooting and climbing; and, for day visitors if the farm is on the way to beautiful country, picnic sites, rare breeds, museums, catering, sales of produce, farm trails, country crafts and occasional events like steam rallies and motor-cycle scrambling.

In the Lake District, where farmhouse accommodation has been common for many years, the Special Planning Board supports the principle of farm tourism but pays particular regard to the scale of the proposal, access, the effect on services and the impact on the landscape. It expects farmers to enter into an agreement to ensure that their farm tourism project remains an integral part of the farm system and it will prevent new or converted buildings becoming second homes by restricting their use to tourist accommodation based on short-term lets. Stables and Gilchrist, architects in Windermere, have carried out a number of farm conversions. One of these, illustrated here, includes a variety of buildings from the main house to an apple store, which provided 11 family units. The farm now comprises 88 acres and stock includes 20 hill suckler cows, 100 ewes, fell ponies, free-range hens and certain exotic wildfowl. The retention and use of traditional local field names has identified special buildings and a guided nature-cum-farm trail is being formed in co-operation with the

[8]*The Times*, 2 September, 1978
[9]'Profit from Pleasure', a *Farmers Weekly* supplement, 11 March, 1977

5, 6. Two barns near Bolton Abbey in Yorkshire, which are still in use. But for how much longer?

National Park Centre at Brockhole and with assistance from the Job Creation Programme/Task Force North.

Not all conversions, however, need be as thorough and complete. Indeed barns, of which there are more in Britain than any other farm building type, are difficult to convert to a new use without depriving them of their character. The two examples, illustrated in this chapter, the barns at Lacock and Dersingham, were fortunate in their new use and have resulted in unusually successful conversions. But other, much simpler proposals have been carried out or suggested. In the appendix, Found Space, there are two examples of barns adapted at minimum cost and largely by self-help methods to various forms of community use. Of the more imaginative there is the Duchess of Devonshire's and the Derbyshire Historic Buildings Trust's proposal to adapt the dry-stone barns of the area for the use of hikers, in other words to treat them as stone 'tents', and to do the minimum of conversion work. Water would have to be laid on, an elsan or earth closet installed and a sleeping area provided, raised off the ground. Otherwise the structure would be made wind- and water-tight, but there would be no question of blocking up the dry-stone walls. Openings would have a single pane of fixed glass and doors would provide the ventilation. Cooking and lighting would be by calor gas. None of this complies with the bye-laws and local authorities would have to be persuaded to issue 'waivers'. Two pilot projects will shortly be instigated by the Trust and eventually it is hoped that the idea will catch on and lead to the establishment of a network of stone, brick and timber 'tents' throughout the country.

Like barns, churches are single-space structures and it is this that makes them so difficult to convert to new uses without changing their original character out of all recognition. To convert a church into a house is to change a single-space structure into a cellular one or, quite simply, to deprive the original building of its essential characteristic. Nevertheless we have included one example of such a conversion, the church at Langdon Hills in Essex, because we believe it to be the exception to the rule where client and architect successfully preserved the space of the church. In general, however, churches are much better not converted at all if a single-space use cannot be found for them, and we support that section of the rural community which would like to see the nave, aisles and churchyard 'returned' to the people. Early in the nineteenth century high-church parsons, whose province had previously been the chancel only, declared the whole church and churchyard to be hallowed ground. 'In the late medieval period,'

142

according to F. F. Cartwright,[10] 'the parish church was the focal point of village life. The nave served as a meeting place for debate, manorial business, or for plays and other entertainments. The side aisles were refuges, in which people burned out of their houses could be accommodated or which sometimes served as hospitals in pestilence. The strong tower afforded lodgement for valuables. Games, predecessor of the modern fives, were played against the north wall. The walled churchyard provided emergency herbage for cattle in times of trouble and was pastured by sheep in times of peace'.

A more specific example comes from Hugh Johnson[11] writing about the church at Saling in Essex. He points out that for some 500 years the church, the only stone building in the village and the most valuable thing the people possessed, was looked after by their cooperative effort for their general use. 'Since the holification of the whole church', he continues, '. . . the village has had to look elsewhere for the old facilities . . . Like many village halls, ours is a poor building, which cannot last long. At the same time the size of our congregation suggests that our church is likely to be decommissioned at some time in the next generation. Surely the answer must be to demolish the village hall, "develop" its site, and use the proceeds to reconvert the church for general use—thus giving back to the village its original community centre and spending our sparse funds on maintaining an ancient monument rather than a prefab. My guess is that it would also increase attendance at worship'.

If churches are difficult to convert and if the kind of extended use suggested by *The Times* correspondents is a way of keeping the village church alive, the village school is relatively easy to convert into one or more houses for commuting or retired residents. But we have deliberately not included any village schools because we believe that none should be closed. Somerset, for example, is committed to closing no more schools despite the fact that none of the £1·7 million given by the government for school building over the next three years will go to the village primaries. Some 800 village schools were closed in the decade 1968–78, and another 1,000 are now threatened. The Plowden Report (1967), which recommended a minimum size of 50 pupils and three teachers, accelerated closure, though it had begun in earnest after the 1944 Butler Education Act, which abolished the all-age village school, leaving it only with a few children up to the age of 11.

The main reason for village schools closing today and in the foreseeable future are three. There is, first, a considerable fall in the birthrate: the primary school population in England and Wales is expected to fall from 4,600,000 to 3,400,000 by 1986. Second, there have been cuts in public spending, with the Rate Support Grant to rural areas, for example, reduced substantially since 1974; and, third, there is the change in the village population which we have already noted.

The argument often hinges on economics, and the village school, if there are less than 20 pupils per teacher, can indeed cost twice as much to run per pupil as a town school. But as a whole rural schools are more economical to run than urban schools, so that the larger villages could 'cross-subsidise' their smaller neighbours without help from central funds. Rural communities also take some 10 per cent less out of the public purse than urban areas, so that the smaller communities may feel entitled to their 'expensive' school.[12]

[10]In a letter to *The Times*, 31 August, 1978
[11]In a letter to *The Times*, 2 September, 1978
[12]*The Decline of Rural Services, op. cit.*

With the benefit of hindsight the disadvantages of large schools are now familiar. Conversely there is also better appreciation of the small village school's educational and social value, of the need for close ties between such a school and the community it serves. In Leicestershire community centres, with the community taking a share of their management, have recently been created in some 20 schools. They take the form of a spacious common room, with refreshment bar and storage, available all day long and every day of the week, and a room for local clubs or the parish council.

In the past the lack of teachers used to contribute to school closures. But there is no shortage today, especially as peripatetic teachers and even peripatetic headmasters are becoming more frequent. When a village school is threatened, parents should get together and provide part-time ancillary help. Madingley, Cambridgeshire, is an example where a parent-teacher cooperative was formed to keep the school going through a charitable trust which doesn't charge fees. The parents do much of the work to keep costs down and raise money to pay the teachers.

In conclusion we would like to list a number of remedies, many of which were first proposed by the authors of *The Decline of Rural Services*. They are mostly of an official kind because enough has already been said about voluntary self-help methods and because self-help, as Graham Moss[13] points out, is no substitute for government finance or local authority provision:

1. The Government Rate Support Grant to rural areas, which was cut in 1974, should be increased to redress the imbalance between town and country.

2. A special grant, paid through district councils, should be made available for private operators who intend to close their service to delay closure so that an alternative way of providing the same service can be worked out. With the same purpose in mind there should be an early warning system by which all public and private agencies have to notify their district and county councils at least six months in advance of their intention to close a service.

3. Parish councils should make greater use of their power to levy up to a 2p rate to support local services. Fernhurst in West Sussex has done this to keep its primary school going and there are other cases where the local bus service has been maintained in the same way. Parish councils should generally be given more responsibility, with statutory bodies like the GPO, for example, consulting them over closures.

4. A European rural fund should be established, replacing in a rural context the regional and social funds at present concentrated on urban industrial areas.

5. The selective 'key settlement' policy should end and a planning policy which encourages small developments in council housing and a rich variety of activities in villages—farm tourism, small factories, independent craftsmen, local business and trades—should take its place. Not only does this imply the conversion of derelict farm buildings or the multi-use of buildings which are under-used, but it also establishes a sound base for local employment. A percentage levy on the purchase of second homes to assist locally employed people to buy houses should also be considered.

6. Because in Britain no direct financial aid to rural shops is available from any statutory body, local authorities should consider buying

[13]Graham Moss, *op. cit.*

village shops and either leasing them at a peppercorn rent or running them themselves. Low-interest loans should also be available to country shopkeepers to finance stock-holding and to allow them to offer credit. The salaries of lower-tied sub-postmasters should be substantially increased.

7. The principle of multiple services should be developed. Traditionally the post office is often combined with the village shop and country doctors often double up as dispensing chemists. But the shop *cum* post-office could also be a garage, or the shop could be part of the pub. The greatest potential is perhaps in the post-office van which could share its postal deliveries with paper, milk, groceries and other deliveries as well as provide a post-office counter and information services. The principle of part-time services should also be developed. It means providing part-time services in as many places as possible rather than full-time services in one central place which may be out of reach to the elderly and less mobile residents of the villages. There are examples of sub-postmasters operating on a part-time basis. Or a sub-postmaster could be appointed to serve a number of villages, as parsons and doctors already do. The same principle can be applied to school teachers.

Recommendations such as these, however, must remain random or tentative for lack of proper information. In contrast, our comparative inner city study on Bologna in Chapter 1 shows that the plan there is based on a sound and thorough survey. No rural policy can be formulated in Britain until much more is known about the state of the villages and the countryside as a whole.[14] Not long ago the *Architects' Journal*[15] reminded us that the last survey of the state of the nation's villages was held in 1086 and called for another Domesday, because 'no sensible planning proposals can be produced without going through the time-honoured sequence of survey-analysis-plan'. There is still no sign that this fundamental principle has been understood.

[14]The Department of Education and Science, for example, have only been keeping a record of school closures since January 1977
[15]*Architects' Journal*, 20 September, 1978

8 Small buildings converted to a new use

WATERMILL, WADENHOE, NORTHAMPTONSHIRE

New use House

Architect Martin and Weighton

Client Kit Martin

Site Wadenhoe in Northamptonshire is typical of the stone-built settlements which follow the east-west stratum of oolitic limestone from Gloucestershire to Lincolnshire. The watermill is part of a group, together with the neighbouring stable and cottage situated beside the river Nene. Like other farm groups, it forms an important part of the village scene.

History The village still belongs to a single squire and until recently the majority of its inhabitants worked on the land. But today modern agricultural machinery has made most of the farm labourers and buildings redundant.

Kit Martin bought the mill, and associated buildings. The group became the first in the village to be converted to residential use. The buildings date from the seventeenth century and were in continuous use until the 1920s. From that date until their conversion, the buildings stood empty.

Character The mill is a tall L-shaped four-storey structure. Grain was stored at the third and fourth levels and fed from the grain bins on the third level through openings on to the millstones on the second level, which were driven by a wheel and turbine at ground level. These not only drove the millstones and other machinery, but pumped water to houses in the village. There are three water courses under the building so that the water can be controlled. The structure is of stone and timber with pitched roofs covered with Colleyweston slate. Windows are small and few, and, in the original building, non-existent on the upper levels.

Work done Because there was no daylighting to the top floors, extra windows were made just below the eaves, marginally altering the external character of the building, and skylights were let into the new stone-slated roof. New windows were made in old doorway openings on the ground floor. The ceiling levels in the upper storeys were too low for residential use, so the whole of the top floor and the second floor over the living room were removed, and a gallery was made, leading to the bedrooms. The rooms thus created were high, reaching up to the exposed roof trusses. New partitions are not load-bearing, which meant that the plan can be modified as family requirements change. The plumbing and heating are all conducted through two ducts so that radiators and bathrooms can be changed or added as necessary. This system allows ceiling joists to be exposed and stone walls to be left unplastered. The heating is zoned so that areas of the house can be controlled independently. The stone work was repaired and the roof was repaired with old stone slates found locally which matched the existing. A new terrace was built over the water on the south side. Kit Martin also designed some of the furniture and the interior finishes, which were all made by Ray Barnes, the main contractor who has worked with the architects on a number of other conversions to new uses.

Accommodation Ground floor—hall, cloakroom, stores, three garages.
First floor—kitchen playroom, dining room, living room.
Second floor—seven bedrooms, three bathrooms.

Date of completion Work on all three buildings (watermill, mill stables and mill house) started in January 1972 and was completed in December 1972.

Cost £18,500 (water-mill conversion only, not including external works, garden, swimming pool and stable block); rate—£3.56 per square foot. A discretionary grant of £100 was obtained.

3. View of the mill from the back, with the garage and kitchen wing on the left.

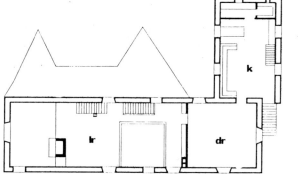

1. First floor plan. This shows the main living level.

2. Cross-section through the double-height part of the dining/living area and second floor gallery which gives access to the bedrooms.

4. The bedroom passage on the second floor. (PHOTOGRAPH: BILL TOOMEY)
5. The dining-living area.

147

LOWER TREVOLLARD FARM, CORNWALL

New use Two houses

Architect Howell, Killick, Partridge and Amis

Client Stanley Amis

Site The buildings are set in a rural site near Saltash, Cornwall.

History The buildings ceased to be used as a farm in 1972, and were sold separately from the surrounding land by public auction in 1972. Planning permission was granted in 1973 for conversion to residential use. The conversion won an award for popular architecture given by the Plymouth branch of the R.I.B.A. in 1978, and commendations by the R.I.B.A. and the Civic Trust in 1979.

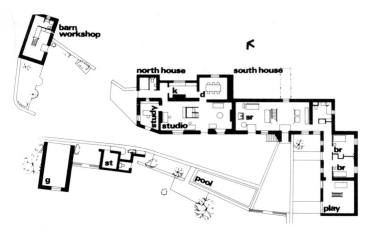

1. Ground floor plan.
2. Long section.

Character The stone buildings are L-shaped on plan, and divided into two. The north wing was the original farmhouse and the south wing was an L-shaped barn adjoining the south-eastern wall of the house. The roof coverings were of varied materials—Delabole slate, asbestos slate, corrugated asbestos, iron, slurry, and felt. There was a single outside lavatory, and the water supply was pumped from a well off-site. The farmyard contained various other buildings of concrete blocks and rusted corrugated iron which served as stables and a dairy.

Work done The outhouses not of stone were demolished, leaving the farmhouse and the adjoining barn, and three additional small buildings. The existing stone walls were repaired and the entire complex re-roofed in second-hand Delabole slate. Care was taken in the slating to achieve diminishing courses and a random bond. The ridges were of second-hand slate wing and roll. A transfusion damp-proof system was installed and the roofs were well insulated. The exterior character of the buildings was retained by using bargeboards at the eaves and by treating the verge with dark green preservative. In the original farmhouse (the north house) the first floor was reconstructed and a new staircase positioned to allow access to the new bathroom in the roof space. In the L-shaped south house, a service core was situated at the 'elbow', with bathrooms at both levels. A new staircase was sited in the centre of the living space

and, by changes of level at both the ground and first floors, it was possible to achieve an entrance under the granite landing on the first floor. The floor of the main bedroom, originally the hayloft, was lowered to make sufficient headroom under the exposed king-post trusses. The floors at ground level were finished with composite slate tiles over electrical underfloor heating. On the first floor they were finished with rush matting on plywood and tanalised boarding.

The structural walls were left exposed, except in the smaller bedrooms and the playroom, where they were painted white. New partitions were of timber stud, clad both sides with board-

3. The south side, with the front door under the old external granite stair which gives direct access to the first floor dining-kitchen.

ing. Ceilings were faced with boarding, leaving the joists, rafters, tie-beams and purlins exposed and treated with dark green preservative. The inward opening tilt-and-turn wooden windows of extreme exposure rating have non-ferrous hardware, essential in the local weather conditions.

The pine four-poster bed and cupboards in the main bedroom of the south house were designed by the architect. The three remaining external buildings were converted into a garage, a store and a studio with a sleeping gallery.

Accommodation North house—ground floor studio/living room, study, kitchen, dining room, lavatory.
First floor: four bedrooms, bathrooms, store.
South house—ground floor; living room (partly double height), two bedrooms, bathroom, playroom (partly double height).
First floor: kitchen/dining gallery over living room, bathroom, bedroom, sleeping gallery over playroom.

Date of completion April 1975 for houses; December 1975 for remaining outbuildings.

Cost £46,000 including all buildings.

4. The living room on the ground floor. The stair leads to the dining-kitchen.

5. The dining-kitchen on the first floor overlooks the double-height living room.
(PHOTOGRAPHS: MARTIN CHARLES).

LACOCK BARN, LACOCK, WILTSHIRE

New use The Fox Talbot Museum, primarily to commemorate the invention of positive/negative photography by William Henry Fox Talbot, but also to house a collection of memorabilia and a reference system through which any work of his can be located.

Designer Robin Wade Design Associates

Client The National Trust

Site Lacock is a picture-book village in Wiltshire belonging entirely to the National Trust. Fox Talbot's family lived here for generations and members of the family still live in Lacock Abbey. The barn is situated at the gates of the Abbey and forms a landmark in the village street.

History The Abbey Barn dates from the seventeenth century and was in use until the nineteenth. When the National Trust took the village over in 1944, the barn was already redundant and housed old building materials and junk. Cleared of these, it was used as a meeting hall for boy scouts. In 1972, the Trust gave Robin Wade Design Associates a brief which included not only setting up a museum, but also designing the exhibitions, involving research and organisational work not normally entrusted to a design team. Fox Talbot, (1800–77) to whom the museum is dedicated, was a remarkable polymath. Besides his photographic invention, he also devoted himself to botany, mathematics, optics, astronomy, Egyptology, philosophy and theology, and was a Member of Parliament in 1833–4.

Character The barn is a large stone-built structure. It is rectangular on plan, with a single interior space, rising up to the king-post roof trusses. Typically, windows are few and small. There are two high and wide entrances on the northeast side and two small man-sized ones on the south-west side, which fronts on to the road. The pitched roof is covered with stone slates. There is an early photograph (taken by Fox Talbot) showing Gothic blind tracery which has now disappeared. This was probably done in the eighteenth century at the same time as the Gothic alterations at the Abbey.

Work done To make full use of the height of the building, a new floor was inserted in the form of a gallery standing

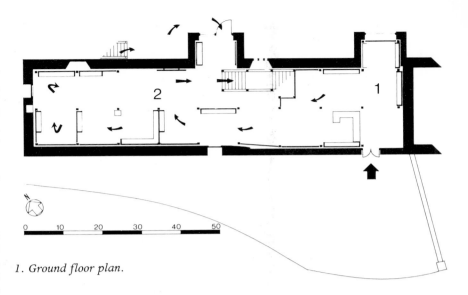

1. Ground floor plan.

2. First floor plan.

1. PUBLICATIONS AND SALES
2. MAIN EXHIBITION
3. TEMPORARY EXHIBITION
4. AUDIO-VISUAL ROOM
5. OFFICES AND ARCHIVES

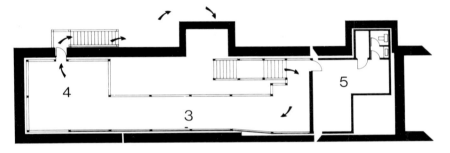

3. The barn seen from the village road, (PHOTOGRAPH: WYKAMOLDID).

150

4. Exhibition bays on the ground floor formed by the new gallery structure. (PHOTOGRAPH, CRISPIN EURICH).

5. At one end of the building solid partitions enclose the offices and archives on the first floor. (PHOTOGRAPH: CRISPIN EURICH).

quite separately from the old walls and roof trusses. It is made of heavy oak and elm timbers, continuing the functional character of the barn. One end of the gallery was closed off to provide space for offices and storage. The dividing wall has small slits, echoing those in the external walls and giving a view down into the museum space. The exhibition space is for conservation reasons artificially lit, which also obviates the need to create more window openings. The museum is also fully equipped with humidity and temperature control systems.

Accommodation Ground level—Main exhibition space, bookshop.
Upper level—Audio-visual room, space for temporary exhibitions, offices and archives.

Cost Approximately £50,000

CURTIS MILL, LOWER KILCOTT, GLOUCESTERSHIRE

New use House

Architect Jeremy Johnson-Marshall

Client Stirrat and Joan Johnson-Marshall

Site The mill is situated in the confluence of two valleys which are steep-sided, wooded and typical of the many that cut into the Cotswold escarpment—a little short on sunlight but abundant in water.

History The earliest records of the mill date from 1777, and they indicate that it was functioning well before that, one of thousands built to mechanise the fulling (cleaning) of Gloucestershire wool. At some stage it changed to a corn mill and in 1890 the owners moved into the prefabricated bungalow which they had built against the mill. Finally great visual damage was caused by pulling down the miller's house. The length of the building was halved so that it no longer appeared to form the whole dam to the pond.

Character Before conversion, the building retained an industrial air with a functional arrangement of features. Only the odd cosmetic chimney stack conceded to the picturesque character of the setting. The building is divided into two

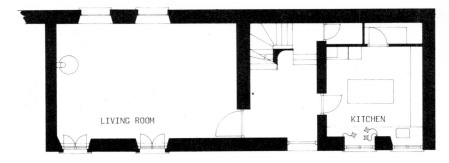

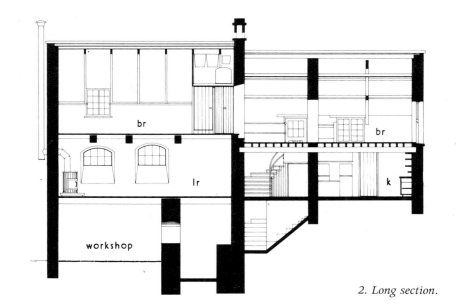

1. Ground floor plan.

2. Long section.

3. View from the mill pond.

152

halves, with one roof slightly lower than the other. Because of the sloping ground, the building is three storeys high on one side and only one-and-a-half storeys high on the other. Windows were small and few in the original buildings which, when acquired, was in very bad condition, with the roof falling in and many of its stone slates lost.

Work done The building was gutted and reduced to four walls and principal beams before rebuilding. An unwanted oak-framed barn was bought and its components converted on site for both structural and joinery timber. Conversion to a home meant increasing the fenestration but, to make the building look more like a mill that was lived in than a house that had once been a mill, only dark timber or cast iron windows were installed and the complexity of levels, windows and doors was increased rather than simplified.

Internally, partitioning of the original masonry spaces was avoided except to form bathrooms. This led to a simple two-bedroom, living room and kitchen layout on the upper floors, and a workshop and store on the lower floor.

The internal finishes are render, sawn and reclaimed timber, and slate. The lean-to bungalow was demolished, the pond dredged, streams moved and extra ponds built. Finally, a large open store was built, roofed in the original stone slates which for economy had to be replaced with imitation ones on the main building.

4. View from the entrance side.

Accommodation Lower ground floor—workshop and store.
Ground floor—living room, kitchen.
First floor—two bedrooms, two bathrooms.

Date of completion 1976

Cost £32,000 including landscaping

SEVERN WHARF AND WAREHOUSE AND COALPORT CHINA WORKS, NEAR TELFORD, SHROPSHIRE

New use Museum

Architect Ironbridge Gorge Museum Trust and Robin Wade Design Associates

Client Ironbridge Gorge Museum Trust

Site The site covers an area of some 6 square miles of the Severn River Valley in Telford, Shropshire between the village of Coalbrookdale in the northwest and that of Coalport in the southeast. In the valley are a number of buildings and other structures which together form a unique legacy from the beginnings of the Industrial Revolution. The whole area is being restored to make an open-air museum which contains, among other things, the world's first iron bridge, the blast furnace where iron was first smelted with coke, and an inclined plane which could raise a six ton boat 207 feet from the River Severn to the Shropshire canal in 3 minutes.

Two parts of the museum, designed by the museum's consultant designers, Robin Wade Design Associates, are the Severn Wharf and Warehouse, situated on the north bank of the River Severn, a quarter of a mile upstream from the iron bridge, and the Coalport China Works, two miles downstream from the bridge.

History The early industrial importance of the Severn Gorge was based on an abundance of minerals—coal, iron ore, limestone and clay. It derived from the breakthrough made in 1709 by Abraham Darby, who perfected in Coalbrookdale a technique for smelting iron, using coke as a fuel instead of the traditional charcoal. William Reynolds (1758–1803), one of the most inventive of the Shropshire ironmasters, was also one of the ablest of the entrepreneurs to exploit the area's natural resources. He was responsible for the Shropshire canal, and its link with the River Severn, and for building the town of Coalport around this junction. Besides iron, one of the major industries was the manufacture of china which once spread along both sides of the canal for nearly a quarter of a mile. China was manufactured there until production was transferred to Stoke-on-Trent in 1926. By the late nineteenth century many of the new materials were exhausted, and the Severn Gorge was declining. Between the wars the workforce in the collieries

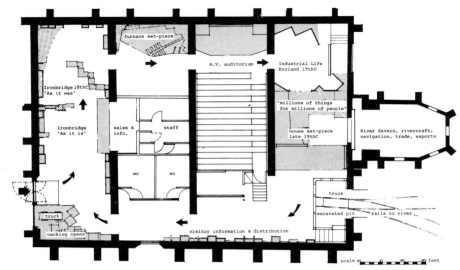

1. *Plan of the warehouse showing its conversion into a visitors' centre.*
2. *View of the warehouse and wharf from the river.*

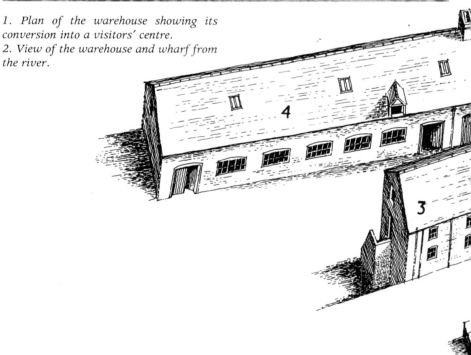

3. *Bird's eye view of Coalport China Works Museum.* (FROM A DRAWING BY PATRICIA READ).

154

4. One of the bays in the warehouse serves as an auditorium for audio-visual shows (PHOTOGRAPH: MARTIN CHARLES).

5. The Coalport China Works with one of the old biscuit kilns in the foreground. The other conical kiln, 6, now houses a display of fine Coalport china. (PHOTOGRAPHS: WEDGEWOOD AND MARTIN CHARLES).

1. ENTRANCE AND SHOP
2. 'CREATED FROM CLAY'
3. 'A LANGUAGE OF THEIR OWN'
4. THE WORKSHOPS
5. THE COALPORT YEARS
6. THE PEOPLE OF COALPORT
7. DISPLAY OF PORCELAIN
8. ARCHAEOLOGICAL DISPLAY
9. FORMER CANAL TO BE RE-EXCAVATED

7. *Iron Bridge*. (FROM A DRAWING BY PATRICIA READ).

became a mere handful and many buildings were demolished (the remaining china works represent only one-sixth of the original). In the 1950s the last brick and tile works folded and in 1960 the last active feature of the area, the railway line, was closed down. It was this dereliction which led to the inclusion of the Gorge within the designated area of Telford New Town set up in the mid 1960s to revive the fortunes of the area. In 1968 the Ironbridge Gorge Museum Trust was set up to preserve and restore the area. Volunteers cleared away the undergrowth and started excavating the surviving remains. The canal was cleared, brickwork was repaired and pathways were laid. The whole lower section of the canal was uncovered from the bottom of the inclined plain through to the Coalport China Works. Many of the buildings were restored to working order. In addition to the work of the Museum Trust the New Town Development Corporation has been engaged in major renovation works in the Gorge, including the restoration of numerous dwellings and the installation of such things as main drainage which the area had hitherto lacked.

In 1977 the Ironbridge Gorge Museum Trust won the European Museum of the Year Award.

Character *The Severn Wharf and Warehouse* In form it is an example of Victorian Gothic, built in the 1840s and a very odd building by any standards. Crenellations adorn the heavily buttressed walls and two false tall chimneys, complete with arrow slits, rise up either side of an apsidal projection at the east end. From here the warehouse foreman could view the activity on the wharf and the river. The plan is basically rectangular, divided into four interior bays for storage of goods. The structure is of brick and timber. The roof is pitched over each bay and the rafters are exposed to view. High, wide doorways, with ramped access to the quay, allowed loaded vehicles to come in and out.

Coalport China Works This consists of several buildings including three conical brick kilns (two are still intact, the third is a ruin), and a number of other structures, all of which housed various aspects of the china manufacturing process. Their common characteristics are pitched, tiled roofs; small, regularly-spaced windows; and a construction of brick and wood, or iron.

Work done *Severn Wharf and Warehouse* The Warehouse and Wharf first had to be cleared of the earth which came right up to the window-sills. They were restored partly by contractors and partly by the Trust's own craftsmen to a design developed jointly by the Museum Trust and Robin Wade Design Associates, and made into an interpretative centre introducing the Gorge and its extraordinary past. Displays, some of which are mounted on brown wooden packing cases, blend well with the industrial character of the building. Other displays include a reconstructed and cut-away interior of a Victorian house containing industrial objects, the reconstruction of the mouth of a blast furnace, and various view points interpreting the river, the wharf and the neighbouring hills. One of the bays is devoted to an auditorium in which an audio-visual presentation is housed.

Coalport China Works Restoration was undertaken by the Telford Development Corporation's building surveyor, working to a conservation specification prepared by the Museum Trust. The museum, showing how Coalport china was made, was designed by Robin Wade Design Associates. One of the bottle kilns now holds a circular brick-built display which is based on the form of the kiln's inner chamber in which pots were once glazed.

8. Pit-head-winding gear at the Blists Hill Open Air Museum. (FROM A DRAWING BY PATRICIA READ).

9. The Great Warehouse at Coalbrookdale, recently converted into a museum of iron. (FROM A DRAWING BY PATRICIA READ).

Accommodation Galleries showing the history of Ironbridge Gorge, its manufacturing activities and its part in the British Industrial Revolution.

Date of completion Severn Wharf and Warehouse—1977
Coalport China Works—1976

Costs Severn Wharf and Warehouse (including landscaping) approximately £60,000
Coalport China Works (including landscaping) approximately £100,000

10. Cottages off Wellington Road, Coalbrookdale. (FROM A DRAWING BY PATRICIA READ).

No. 34 HIGH STREET, IRONBRIDGE, SHROPSHIRE

New use Shop and flats

Architect George Robb

Client The Landmark Trust

Site In the Market Place, on the river side and overlooking the bridge.

History The Market Place was laid out as a direct consequence of the building of the bridge in 1779, and the bringing of new wealth and increased population to the village of Ironbridge. No. 34 was the establishment of a substantial grocer, consisting of a large house over a double-fronted shop; three floors of store rooms with trap doors in each floor and the original crane still in the roof; an office, stables, coach house, cart house, 'bacon drying house'; and two cellars, one under the other, the lower one communicating by a tunnel with the bank of the River Severn, up which, until the late nineteenth century, cargoes were brought by barge.

Character The brick building is almost square in plan. It rises three storeys above the Market Place level, and is crowned by a hipped roof with a flat lead-covered top. The slope of the ground down to the river permits access from a terrace on the river side of the building to the upper cellar. Ground,

1. 34 High Street with the market place on the left.

first and second floors are of timber construction. The roof is framed timber and covered with tiles.

Work done General repairs to the building were undertaken. On the High Street frontage, double doors on the ground floor were replaced by a window. Some windows were renewed, one was bricked up and three openings, which had been bricked up, were re-opened and fitted with new windows.

Internally the ground floor and upper cellar were improved to form shop and storage accommodation and the two upper storeys were formed into two flats.

Accommodation The ground floor shop and cellar have been let to the Ironbridge Gorge Museum Trust. One of the living units above is let to a permanent tenant and the other is for Landmark visitors.

Date of completion 1976

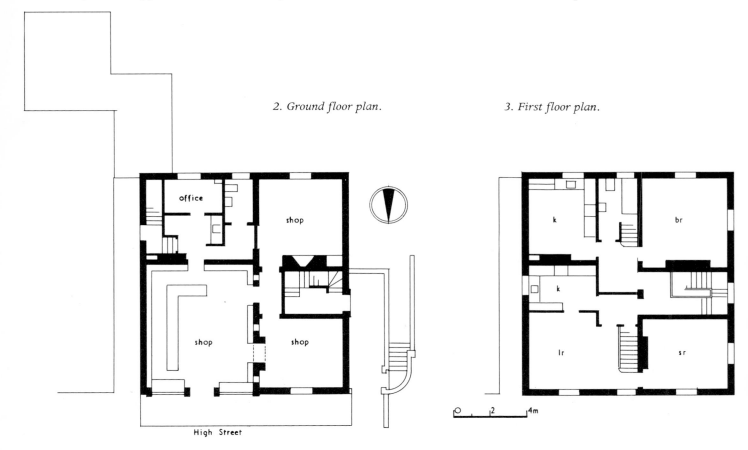

2. Ground floor plan.

3. First floor plan.

BARN, FRIESLAND, HOLLAND

New use House

Architect E. J. Jelles

Client J. Bakkum

Site A rural site in the flat lands of Friesland in north Holland. The nearest village is several miles away.

History The nineteenth-century building was in use as a barn until 1975 when the farmer died. The farm was too small to be an attractive proposition to a young farmer, so the land was sold to neighbouring farmers, none of whom wanted the decaying barn. The client at first commissioned the job for a friend whom he had persuaded to buy the barn. But he later bought it from the friend and took over the restoration work himself, completing it at weekends with the help of family and friends.

Character The building was originally a single-space red brick barn with a steeply pitched thatched roof reaching down to a few feet from the ground. It had an addition at the rear with higher walls and a tiled roof of similar pitch. It had two doorways at the front—a high, wide one slightly to left of centre and a man-sized one to the right. Window openings were small and few.

Work done The walls were repaired and re-pointed, decayed beams were replaced with new timber and new timber windows and doors were inserted mainly in existing or enlarged openings; the thatch was stripped off and completely replaced. A new H-shaped timber frame was inserted into the roof to provide three bedrooms

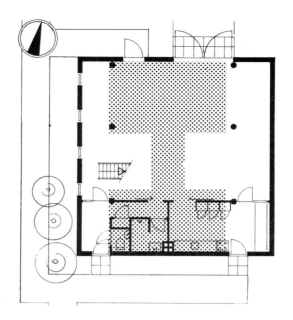

1. Ground floor plan.

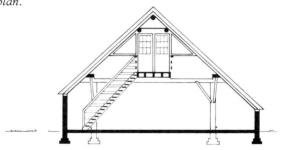

2. Section.

joined by a small corridor and a staircase. Heating pipes were laid under the ground floor and covered with red tiles, and the whole house was painted in light and dark shades of blue and red with very little white—the traditional colour scheme for rural buildings in this area.

Accommodation Ground floor—living room, kitchen, bathroom.
First floor—three bedrooms.

Date of completion 1975

Cost Approximately 100,000 Dutch Guilders

3. The barn before and, 4, after conversion.

TITHE BARN, DERSINGHAM, NORFOLK

New use Store for historic building materials.

Architect J. M. Shaw (County Planning Officer, Norfolk County Council)

Client Norfolk County Council

Site Dersingham is a small village in Norfolk about a mile from the Queen's estate at Sandringham. The tithe barn is situated in the heart of the village, next to the church.

History The building is dated 1671, and was used by the church to collect tithes until this practice fell into disuse at the beginning of the nineteenth century. It was owned by the Queen as part of the Sandringham estate and was used as a grain store by a farmer until 1973 when the Queen presented it to Norfolk County Council. The barn is now used as a store for salvaged historic building materials. An existing internal timber partition is used to provide a secure store for valuable items.

Character The structure consists of large chalk blocks for the front and back walls, and carstone (a local sandstone) which is mainly used in small rectangular blocks laid coursed in the gable walls and below the chalk blocks at the front and back. Larger blocks of carstone are used in the plinth and lower in the gable walls. Red brick dressings attractively frame the window slits and decorate the crow-stepped gables. The steeply pitched roof is covered with red pantiles, but was originally thatched. There are two high and wide doorways to allow access to laden farm carts. Internally the structure is open to the roof with exposed timber trusses and rafters supported on brick corbels. The interior is divided into two unequal parts by a timber partition.

Work done When the barn became the property of the County Council in 1973, the building was structurally sound but subject to vandalism. The chalk blocks had weathered badly and required careful repair. The doors were replaced with new ones, and electricity was installed. An area was cleared in front of the building to allow easy access to lorries and to improve the setting. Gravel has been laid around the sides abutting on to the churchyard in an effort to keep the weeds down.

Accommodation Store for historic building materials

Date of completion 1976

Cost £4,900

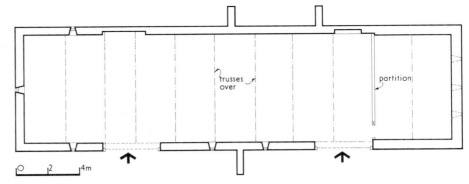

1. Plan.

2. View from the cemetery.

3. View of interior towards the partition. (PHOTOGRAPHS: BILL TOOMEY).

ST. FAITH, NEWTON IN THE WILLOWS, NORTHANTS

New use Field studies centre in regular use by groups of school children on day courses and by adult residential students on weekend courses.

Architect John Stedman Design Group; mural of knights and their ladies by Chris Rowlatt

Client The Newton Trust

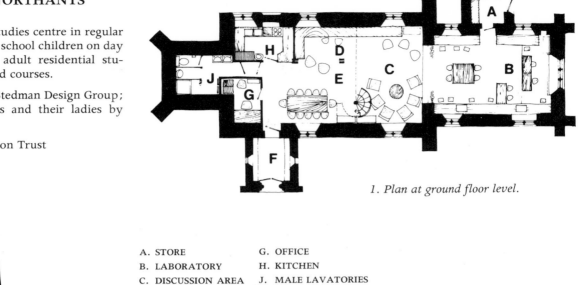

1. Plan at ground floor level.

A. STORE
B. LABORATORY
C. DISCUSSION AREA
D. LIBRARY
E. DINING
F. PORCH

G. OFFICE
H. KITCHEN
J. MALE LAVATORIES
K. DORMITORIES
L. FEMALE LAVATORIES
M. FUTURE VIEWING PLATFORM

2. Long section looking north.

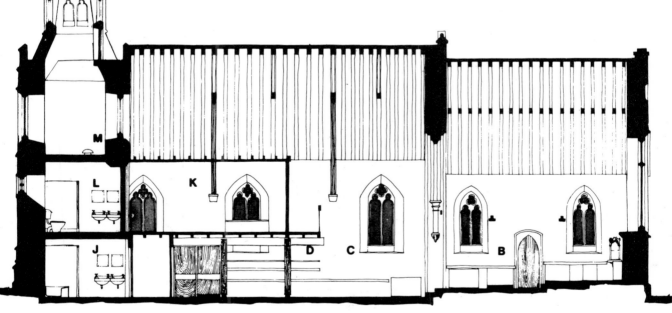

Site A rural site just outside a village mid-way between Corby and Kettering in an area where quarrying activities, the River Ise, reservoirs, farmland and woodland are all within easy reach.

History The church was founded in the thirteenth century, but all of it except the tower was rebuilt in 1858. Because of its isolated situation, attendances declined, and worship ceased in 1958. During the 1960s it remained unused, but was maintained in reasonably good order by the Newton Trust. In 1972 the management committee of the Trust approached the architects for preliminary designs for the conversion of the church into a field studies centre.

Character The tower and spire date from the fifteenth century but the nave and chancel are Victorian, although some of the old windows with their geometrical tracery were used in the rebuilding. The simple interior space is undivided by columns and the chancel is somewhat narrower with the roof lower than the nave. The structure is of stone and timber, with the roof trusses exposed on the inside. The pitched roof is covered with stone slates.

Work done The fabric of the church was fairly sound although all the windows had been broken or removed. A certain amount of beetle infestation was present in the roof timbers. As a result of an archaeological dig to explore tombs of the Tresham family, a large proportion

161

of the nave floor had been disturbed. The initial work consisted of re-laying the floor, using existing stone flags supplemented by a small amount of new stone. All accessible roof timbers were treated with preservative and the walls of the tower and nave were re-plastered on ventilated Newtonite lath up to a height of at least 7ft.

The chancel was equipped with work benches and sinks to form a lecture room and laboratory. A gallery was constructed in the west end of the nave to provide two dormitories, and lavatories were constructed at the ground and first floor levels of the tower. Below the gallery is a small kitchen, an office and a library. A nature trail was created, centring on the church, to lead through the varied landscape of the area.

Accommodation Ground floor—(chancel) laboratory/lecture hall, store; (nave) library, kitchen, office; (tower) at ground and first floor levels, lavatories. Gallery—two dormitories.

Date of completion July 1975

Cost £21,000

3. *View from the south.* (PHOTOGRAPH: ROBERT WILSON).

4. *The west end of the church with its new gallery over the library, dining area and kitchen.* (PHOTOGRAPH: JOHN MCCANN).

5. *The chancel now houses the laboratory.* (PHOTOGRAPH: JOHN MCCANN).

NEW MELLERAY ABBEY, DUBUQUE, IOWA

New use Church, chapter house and chapel

Architect Hammel, Green & Abrahamson Inc.

Client New Melleray Abbey

Site A rural one near a small town in Iowa, in the American mid-west. 3,000 acres of surrounding farmland belong to the Abbey and are farmed by the monks.

History The Abbey was built in the 1870s by a community of 50 Cistercian Trappist monks who came in 1849 from Mount Melleray Abbey in Ireland. The Abbey was designed by a local architect, John Mullany who was a disciple of A. W. Pugin. In the original plan, the north wing had a two-storey interior which accommodated the library, the refectory and store rooms on the ground floor, and a dormitory on the first floor. Projecting from it was a kitchen wing which is now the chapter house. The church was located on the first floor of the east wing until the 1920s when it was relocated on the first floor of the north wing. The church was ultimately meant to occupy the south wing which now closes the quadrangle (not shown on the drawing), but by the time construction was resumed on the south wing in the 1950s, the original plan for the church had been set aside. In the 1960s the monks decided they wanted to redesign their church, at first as a new structure in place of the north wing, but later as a new use for the north wing. The architects were commissioned in 1973. The project won an Honor Award from the Minnesota Society of the American Institute of Architects. The jury commended the design for being 'entirely appropriate to the spirit of the monastic life, an attempt to get to basic essences with frugal means'.

Character The building is a Neo-Gothic quadrangular structure of rough-cut local sandstone blocks, with limestone quoins and dressings around the window openings. The single-storey kitchen wing, now the chapter house, has a tiled pitched roof supporting a steepled bell-tower. The north wing of the quadrangle, now the church, is a double-height structure with a pitched

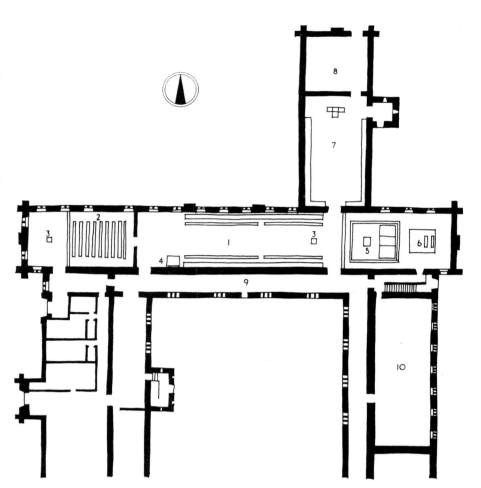

1. Part ground floor plan.

1. CHOIR	6. TABERNACLE HOUSE
2. GUEST SEATING	7. CHAPTER HOUSE
3. FONT	8. CHAPEL
4. ORGAN	9. CLOISTER
5. ALTAR	10. SACRISTY

2. View from the west with the library and refectory building (now the church) on the right, and the single-storey kitchen wing (now the chapter house) in the background on the left (PHOTOGRAPH: LES TURNER).

4. The tabernacle house behind the altar.
(PHOTOGRAPH: LES TURNER).

3. The choir seen from the guest seating.

roof surmounted by several ornamented chimneys. Lancet windows pierce the thick walls on the north side of the building at ground and upper level, and on the south side at the upper level only. The lights are of clear glass.

Work done The interior of the north wing was completely gutted and the plaster stripped off, exposing the masonry walls and the roof trusses which were sandblasted. A new floor of buff-grey brick tiles was laid, new casements were inserted and new furniture, made of butcher-block red oak, was designed specially for the church. At either end of the church a dais was installed, one for the sanctuary and the other for visitors. These enliven the bare interior and improve visibility. The church was rewired and heating was installed. A structure of the same wood as the furniture stands behind the altar and houses a tiny chapel for private prayer.

The kitchen wing was similarly converted into a chapter house and chapel.

Accommodation Church, chapter house and chapel

Date of completion July 1976

Cost $500,000

OLD ALL SAINTS, LANGDON HILLS, ESSEX

New use House

Architect Colin Dollimore (of Trevor Dannatt and Partners)

Client Private owner/occupier

Site The church is situated in a church-yard on the western slope of Langdon Hills. It is a distinctive landmark and there are good views from it to the north-west. The immediate landscape is a combination of wooded hillsides and arable farmland. A right of way through the churchyard and a narrow strip of land around the building form part of the lease.

History The church consisted of a nave, chancel, chapel and porch, and a bell tower with spire. The nave and chancel were built in the sixteenth century, but evidence of flint rubble at the base of the walls and jamb stones on the south doorway indicate the existence of an earlier building. The north chapel was rebuilt in 1834 and the bell turret with spire are comparatively modern. Notable internal fittings include the royal arms dated 1660, painted on a plastered tympanum over the entry to the chancel, and two floor-slabs dated 1630 and 1669. The church became disused in the 1960s and under the Pastoral Measure of 1968 it was made redundant. The building became derelict, the spire turret decayed. The interior was badly damaged by vandals who smashed all the windows and made a hole in the nave roof.

Character The long axis of the building is set parallel to the slope of the hill, the western end riding out above the contour establishing a strong brick-buttressed base to the bell tower with its spire. At the eastern end the floor level is set some 3ft below ground.

The nave and chancel walls are finished externally in a two-inch red brick with variegated 'stitching'; internally they are plastered. The windows are of brick arch and tracery construction and the west window and north door are modern. The chancel is square in plan divided from the rectangular nave by a plastered tympanum. The nave has at its western end a stepped choir gallery with a plastered raking soffit.

Work done The kitchen/dining room and bathroom were accommodated within the old Victorian chapel. The bathroom and kitchen, ventilated lobby, boiler and washing machine alcoves, were designed as a single joinery unit set

1. Ground floor plan.
1. ENTRANCE LOBBY
2. STUDY, WITH BEDROOM BALCONY ABOVE
3. SITTING AREA
4. DINING AREA
5. DINING-KITCHEN
6. BATHROOM, WITH STORAGE PLATFORM ABOVE

2. Long section looking south.

in a double-height space. Three new window openings were cut, from which the only outside view from within the church is obtained.

The existing stepped choir gallery was used as the bedroom and incorporated a purpose-made bed with legs of differing lengths and storage units. A new staircase was built rising from a brick podium at the west end. The library was located under the gallery. The existing south porch was retained as the front entrance but a lobby was created by the provision of an outer entrance door. The windows were reglazed with clear glass and leaded. The existing door opening in

165

3. View from the north-west. (PHOTO-GRAPH: MARTIN CHARLES).

4. The sitting area looking towards the dining area and east window. (PHOTO-GRAPH: MARTIN CHARLES).

5. The kitchen occupies the former Victorian chapel. (PHOTOGRAPH: MARTIN CHARLES).

the nave north wall was fitted with a solid-boarded stable-type door. Extensive re-plastering to old walls was carried out in a soft plaster to marry with the existing in texture and contour. The new ground floor was finished in a red/brown quarry tile throughout, apart from the bathroom which is in cork. Existing monuments in the floor were raised and re-set.

New openings were formed with an Essex soft red brick to match the old as closely as possible and splay bricks were used on jambs similar to the earlier openings. To avoid new and unsightly rainwater gutters and down pipes, brick paving was laid around the edge of the building forming a ground gutter discharging into gullies. Extensive structural repairs were necessary to the bell turret and the spire was entirely reconstructed. The turret was clad in oak weather-boarding and the spire in cedar shingles.

Grants were obtained from the Historic Buildings Council and Monument Trust.

Accommodation Ground floor—entrance lobby, study, sitting area, dining area, dining-kitchen, bathroom. First floor—bedroom balcony, storage platform.

Date of completion 1976

TINTERN RAILWAY STATION, GWENT

New use Visitors' centre

Architect Gordon Probert, County Planning Officer, Gwent County Council; K. P. Jones, County Architect

Client Gwent County Council and The Countryside Commission

Site The station is situated in the Wye valley, an area listed as of outstanding natural beauty. The railway line it served was the 13-mile single-track line from Wye Valley Junction to Wyesham Halt and linking Chepstow and Monmouth. The long site includes a ¾-mile stretch of the old railway line (long since removed) extending between two bridges and running roughly parallel to the River Wye.

History The Wye Valley Railway was opened to the public on 1st November 1876, but the line never fulfilled expectations, losing money continually until it was amalgamated with the Great Western Railway Company in July 1905. Rail traffic continued to fall until the line was closed to passengers in 1959 and to goods in January 1964. Soon after this the rails were taken up and sold for scrap. The site changed hands several times over the next ten years until the County Council bought it in 1970, and three years later bought an adjoining site of 0·8 hectares (2 acres) with a view to providing a tourist centre with picnic and walking facilities, light refreshments, a tourist information service and a permanent exhibition of the Lower Wye Valley line and other features of the locality.

Character Originally the buildings involved were the station building, the signal box, the water tower and the engine shed. The shed had deteriorated so badly that it had to be demolished.

The station building is typical of a small wayside station of the late nineteenth century. It is a single-storey structure of local stone with attractive fretted bargeboards. Outside the front door a canopy overhangs what was once the station platform. Inside is one large main space incorporating the booking hall and the waiting room, with a floor and ceiling of wood.

The signal box is a two-storey building of similar construction. An external staircase leads up to the control room on the first floor, which has almost continuous windows on three sides, commanding good views of the tracks. On the ground floor are two round-headed windows and openings which allow the

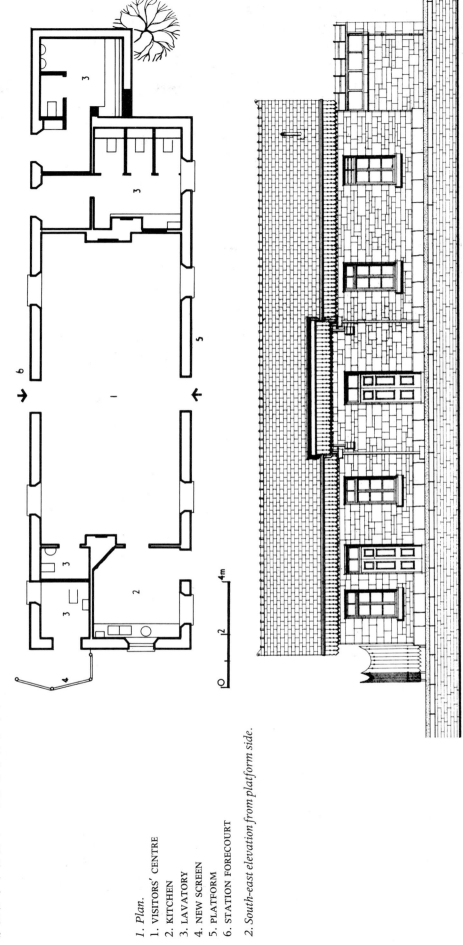

1. Plan.
1. VISITORS' CENTRE
2. KITCHEN
3. LAVATORY
4. NEW SCREEN
5. PLATFORM
6. STATION FORECOURT

2. South-east elevation from platform side.

167

rods controlling the rails to connect with the controls upstairs. The water tower is a fairly massive solid stone structure.

Work done Gwent County Council showed considerable ingenuity in tapping the goodwill and resources of the community. Local schoolboys voluntarily cleared the site of undergrowth and building débris. The demolition of the old engine sheds was undertaken as a Territorial Army exercise. Repairs were carried out by a local building firm. In the station building these involved new quarry tiled floors instead of the old wood, internal re-plastering, new doors and casements throughout, a new roof of dark blue asbestos-cement slates and, where necessary, new fretted bargeboards. Lavatories were put into the north end of the building, and a kitchen and a disabled persons' lavatory at the south end. New electrical, water, heating and drainage installations were provided.

The signal box was repaired and re-roofed, using slates from the main building and the engine shed. The lower floor was cleared of débris, and the window and rod openings were filled in with matching stonework. The tower has been cleared of ivy and re-pointed. A high-level floor will provide good views of the valley.

Externally the area has been tidied and landscaped. Picnic furniture has been provided and the original garden re-planted. Two new car parks accommodate 70 cars between them.

Accommodation Station building— display/information area, kitchen and refreshments counter, lavatories.
Signal box—ground floor: tool store
first floor: Warden's office.

Date of completion September 1975

Cost Approximately £30,000

3. The station and signal box.
4. The station hall converted to a visitors' centre.

9 Case study: the Landmark Trust and the Little Houses of the National Trust for Scotland

Introduction

This chapter examines the modest but remarkable operations of two charitable trusts, the Landmark Trust, whose activities encompass the whole of the British Isles, and the National Trust for Scotland's Little Houses Scheme which is restricted to Scotland and largely concentrated in the County of Fife. Although both operations are mainly concerned with the conservation and continued use of small but worthwhile buildings, there is considerable difference in the methods of finance and in the principles on which each is based. Both operations are illustrated with examples and a number of Landmark Trust conversions are also included in Chapters 8 and 11.

The Landmark Trust was started by John and Christian Smith in 1965 'for preserving small buildings, structures or sites of historic interest, architectural merit, or amenity value, and where possible finding suitable uses for them; and for protecting and promoting the enjoyment of places of historic interest or natural beauty'.[1] Today Landmark owns some 60 properties, most of which have been converted with the help of local architects for letting to holiday-makers. The income derived from the 10,000 people a year now staying in these is sufficient for maintenance only. Some of the cost of rehabilitation and restoration—approximately 9 per cent of the money spent—has been met by grants from the Historic Buildings Council, the tourist boards and local authorities. Buying and converting, however, has been financed mainly by the Manifold Trust, another charitable foundation started by Mr and Mrs Smith, which has distributed some £4 million since its inception in 1963 to environmental and educational causes. Some 70 per cent of the revenue has gone to the Landmark Trust, but it also paid to establish HMS Belfast in the Pool of London and has given generous support both in the field of industrial preservation and to organisations as diverse as the Maritime Trust, the London Library, the Bate Benefaction and the Victorian Society.

It is the policy of the Landmark Trust not to take out of the 'housing stock' any cottage or house which could provide a permanent home. Even when a building is saved from demolition, like the New Inn at Peasenhall in Suffolk (page 179), the Trust will only keep for letting

[1] From the Trust's handbook, *The Landmark Trust 1972.*

169

those parts which are difficult to convert for permanent occupation. At Ironbridge (page 158), a former grocer's establishment now incorporates a small holiday flat, but is still essentially a shop with living accommodation above which is let to a tenant.

The Trust's choice has fallen on 'minor but handsome buildings of all kinds, into whose construction went much thought and care, which are part of our history, and which contribute greatly to the scene; but whose original use has disappeared and which cannot be preserved from vandals, demolition or decay, unless a new use, and a source of income, can be found for them'.[2] These principles have been extended to buildings that may not be outstanding in themselves but occupy an important position in fine surroundings that could easily be spoilt. Often the buildings acquired by the Trust are in an advanced state of decay. Tixall Gatehouse (page 182) was 'an Elizabethan ruin, without roof, floors or windows, standing in a field and used as a shelter for cattle'[3] The Music Room at Lancaster (page 177) had been not only grossly misused inside but engulfed outside by shacks which had to be bought in order to be demolished. Wortham Manor in Devon (page 213) is a fine medieval structure, belonging to the category of small country houses that is so particularly at risk today. Too much of a responsibility and probably too large for a private owner, it is also not the kind of house that the National Trust would like to look after, much as it would like to see it looked after by others. Wortham Manor has cost the trust more than any other building, a fact which it has celebrated by acquiring the disused farm buildings on two sides of the house so as to preserve its setting. In the case of Clytha Castle, a Gothic Revival folly near Abergavenny (page 202), Landmark took a long lease at the suggestion of the National Trust who own the building. It is a good example of an eccentric plan which makes an interesting holiday home but is too inconvenient for permanent occupation.

Characteristic if not typical of the Landmark Trust is its involvement in Lundy, a small island in the approaches to the Bristol Channel. Rising over 400ft out of the sea, its western range of cliffs slope steeply down to the more sheltered east coast facing the mainland. Three lighthouses, a castle, a church, a farm and a population of about 25 are concentrated at the south end of the island. Lundy offers nature almost untamed, buildings and field walls made of the island's granite, no traffic and the likelihood of a hazardous landing on the open beach. When in 1969 Lundy came up for sale, John Smith recognised 'that slow decline is probably the most agreeable and natural state of affairs for a small island, but decline, if it is to continue, has to be reversed occasionally'.[4] So he offered to underwrite an appeal (the National Trust having decided reluctantly that it could not buy it) to raise the purchase price, and then restore and run the island if the National Trust would accept ownership. Since then the Landmark Trust has been rehabilitating the island's buildings and services, a not inconsiderable logistical exercise in a place where everything has to be brought in by small boat. There is accommodation for nearly 90 visitors in some ten buildings, including a 12-bed hotel.

There are basically two objects which the Landmark Trust sets out to fulfil, one of which, that at least part of a building should be let furnished for short periods, has already been mentioned. This enables

[2] *ibid.*

[3] Quoted in *The Landmark Handbook 1977*, The Landmark Trust, Shottesbrooke, Maidenhead, Berkshire.

[4] *ibid.*

the Trust to keep the work simple and to avoid having to make the sort of changes and additions which are needed for a permanent home and which often spoil the building. At the same time it enables the Trust to concentrate on the repair and restoration of an old building, fighting as it often does against the tendency of architects, builders or local authorities to renew and replace when the existing is by no means beyond salvation. Referring to timber-framed buildings, of which the Trust owns a fair number, John Smith has said that 'to repair these is like patching a cobweb; and although we set our face against conjectural restoration, the urge is often irresistible to replace missing timbers whose original appearance can be deduced with certainty, instead of carrying out such repairs in a different material which is what a purist would do'.[5] He admits that the Trust has made mistakes, but points out that it won 11 awards in European Architectural Heritage Year 1975, several more than any other recipient in Britain, including the government.

The second object, 'promoting the enjoyment of places of historical interest or natural beauty,' implies something more than preservation for the tourist who pays a brief visit by day. It implies education, opening the visitor's eyes, transforming his ideas, so that more and more people will appreciate the need to preserve and organisations like the Landmark Trust will no longer be needed. Some of this 'education' is achieved by asking people to stay for at least a week so that their visit becomes 'not just a holiday but an experience, of a mildly elevating kind'.[6] The properties, moreover, are carefully furnished, mainly with good, old furniture; curtains specially designed and printed for each place; attractive old rugs and carpets; pictures with a special reason for being there; a shelf of books, including fiction and poetry, to do with the district; an album of historical notes, plans and photographs; and large-scale maps of the area marking the footpaths.

The work of the Landmark Trust is an exceptionally intelligent response to the growth in tourism and leisure activities. The potential is enormous, not only for Landmark, which is now recruiting local secretaries to expand its activities, but also for like-minded organisations for whom Landmark represents an example and an inspiration.

The National Trust for Scotland has been concerned with the preservation of vernacular architecture since its foundation in 1931. Hew Lorimer, the Trust's representative in East Fife, has described the Little House as 'the typical building of the "burghal" domestic tradition of architecture. It was a product of the plan of the Scottish burgh, the main lines of which were established in the twelfth century, and which have influenced the development of the burgh ever since. Thus our Little Houses are a most valuable element in our heritage and reflect national character perhaps more directly than any other type of building'.[7] Their walls are usually white harled or of local stone, their roofs of red pantiles or grey slates. Other characteristics are gables, often crow-stepped, and standing at right-angles to the street; and outside steps leading to entrance doors headed by marriage lintels or biblical texts.

By 1936, when the Trust numbered a mere 500 members, 20

[5]*ibid.*

[6]*ibid.*

[7]*Little Houses of the National Trust for Scotland*, The National Trust for Scotland, 5 Charlotte Square, Edinburgh EH2 4DU.

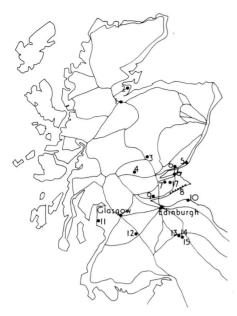

1. *Map of Scotland showing the Little Houses projects of the National Trust for Scotland.*

1. INVERNESS
2. CROMARTY
3. DIMKELD
4. FOWLIS-WESTER
5. BROUGHTY FERRY
6. DUNDEE
7. FALKLAND
8. FIFE COAST: DYSART, ST MONANS, PITTENWEEM, ANSTRUTHER, CRAIL, KINGSBARNS, ARNCROACH
9. CULROSS
10. NORTH BERWICK
11. WEST KILBRIDE
12. DOUGLAS
13. BEMERSYDE
14. BOWDEN (NEAR MELROSE)
15. ST BOSWELLS
16. TAYPORT
17. CERES (NEAR HILL OF TARVIT)

(In the case of 16 and 17 help was given to local preservation societies to carry out similar work.)

2, 3. Powrie Castle, near Dundee, was bought by the National Trust for Scotland in 1978. The Trust then found 'a restoring purchaser' in Peter Clarke, who undertook to restore and rehabilitate the castle to the Trust's specification (architects: Datum Design of Aberdeen) and entered into a 'Conservation agreement' with the Trust. There are two distinct buildings which were once connected by an enclosing wall on the west side and by a range of building on the east. The southern building dates from the first half of the sixteenth century and contained the great hall on the first floor. The northern building, a fine example of early seventeenth-century domestic architecture, is a long narrow structure, two storeys high, with a round tower at the north-west corner. When Peter Clarke became 'the restoring purchaser' he found the building falling into ruins. The upper storeys of the south building were lost and the ground floor had been used as a piggery. The northern building, still in reasonable repair, had been inhabited by labourers. As a result of the restoration work which cost £30,000, the southern building now provides three basement store rooms and one bedroom; and the northern building a dining-kitchen, drawing room, cloakroom and bathroom on the ground floor and two bedrooms, a dressing room and a study on the first.

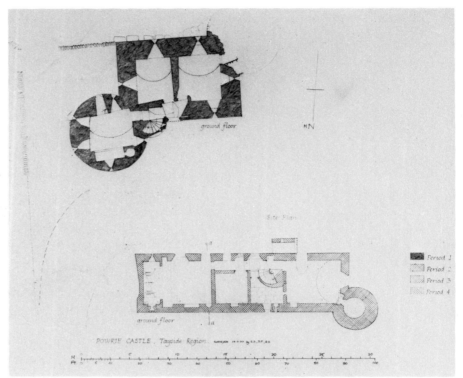

4. Pan Ha', Dysart, Kirkcaldy, before the start of the £100,000 scheme in which the National Trust for Scotland acted as agent for the Crown Estate Commissioners. St Serf's Tower (left) dates from the sixteenth century. The Anchorage, the large white house with crow-stepped gables (right of centre) was the first building to be restored by the Trust and prompted the undertaking of the whole project.

5. Pan Ha', Dysart, after restoration.

6. Part of the Little Houses scheme at Culross.

properties had been acquired in Culross, one of the two towns in which the Little Houses project began. In the same year an appeal for £500,000 was launched by the Marquess of Bute, who also initiated a survey of the buildings in Scotland worth preserving. This pioneering work has been called 'the first step . . . towards a national census of vernacular architecture',[8] and by the time the war stopped it, 100 burghs had been surveyed and 1149 houses had been 'listed' as of architectural merit.

But the time was not ripe for rehabilitation: little distinction was made by the public between old houses and slums. It was not until 1952, when the Trust celebrated its coming of age with a 'Little Houses' conference, that the project really got under way. In Culross the programme of buying and rehabilitating houses was expanded; and in Dunkeld the restoration of the street leading to the Cathedral was begun with the collaboration of the County Council. Large capital sums had to be raised and, because the law as it then stood required each completed house to be let at a rent comparable to that of a council house, the Trust found this way of financing the project too expensive and too slow. As a result, in 1961, the Little Houses Improvement Scheme, based on the simple idea of buying, restoring and selling, with the capital from the sale used again and again in a 'revolving

[8]*ibid.*

fund', was initiated with the basic capital sum of £20,000 provided in equal parts by the Pilgrim Trust and the National Trust for Scotland. To this was added later £5000 from the County Council of Fife, a £20,000 interest-free loan from a Trust member and additional loans from the Pilgrim Trust and Fife County Council of £4000 and £2500 respectively.

By the late 1960s the virtues of rehabilitation had become understood. Referring to the Customs House at Crail, the Trust's booklet on the Little Houses remarked on the fact that such a building restored by the Trust, could cease to be a 'problem' and become, after rehabilitation, 'the centre-piece of countless calendars and postcards . . . And there is also the local lesson that the former centres of communities do not degenerate into slums, nor yet do they become museum pieces, for when the occupants move into the renewed buildings, they bring renewed life'.[9]

Variations to the 'revolving fund' principle were introduced, among them the concept of 'the restoring purchaser' who undertakes to rehabilitate to the Trust's specification, sometimes with supervision from the Trust's technical staff, and enters into a Conservation Agreement over the property with the Trust. By 1970, when restoration work to more than 60 properties in the East Neck of Fife was either under way or completed, £63,000 out of a total of £115,000 for work in hand was being financed by 'restoring purchases'.

Illustrated here among other examples is the largest single project yet undertaken, which was completed in 1969, and in which the Trust acted as agent for the Crown Estate Commissioners. It was the rehabilitation, in collaboration with the Kirkaldy Town Council, of a stretch of shore at Dysart which included restoring six derelict sixteenth-century houses and filling a gap with five new ones. The work re-established a community in an abandoned area. Most indicative of the change of mood was the response in 1971 to an advertisement—a rush of over 1000 applicants—announcing the sale by the East Kilbride Development Corporation of 23 weavers' cottages, on the condition that they were restored by the buyers. Today properties restored by the Trust house well over 100 families and the work continues apace.

In recent years inflation and rising building costs have reduced the real value of the Trust's Revolving Fund which now stands at £140,000. There has also been the problem that local authority 'improvement grants', which often represent the difference between profit and loss on a restoration, now have to be repaid if the property is re-sold within five years.

To counter these problems, the Trust has switched its strategy and is now using its funds to buy up suitable derelict property and devoting more time to finding 'restoring purchasers', rather than restoring itself. The end result is exactly the same and the overall number of restorations achieved has in fact accelerated to about ten a year.

Looking to the future, the Trust have been most encouraged by the growing interest and support from local authorities. Following the Fife region's lead, both the Borders region and the Strathclyde region have now given sums to the Trust to establish local regional revolving funds to further this work.

[9]ibid.

MARGELLS, BRANSCOMBE, DEVON

New use Holiday house

Architect Pearn and Procter

Client Landmark Trust

Site Branscombe has been described as a long straggling village along the bottom of the combe for the most part, and containing a remarkable number of 'good' houses, many apparently of the sixteenth and seventeenth centuries. Church records show that it was a village which housed a number of minor gentry, and Margells was almost certainly a house belonging to one of these families. The house is too far from the parish church to have been the original vicarage.

Character Margells is a thatched sixteenth-century house with magnificent carved floor beams, plank and muntin screens, joined crucks and collars, small oak framed partitions with wattle and daub filling and the remains of a wall painting in one of the upper rooms which gives an indication of the colour and richness of the original interior.

The house is probably older than mid-sixteenth century and originally consisted of an open hall with a screen passage and sleeping platform over. Unfortunately only one of the earlier windows, with its Beer stone hood mould, jambs, sill and mullion, remains (the one facing east which has been reinstated); there are only a few stones of the window in the south wall in position, which are sufficient to indicate the original form. The chimney stacks have also been altered over the years.

Work done The aim of the Landmark Trust was to keep alterations, involving installation of bathroom and kitchen fittings, to a minimum. The major part of the work was concerned with masonry repairs, including stabilisation of the wall by underpinning, repair of the timber screens and roof trusses; the opening up of fireplaces, treatment of timber infestation and insertion of an electro-osmotic damp-proof course. The roof was re-thatched and a former window in the east elevation reinstated.

The existing ground floor was of lime-wash in poor condition. This was taken up and replaced with concrete and a damp-proof membrane with Blue Lias paving slabs incorporating electric under-floor heating. Since the link between Margells and the adjoining cottage was found to be a hazard with no barrier in the roof space, a fire curtain was installed.

During the work a wall painting, approximately 7ft square, was uncovered in the west upper room and restored. It had been painted in a lime and skimmed milk medium with dry colour directly on to the lime and sand support of the wall. Over the centuries this had been covered over by a number of layers of colour wash and finally by layers of wallpaper. The painting is typical of the late sixteenth century and consists of a foliated pattern in several colours, including red, black, green and white, with a chevron patterned border and frieze. It is possible that the whole was decorated in this way, but the remaining areas of wall surface were re-plastered at some later date. The restoration and stabilisation of the painting was carefully carried out, ensuring that the new infill pieces are easily distinguished from the original.

Accommodation Ground floor—sitting room, screens passage, kitchen and bathroom.
First floor—three bedrooms.

Date of completion October 1976

Cost £41,000

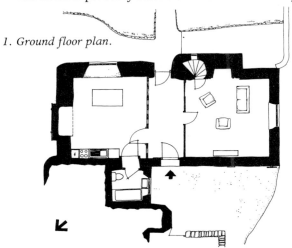

1. Ground floor plan.

2. View from the west showing the entrance on the road side.

3. View from the south-east.

175

THE EGYPTIAN HOUSE, PENZANCE, CORNWALL

New use Holiday house

Architect Pearn and Proctor

Client The Landmark Trust

Site The Egyptian House stands facing north-east at the higher end of Chapel Street just below the junction with Queen Street and forms part of the development which took place during the first 30 years of the nineteenth century when the population of Penzance doubled from nearly 3,400 to just over 6,500. The expansion of the town followed what was then the main route, which climbed from the harbour past the church and the site of the old chapel of St. Anthony, from which the road received its name. Many of the houses erected at that time were faced with brick, the newly-introduced and fashionable material, whilst the local granite was relegated to the backs. But the street possesses many excellent examples of the simple but decorative architectural details of this period, which are to be found on many West Country urban domestic buildings.

History The Egyptian House was built by George Lavin in about 1830 to house his collection of minerals and, so a page in Murray's *English Handbook Advertising* of 1858 tells us, from it Lavin sold articles manufactured by the Lizard Serpentine Company, views of Cornish scenery in photographs, stereoscopes, handbooks, pocket maps, etc. The Landmark Trust bought the property in 1968.

Character The building is similar in many respects to the London Museum, also known as Bullock's Museum or the Egyptian Hall, which was erected in Piccadilly in London in about 1811 to the design of P. F. Robinson. The two are almost identical externally, and it would seem possible that P. F. Robinson, or someone from his office, was responsible for the design of the replica in Penzance. But the Egyptian House differs in its plan and internal accommodation for, instead of galleries and lecture hall over the shops, there were two maisonettes.

Work done When the Landmark Trust requested a careful and accurate re-instatement, a detailed survey of the structure revealed damp penetration from a defective gutter behind the cornice and dry rot infestation arising from a poorly maintained drainage system.

It was decided to divide the interior horizontally into three flats with access from the central staircase. The upper floors were removed and repositioned, the timber ground floor was replaced with reinforced concrete, and steel beams were inserted under the ground and first floors. The larger staircase was rebuilt in reinforced concrete and the existing wooden stairs were placed over the new fire-resisting construction.

The new flats each have a sitting room, two bedrooms, kitchen and bathroom, and drying cabinets are provided in the basement for each unit.

The plate glass was removed from the ground-floor shop windows and the frames carefully examined to establish the position of the mortice and tenons of the glazing bars. A design for the windows was made based on this information and on the details shown in an aquatint of the Piccadilly building. Finally the stucco and Coade stone of the front were repaired and decorated in colours which were chosen after an investigation of the layers of paint on the several surfaces of the elevation.

Accommodation Three flats

Date of completion 1972

Cost £25,141

3. The street façade restored. (PHOTOGRAPH: RICHARDS BROS).

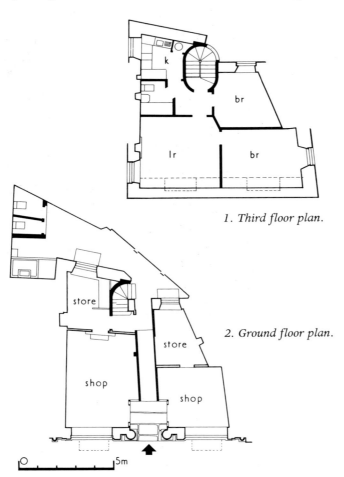

1. Third floor plan.

2. Ground floor plan.

176

THE MUSIC ROOM, LANCASTER

New use Bookshop and holiday flat. The Music Room on the first floor, now restored, is open to visitors by appointment with the caretaker.

Architect Charles B. Pearson Son & Partners

Client The Landmark Trust

Site An urban site in Sun Street, Lancaster.

History Until comparatively recently this small eighteenth-century garden folly was very little known, as it was completely hemmed in by nineteenth- and twentieth-century accretions. In 1972 it was acquired by the Landmark Trust who also had to buy the accretions so that they could be demolished to allow access to the Music Room. The space that they previously occupied has now been paved by the Lancaster City Council to form a small pedestrian square.

Work done The rich plaster work in the Music Room itself on the first floor was restored to its original condition. Stone on the external face of the building which was in good condition was carefully cleaned and pointed. Damaged or missing stones were replaced with stone from Longridge quarry which closely matches the original, although it will take some time to weather in. Small areas of detail were repaired with plastic stone. All windows were replaced and the large archway on the ground floor, which originally must have been open, was glazed with one large sheet of plate glass. The boundary wall on the north side of the building, which had previously overlapped one of the pilasters, was rebuilt. The wall on the south side was tidied up.

Accommodation Ground floor—second-hand bookshop.
First floor—the Music Room.
Second floor—holiday flat.

Date of completion July 1976

1. First floor plan (music room).

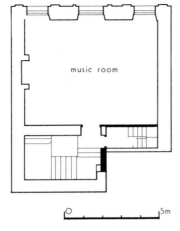

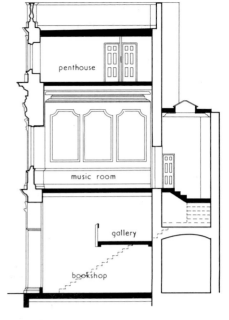

2. Section.

3. Second floor plan (penthouse flat).

4. The façade on to the newly formed pedestrian square. (PHOTOGRAPH: JOHN MILLS).

5. The music room with its rich plaster-work restored. (PHOTOGRAPH: JOHN MILLS).

THE NEW INN, PEASENHALL, SUFFOLK

New use Permanent and holiday accommodation

Architect John Warren of the Architectural and Planning Partnership

Client The Landmark Trust

Site The Inn fronts on to the village green at Peasenhall near Yoxford in Suffolk, and is flanked by cottages on either side. Since its restoration the area has been listed as a conservation area.

History In 1464 the Abbot of Sibton sold to John Kempe the triangle of land at the eastern end of the green on which the whole group of cottages now stands. Sibton Abbey, now ruined, lay nearby, and such little of its creamy stone as now survives is hidden in woodland. The timber-framed open-hall building dating from the late fifteenth century was apparently built as an inn and was known as such—the name 'New Inn' goes with the earliest records of the extant building.

By the nineteenth century the land on both sides had been taken up with cottages and the New Inn itself had been parcelled up into several small dwellings. More recently the New Inn and the cottages deteriorated to a level where they were uninhabitable and became candidates for slum clearance. It was the architectural significance of the New Inn which caused the Trust to purchase the whole group and to conserve it in its entirety.

Character The Inn is a timber construction which originally contained a large hall open to the ceiling. (In a medieval hall house the standard plan allowed for the high table to be placed at one end of the hall. This end was known, therefore, as the 'high' end. At the opposite end were the opposed entrances and doors leading to service rooms. This was the 'low' end.) In the sixteenth century an upper floor was put across the open hall and an ad-ditional timber-framed building attached to the low end. Two massive brick chimneys were inserted into the timber framing, one at the high end of the hall itself and the other in the outer wall frame at the low end.

The cottages attached to the Inn are nineteenth-century brick-built artisans' houses. Their two-up two-down accommodation was minimal and of flimsy construction.

Work done It was decided that the New Inn should be turned into two holiday lettings, each of which was to be self-contained within the high and low ends. It was felt that re-opening the hall to the roof, which involved the removal of the inserted sixteenth century floor and chimney stack, was justified by the poor condition of the later accretions and by the fact that so few medieval halls can be seen in their original condition. There was one variation to the plan, however. In stripping the building down it was discovered that the false cross-wing,

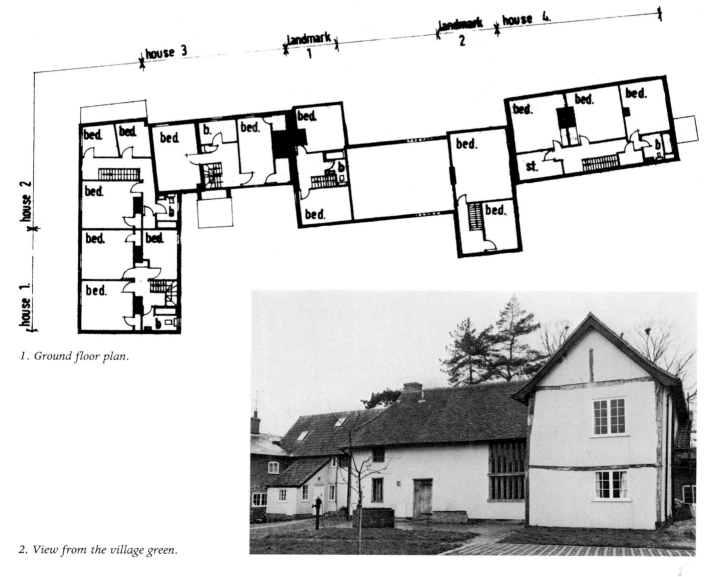

1. Ground floor plan.

2. View from the village green.

179

added as part of the extensions to the low end, was in fact of high calibre and in reasonably good condition. The original decision was modified and the whole of this additional building was kept to form a further holiday letting and to extend the low end to give much needed additional space. Some later windows were also kept, together with a few timbers in the high end upper chamber, which remain as evidence of the inserted seventeenth-century ceiling. This chamber, originally open to the roof, was a further medieval hall in miniature, with a fine octagonal crownpost concealed subsequently by a heavy inserted ceiling. In the high end wall of the hall the framing had been cut away to allow the insertion of a chimney stack and in this section of the building part of the stack has been retained as evidence of the alteration and to avoid speculative insertion of timber.

The main framing of the hall had been racked and twisted by uneven settlement and by the loss of structural integrity when dormer windows and doorways had been cut through the timber. Parts of the exposed wall framing had settled as much as 18in while others had not moved at all, and some rafters were bent out of alignment as much as 2ft 6in in 13ft. While the high and low ends kept in position and much of the panelling was retained, the roof and the walls of the hall itself were completely stripped, missing soleplates were replaced and the walls were reframed on their correct alignment. A new courtyard was formed on the south side in the position of the original medieval court.

Some twelve cottages have been converted to four houses and three holiday lettings, and the Trust's concern has extended to the green itself, which it has purchased. A wooden hut was removed, dead trees and undergrowth were cleared, electricity lines put underground and the road in front of the Inn was replaced with a footpath to re-establish the position of the ancient green.

Accommodation Four permanently tenanted houses, each with two or three bedrooms; shop and store; three lettable units for use as holiday dwellings, each containing two or three bedrooms, bathroom, kitchen/dining room and living room.

Restored medieval hall open to the roof for common use and exhibition purposes.

Date of completion 1974

Cost Approximately £38,000 (timber-framed buildings only)

3. The hall-reopened to the roof after the removal of a sixteenth-century floor and chimney stack.

Below, Appleton (see facing page).
4. Detail of the spiral stair turret. (PHOTOGRAPHS: BILL TOOMEY).

APPLETON WATER TOWER, NORFOLK

New use Holiday house

Architects Michael and Sheila Gooch

Client The Landmark Trust

Site At Appleton, an almost vanished village consisting of a ruined church, farm, and a handful of cottages about one mile south-east of Sandringham House. The tower occupies the highest point on the Sandringham Estate on the edge of the chalk downland of north-west Norfolk, with views to the North Sea and the Wash.

History Part of the development of the Sandringham Estate by the Prince of Wales (later Edward VII) after his purchase of the estate in 1861. Pevsner ascribes the design of the tower to Martin Ffolkes, a local gentleman-amateur. But the estate office still has the original design drawings; the elevations are signed by Robert Rawlinson, 1876, and the structural details by James Mansergh CE, 1877. Presumably this was an Engineer-Architect collaboration, though it is possible Ffolkes may have given advice. The tower was supplied with water by a private pumping station. This later ceased to operate and the tower was then taken over by the Water Authority. It became surplus to their requirements in 1973 and stood empty until the Landmark Trust leased it in 1976. The restoration and conversion work was carried out in 1976–7, exactly a hundred years after the date of the design drawings.

Character The plan consists of two attached brick octagons, the larger supporting the tank and the smaller containing a spiral stair. The tank is of cast iron, and the stair turret continues up past this, giving access to the roof of the tank, and terminates with open arches and a pointed roof on brackets. The exterior appearance is neo-Byzantine, with elaborate polychromy derived from two shades of red brick, contrasted with Carstone, a strongly coloured yellow/brown stone quarried locally. The tank is a sectional cast-iron structure with elaborate applied ornamentation in cast iron and a fanciful balustrade.

The two lowest floors were intended as a caretaker's house, with outbuildings attached on the east side. On the second floor was a lofty octagonal room with

3. View from the west.

four large windows and a fireplace with separate access by the spiral stairs. This was no doubt intended as a picnic and viewing room for royal shooting parties, though one wonders whether their host could have managed the long climb up the spiral stair. Above this is a valve room, full of water pipes and controls, with the fireplace flues piped into a central flue going up through the tank. Above this again, supported on massive cast iron beams, is the tank.

Work done The first job was the thorough repair of the fabric, including new roofs to the turret and the tank, brickwork repair and repointing, repairs to the ironwork of the tank, including making replicas to replace missing ornamental details, renewal or repair of windows and doors. The outbuildings were demolished, to leave the tower freestanding in its clearing. The interior was converted to a lettable holiday house by linking the second floor to the lower floors with an extended internal stair.

Accommodation Ground floor—living/kitchen, shower room.
First floor—bedroom.
Second floor—bed/sitting room.

The interior has been furnished by the Landmark Trust 'in period' with late Victorian furniture, ornaments and pictures.

Date of completion 1977

Cost (excluding furnishing) £24,000

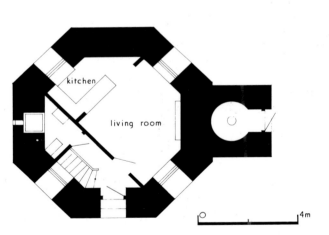

1. Ground floor plan.

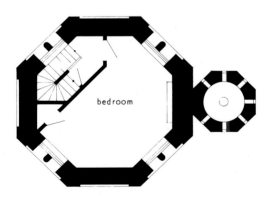

2. First floor plan.

181

TIXALL GATEHOUSE, STAFFORDSHIRE

New use Holiday house

Architect Lawrence H. Bond & Robert W. Read

Client The Landmark Trust

Site In the *Landmark Trust Handbook* the site is described as follows: 'As the traveller by canal comes down the valley of the Sow, and through Tixall Lock, he enters the last and most beautiful mile of the Staffordshire and Worcestershire Canal before its junction with the Trent and Mersey. The cut here broadens into a lake, known to boaters as Tixall Wide. On either side lie most handsome stretches of country—to the south, Shugborough, with Cannock Chase beyond, and, to the north, Ingestre, with Tixall Gatehouse in the foreground. The two houses which were once approached via the gatehouse have disappeared and the gatehouse now stands in a grassy field.'

History The gatehouse was built about 1580 by Sir Walter Aston whose son had just married the daughter of Sir Thomas Lucy of Charlecote (Shakespeare's Justice Shallow), where there is an earlier gatehouse which may have inspired the much grander one at Tixall. The Tudor house, in front of which the gatehouse stood, was replaced in the eighteenth century by another house built to one side of it by Thomas Clifford, a descendant of the Astons. In this, and in his landscape works, he was 'assisted by the taste and judgement of the celebrated Brown'.

Having been used as a cattle shelter for some years, and become all but ruinous, it was acquired by the Landmark Trust in 1968 when the last parts of Lord Shrewsbury's estate were being sold off.

Character The design of the gatehouse has been attributed to Robert Smithson, the architect of Wollaton Park, Nottingham. It consists of a ground stage pierced by the central carriageway, and two floors, with a flat roof. At the four corners are polygonal turrets rising above the balustered parapets, and roofed with 'bottle' domes surmounted with weather vanes. The north and south elevations are identically treated, with three orders of classical columns, in pairs between the large mullioned and transomed windows, each carrying a full entablature. The central windows in the two upper floors project above the archway as a two-storey oriel. The frieze to the ground stage is elaborated with heraldic devices carved on the metopes

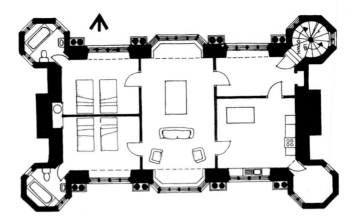

1. First floor plan.

2. Tixall Gatehouse with its manor house, now disappeared (from an eighteenth-century engraving).

and with triglyphs which are fluted. The spandrels of the semi-elliptical archways contain robust sculptures, on the south reclining winged females, and on the north armed warriors.

Access to the upper floors is by a broad stone newel stair in the north-east turret. Nothing remains of the interior details, but the outline of an elaborate stone chimney piece, all hacked away, can be seen on the west wall of the first floor.

Work done New floors and roof of steel and concrete were provided. In the first floor rooms the floors were finished with elm boarding, and in the kitchen with Staffordshire tiles. The flat roof was paved with reclaimed Yorkshire flagstones.

Very conservative repairs and renewals to masonry were carried out by a local mason, who understood the architects' philosophy of renewing only to prevent the spread of decay, or to replace losses which interrupt features of the design.

The weather vanes which, with the stone finials, had fallen from the turret domes were replaced with new ones, the guidons of which were gilded. The windows were glazed with carefully selected glass, some antique reamy, some Cordelais, in leaded lights, as they were originally, and some were provided with specially made iron casements.

The first floor was divided to provide an entrance hall, a central gallery or 'common room', kitchen and pantry, and two bedrooms each with a bathroom in the adjoining turret. The second floor was left undivided, as a playroom, and

3. Tixall Gatehouse before restoration by the Landmark Trust. The external appearance has remained unchanged.

extra sleeping space for a large party, with two small turret bedrooms and a lavatory. The gallery was panelled in elm, and all the doors are also of elm. All other walls, except those of the staircase and playroom where the stone was cleaned, were limewashed. At ground level, no living accommodation was provided; instead there are two large storerooms either side of the open carriageway, which was paved with York stone setts.

Water and electricity supplies were installed, as well as drainage disposal, by means of a septic tank and filter.

The conversion won a conservation award from Staffordshire Council for the Protection of Rural England 1977.

Accommodation Ground floor—two store rooms.
First floor—hall, kitchen, living room, two bedrooms, two bathrooms, store.
Second floor—playroom, two turret bedrooms, lavatory.

Date of completion 1977

Cost Approximately £70,000 (partly funded by a grant from the Historic Buildings Council).

THE PINEAPPLE, DUNMORE, STIRLINGSHIRE

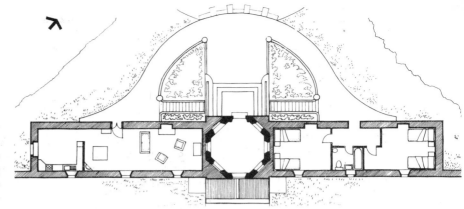

New use Holiday house

Architect David Carr

Client The Landmark Trust

Site The walled garden of a country estate on the fertile lands of the Forth estuary. The Pineapple stands at some distance from the house (now ruined) which is just visible from the Pineapple's north front.

History The Pineapple is an elaborate two-storey summer house built in 1761 for the 29 year old Earl of Dunmore (later Governor of New York and Virginia). The Dunmore Estate was broken up and sold in lots in 1970. The 'Pineapple Lot', including the great walled garden, woodlands and a small lake, were purchased and eventually given by Lady Perth to the National Trust for Scotland. The Landmark Trust have leased the property from the National Trust and carried out restoration work to preserve the Pineapple, a job which won a Saltire award in 1971.

Character An eighteenth-century fruit and vegetable garden dominated by a massive stone folly in the shape of a pineapple. The Pineapple was built in freestone of very high quality and shows no deterioration at all. Though of orthodox classical design at ground level, it grows slowly into something entirely vegetable, conventional architraves put out shoots and end up as prickly leaves of stone, each one drained to prevent damage by frost. The inner low-level entrance doorway is flanked by pairs of Ionic columns with carved timber capitals and timber shafts having perfectly formed flutings with full entasis. There is no connection between the two flanking wings without walking outside past the Pineapple.

The brick garden walls were built to act as heated flues on the north side of the garden and some of the chimneys had their pots disguised as urns. The gardeners' potting sheds and boiler houses containing the bothies were built behind the wall on either side of the Pineapple.

Work done The potting sheds and bothies were in a ruinous state when work was first undertaken. The west wing roof was completely rotten and the east wing roof was missing. Trees were growing in the walls and the roots had found their way along the horizontal flues. The garden walls were bulging and in places had collapsed completely.

1. Ground floor plan.

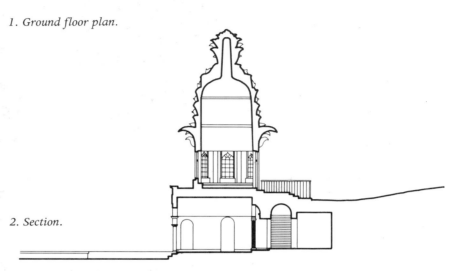

2. Section.

3. The Pineapple before and, 4 (facing page) after restoration. (PHOTOGRAPH: JOHN K, WILKIE, *Courtesy of the National Trust for Scotland*).

Most of the cope needed re-bedding or replacing. The garden was a jungle, adding in a strange way to the fantasy of this folly which reared its pineapple head above the wilderness.

The Pineapple itself was tidied up and cleaned, the walls were cleared of trees, and repaired, the upper floor windows on to the garden were reopened. The roof was completely renewed, the lead flashings replaced and new windows and a new entrance door to match the old ones were installed. Two columns were replaced in the entrance, including capitals and entablature enrichment, all formed of fibrous plaster. Access steps were rebedded and the path relaid. Modern kitchen and bathroom facilities were installed.

The great garden in front was cleared and replanted, the garden walls were rebuilt or repaired where necessary and the potting sheds and bothies were rebuilt.

Accommodation Ground floor—two store-rooms, now housing an exhibition. First floor—west wing: kitchen and living room; east wing: two bedrooms and bathroom.

Date of completion 1976

Cost £76,000 (Part of the cost was met by grants from the Historic Buildings Council and Scottish Tourist Board)

5. The living room.

10 Case study: the paradores of Spain

For nearly 50 years the Spanish government has been converting historic buildings into hotels. With the exception of the Portuguese *pousadas*, the *paradores* are the only example known to us of a long-term government programme of rehabilitation and new use; and the fact that it started as long ago as 1930 makes it all the more remarkable. It is presented here as an exemplar to other countries which are fortunate enough to combine a growing tourist industry with an architectural heritage of castles and monasteries—France, for example, or Austria with 427 of its surviving castles in Lower Austria alone. In England stalwart work of a similar kind, though on a far more modest scale, has been carried out by the Landmark Trust, and some of the larger buildings it has converted are included in Chapter 11, which also contains examples of large country houses and castles converted to uses other than hotels.

The original idea behind the *parador*[1] was to provide a hotel where none existed at a time when increasing wealth and better communications were beginning to encourage would-be tourists. In 1905 a national commission was set up to encourage foreigners to visit Spain through propaganda and the improvement of railways and hotels. And its successor in 1911, the Comisaria Regia del Turismo, established tourism on an organised footing and planned the first *parador* in 1926. This was a new building on the edge of the remote Sierra de Gredos west of Madrid, and was an immediate success. As a result, the Patronato Nacional de Turismo, which had succeeded the Comisaria Regia, established the Junta de Paradores y Hosterias del Reino with instructions to build *paradores* in the more attractive parts of the country that were without adequate hotels.

It was at this point that the idea of converting castles and monasteries was conceived, and in the first five years, out of the eleven *paradores* and *hosterias* which opened, five were in historic buildings. Two of these, the *paradores* of Oropesa (1930) and Merida (1933) are fully illustrated here. The others are the Hosteria Alcala de Henares (1930) north of Madrid, a sixteenth-century cloistered courtyard that once formed part of the Colegio Trilingue; the *parador* at Ciudad Rodrigo in the twelfth-century castle; and the *parador* at

---

[1] The word comes from the Arabic *waradah*, halting place, and has been used since early times to mean caravanserai, inn, etc.

KEY

Paradores in historic buildings
Date indicates year of opening

1	*Oropesa (Toledo)	1939
2	Ciudad Rodrigo (Salamanca)	1931
3	Ubeda (Jaen)	1931
4	*Merida (Badajoz)	1933
5	Granada (Granada)	1945
6	Santillana (Santander)	1946
7	Pontevedra (Pontevedra)	1954
8	*Guadalupe (Caceres)	1965
9	*Jaen (Jaen)	1965
10	Santo Domingo de la Calzada (Logroño)	1965
11	Alarcon (Cuenca)	1966
12	Avila (Avila)	1966
13	Bayona (Pontevedra)	1966
14	Jarandilla (Caceres)	1966
15	Olite (Navarra)	1966
16	Gijon (Asturias)	1967
17	Villalba (Lugo)	1967
18	Alcaniz (Teruel)	1968
19	Arcos de la Frontera (Cadiz)	1968
20	Fuenterrabia (Guipuzcoa)	1968
21	Morella (Teruel)	1968
22	*Zafra (Badajoz)	1968
23	Zamora (Zamora)	1968
24	Benavente (Zamora)	1972
25	Cardona (Barcelona)	1976
26	Carmona (Sevilla)	1976
27	Monzon de los Campos (Palencia)	
28	Sos del Rey Catolico (Zaragoza)	
29	Tortosa (Tarragona)	1976
30	Siguenza (Guadalajara)	1977
31	Almagro (Ciudad Real)	1978

Hosterias in historic buildings

32	Alcala de Henares (near Madrid)	1930
33	Arties (Lerida)	1967
34	Pedraza de la Sierra (Segovia)	1967
35	Del Comendador (Caceres)	1972

Hostals in historic buildings

36	De San Marcos (Leon)	1965
37	*De los Reyes Catolicos (Santiago de Compostela)	1965
38	La Marall (Ceuta, Spanish Morocco)	1967

*Indicates a building illustrated in this chapter.

Ubeda in the Baroque palace of Don Ortega.

Another enlightened aspect of the Junta's policy, though nothing to do with the re-use of old buildings, was the *albergue de carretera*, a small and modest hotel sited either in an isolated spot without facilities or along a main route for the convenience of motorists. The accommodation was limited to four single and four double rooms, and the restaurant and lounge seating to 30. Overnight stays were restricted, as they still are, to 48 hours. But today the increase in tourist traffic has caused many of the *albergues* to be closed, upgraded into or replaced by *paradores* which are able to cope with the greater numbers.

The Republican government which came to power in 1931 endorsed the *parador* programme and by 1936, when the Civil War broke out and put a stop to all building, there were five *paradores*, one hotel, one *hosteria* and seven *albergues*. During the Civil War many of the buildings were used as hospitals while some, like the Hosteria of Alcala de Henares, were seriously damaged. After the war General Franco again approved the *parador* programme and during his long régime many conversions as well as new projects were undertaken. By 1976 there were 64 *paradores*, nearly half of which were in converted historic buildings, 17 *albergues*, five *hosterias*, three *refugios* (in mountain areas for winter sports) and one hotel. Between 1928 and 1972 the accommodation rose from 30 beds and 80 restaurant seats to 3,862 beds and 7,044 restaurant seats.

The first *paradores* were handed over to private management, as are the *pousadas* in Portugal today. The result, no doubt, was unreliable and uneven. So the government soon decided to build *and* run the enterprise, setting up in 1958 the Administracion Turistica Española as a body operating within the Ministry of Information and Tourism and responsible for works, warehousing, accounts and publicity. Individual *paradores*, however, were to be run like privately owned hotels. They were expected to be self-supporting, though not to make large profits. Any surplus would go into central

1. Map of Spain showing paradores *(nos 1–31),* hosterias *in historic buildings (nos 32–35) and* hostals *in historic buildings (nos 36–38).*

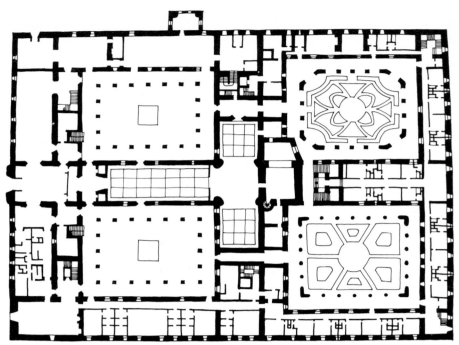

2. *Ground floor plan, Hostal de Los Reyes Catolicos, Santiago de Compostela.*

4. *The great central hall under the tower of the* hostal. (PHOTOGRAPH: ESTUDIOS PANDO).

3. *View of the* hostal *from the steps of the cathedral.*

5. *An armoured plate glass door set in a late Gothic stone surround, Hostal de Los Reyes Catolicos, Santiago de Compostela.* (PHOTOGRAPH: ESTUDIOS PANDO).

funds to meet the deficit of the less profitable establishments. All staff was to be recruited locally, though managers were to be experienced hoteliers, chosen by competitive examination and, once appointed, were to be allowed considerable liberty.

In recent years the government set up a separately subsidised and autonomous body, the Empresa Nacional de Turismo, to provide a competitive element in the construction of *paradores*. In fact the E.N.T. *paradores* are known as *hostals* to distinguish them from the others, and there have so far only been a handful, among them the Hostal de Los Reyes Catolicos at Santiago de Compostela, illustrated here, a vast Renaissance edifice built around four courtyards, which was formerly the Hospital Real. Founded in 1489 by the Catholic Kings and erected between 1501 and 1510 by Enrique de Egas, it stands at one end of the Plaza del Hospital and at right-angles to Santiago's famous pilgrimage cathedral. Conversion to hotel use fitted this essentially cellular building like a glove. More important, it has provided local employment and generally re-animated a dying city.

In converting historic buildings to *paradores* the policy has always been to preserve and, if necessary, to restore the exterior. Important architectural features like courtyards, vaulted rooms or stone staircases are also salvaged and restored. Monasteries, hospitals, palaces—courtyard buildings in general—are easier to convert than medieval castles with their brick, windowless walls and limited

6. *The Castle of Santa Catalina (Jaen).*
(PHOTOGRAPH: BENALDES).

7. *Elevation of the Castle of Santa Catalina showing the remains of the old castle (left) and the new* parador *within the walls (right).*

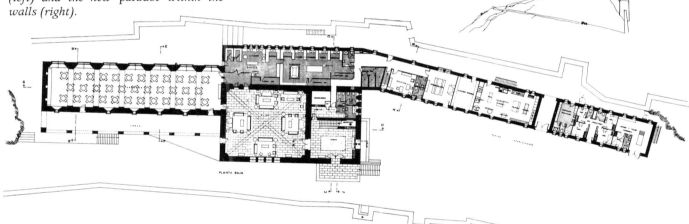

8. *Ground floor plan of the* parador *at the Castle of Santa Catalina.*

9. *The* parador *of Hernan Cortez, Zafra Castle.*

interior space. That is why several *paradores* in castles number no more than 10–15 rooms each and why at the Castle of Santa Catalina de Jaen the architect José Luis Picardo decided to erect a new building inside the castle precincts. This admirable principle, of which history has plenty of examples, is unfortunately compromised by a stylistic approach which we shall criticise later.

Another principle worthy of attention is the respect for later additions. The fifteenth-century castle of Zafra, for example, has seventeenth-century parts which have been preserved and incorporated in the conversion. *Parador* architects, moreover, will readily build on bedroom wings (see the *parador* at Guadalupe) when the existing structure is not large enough or unsuitable. A building must be allowed to grow and change as it has done in the past, and any accretions, old or new become an integral part of this history of the building.

How much more interesting would that history be if the additions of today were built in the spirit of today and not as a pastiche. The Spanish authorities, who were after all the first to appreciate the link between conservation and tourism, argue that if people go on holiday to see beautiful buildings why should they not also be able to stay in beautiful buildings. But the decision to convert old monasteries and castles inevitably brought in questions of style and taste, not only in the matter of architectural additions but in decoration and furnishing. Taste had to be popular and that meant imitating what was already there or what was supposed to have been there. In matters of furnishing it even meant pretending that life in the old building hadn't changed. Above all it meant no experiment, but playing safe with traditional forms and motifs. It meant at best the use of old furniture, though more often reproduction furniture had to serve. Official *parador* architects either believed in this policy or kow-towed to the ministry's wishes, unaware that imitation can never do anything to enhance the original which people come from all over the world to see. No wonder that the architectural profession in Spain is split and that the other half, the modernists, talk derisively of 'the *parador* style'.

The policy is particularly regrettable considering that in the case of many *paradores* the modern hotel might indeed have been planted inside the monument in a stimulating contrast. Often, as at Oropesa, Merida or Guadalupe, only the ruin or semi-ruin of the building survived, crying out for an imaginative rehabilitation appropriate to a modern hotel. The first *parador* conversion at Oropesa in 1930 firmly set the tone for the future with its whimsy timber screens and pseudo-rustic furniture.

Oropesa is a small Castilian town mid-way between Madrid and Estremadura. On the crest of a hill crowning the town stands the castle, home of the Dukes of Frias, Constables of Castile. The castle was probably held in fee for the first time in 1366, during the reign of Pedro I, when it was granted to Don Garcia Alvarez de Toledo, who undertook restoration of the early fortress which had been severely damaged in the wars between Moors and Christians. Having been granted feudal seignory over the town of Oropesa, Don Garcia carried out further work on the castle in 1402, extending it northwards and adding the *patio de armas*. Although twice threatened with destruction in its long history, the castle survived in a good state of repair until the arrival of Napoleon's armies, which left it in almost total ruin.

The castle is joined to the seventeenth-century palace of the Counts of Oropesa and to the walls that used to encircle the town. It is kept as a

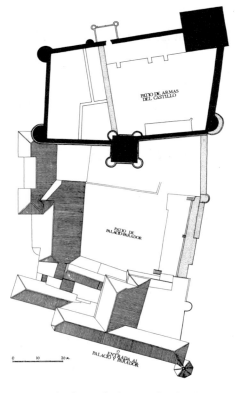

10. *Roof plan of the castle (top) and* parador *at Oropesa.*

190

11. Oropesa: view from the west with the castle on the left and the palace of the Counts of Oropesa, now converted into the parador, on the right.
12. The colonnaded balcony overlooking the courtyard at Oropesa.

13. The balcony on the west front which overlooks the Tagus Valley.

14. The dining room, Oropesa.
15. A pseudo-rustic doorway and screen at Oropesa.

191

16. *The* parador *Via de la Plata at Merida seen from the entrance side on the town square.*
17. *Merida: the diminutive courtyard.*
18. *Merida: the Moorish garden at the back.*
19. *Merida: the former convent chapel, now the main reception area.*

picturesque ruin, while the palace has been converted into the *parador* Virrey de Toledo, named after Don Francisco de Toledo (1512–82), who was for twelve years Viceroy of Peru. The *parador* has 23 double rooms and a series of reception rooms including a dining room seating 100. All the principal rooms face south over the Tagus valley and towards the distant Sierra de Guadalupe. At the back, on the castle side, the rooms give on to extravagantly potted and planted balconies which run nearly the length of the building.

The *parador* Via de la Plata at Merida in Estremadura is also one of the early ones. It was opened in 1933 but redecorated in 1966 and extended by a new wing which gives on to a Moorish garden with tropical trees and fountains. Merida lies near the Portuguese border, on the main road from Madrid to Lisbon, and is the Augusta Emerita founded by Augustus in 25 B.C. It became the capital of Lusitania and the ninth city of the Empire. The evidence is still there, for Merida has some of the finest Roman monuments in Spain: a bridge, an aquaduct, a vast circus, an amphitheatre and a superb theatre built by Agrippa. Even the great Moorish castle was built largely with stones from Roman buildings and today its courtyard is an open-air museum exhibiting a group of tessellated Roman pavements transferred from other sites in the town.

192

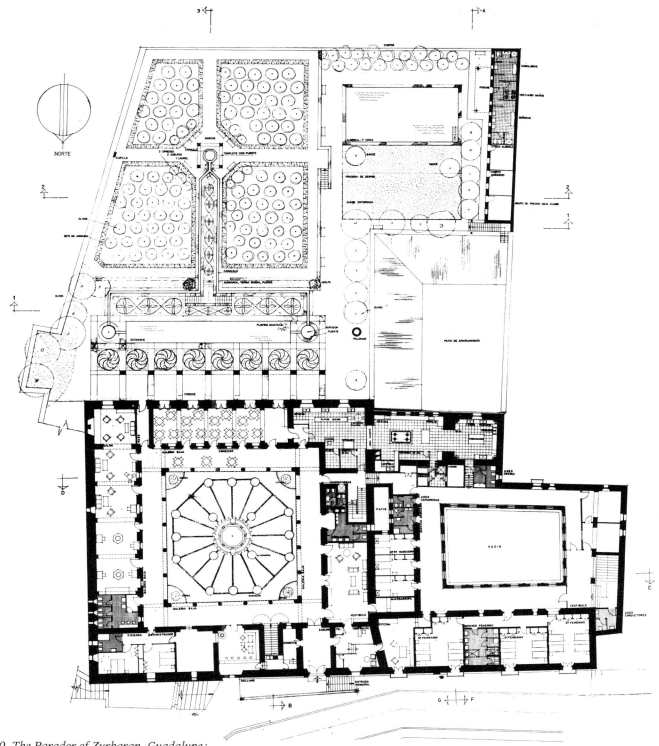

20. The Parador of Zurbaran, Guadalupe:
upper floor plan. The Colegio de los
Infantes is on the left.

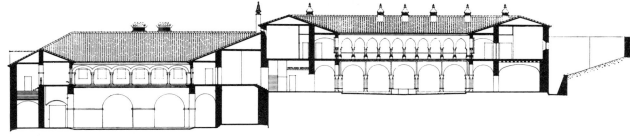

21. Guadalupe: east-west section looking
north.

193

22. *Guadalupe: the portal of a Baroque church seen through the main entrance gate to the* parador.
23. *(Above) Guadalupe: the courtyard of* the Hospital de San Juan Bautista which now houses the service quarters of the parador. *The towers of Guadalupe Castle rise in the background.*

24. *Guadalupe: the Moorish courtyard of the Colegio, now the main hotel premises.*
25. *Guadalupe: the Moorish garden with the new rear façade of the Colegio. The area under the arcade forms a terrace to the dining room.*

The *parador* is around a diminutive but delightful courtyard, which can be covered by an awning in the summer. Its 44 double rooms with bathrooms, dining room seating 120 and impressive sequence of reception rooms which include the old chapel, are housed in an elegant Baroque building which dates from the foundation in 1602 of the Convento de Jesus by the Order of Santa Clara. But on the site of the convent had stood a Roman temple whose white marble columns may be the same as those in the courtyard; and a Visigothic church, which replaced the temple and was in turn destroyed by the Moors, may have left its evidence in the surviving carved capitals.

The last example of a *parador*, and perhaps the most successful, is at Guadalupe, also in Estremadura. It is the Parador of Zurbaran, named

26. *Guadalupe: one of the principal bedrooms.*
27. *Guadalupe: the dining room.*

after the painter who in 1638 went to the monastery at Guadalupe to paint some of his most famous canvases. Among the buildings which were dependent on the monastery were two contiguous structures, the Colegio de los Infantes and the Hospital de San Juan Bautista, which have now been converted into the *parador*. Both buildings are arranged around courtyards and are two storeys high, but the Colegio was built, like the monastery, by artisans with a Moorish background and intended as a residential college for students of grammar and singing to whom the monastery granted scholarships. Architecturally speaking it is the more interesting of the two and houses the main hotel premises, including a dining room seating 200, and all the guest bedrooms (20 double rooms with bath). The Hospital, which steps down the hill so that its first floor is at the Colegio's ground floor, was built in the fifteenth century for the use of pilgrims. It was also a medical school where dissection was first practised in Spain. But the hospital chapel, the most valuable part, no longer exists and the building now houses the kitchens, stores and service quarters.

On the garden side of the Colegio the architect, José Luis Picardo, has taken some liberty by creating a new façade with balconies and pergolas, but without indulging in stylistic fancy. The balconies in fact serve bedrooms which look on what is perhaps the most remarkable part of the whole project—the garden in Moorish style, also laid out by the architect and superbly maintained by the management.

In conclusion it is worth mentioning what Gabriel Alomar, a former Comisario General del Patrimonio Artistico Nacional, has called 'town parador' or '*parador horizontal*'. Referring to the gradual abandonment by its inhabitants of the small historic town, he sees hope in converting the empty buildings into accommodation for tourists. This may stop the others from leaving, he argues, because tourists will bring employment and prosperity. The idea, of course, is not new. In Greece subsidies have been available for many years to householders wishing to convert part of their building to tourist use; and many small towns in France are full of holiday-makers renting rooms in houses rather than hotels. In Urbino an imaginative plan exists which would enable accommodation in under-used buildings to be occupied by students in term-time and by tourists during the holidays. If the Spanish authorities proceed with the idea of the '*parador horizontal*' they will have plenty of precedent on which to base themselves.

195

11 Large country houses and castles

SADDELL CASTLE, ARGYLL

New use Holiday house

Architect David Carr

Client The Landmark Trust

Site The castle stands on the Kintyre shore at the mouth of a little river facing Arran across the Kilbrannan Sound.

History The castle was built by the Bishop of Argyll in 1508. It is a tower house built for strength and under licence from James IV. It is recounted that between 1640 and 1674 'William Ralston of that ilk, who married Ursula Mure, Duaghter to William Mure of Glanderston, was forced to seek shelter from the rage of persecution which at that time prevailed in the Lowlands of Scotland and came to the bay of Saddell, about eight miles from Campbeltown, and having built the ramparts which still remain on the Castle of Saddell, there resided for some time'.

Finally it became the property of the Campbells who held it for over three hundred years.

At the end of the last century it was soundly renovated and lived in by the Laird and his family for many years. Since then it has been deserted and had all but fallen into ruin, saved only by a good roof replacement in the 1930s.

Character It is a fine and complete tower house with a battlemented wall-walk round the roof and part of the original barmkin wall incorporated in the surrounding buildings. The plan is rectangular with a basement and four floors above, reached by a spiral staircase beside the entrance door. The basement is vaulted, the infilling being of pebbles from the shore. During the restoration a second stair was discovered from basement to first floor only, which must have served the kitchen. The original fireplace in the kitchen can still be used and is 5ft 6in deep and 10ft wide. All the windows have deep embrasures and, as is usual in such buildings, there are a number of little closets let into the walls, which are 5ft thick. One bedroom has some eighteenth-century panelling remaining.

Over the years the castle became the centre of a farmyard and the byre, stables, horse mill and bothies remain, though now roofless and bare. Here and there can be seen moulded or carved stones from the ruins of Saddell Abbey, a short distance up the valley. Lying on the ground under the trees are the many graveslabs of the unruly Scots, gripping their long swords or standing in their ships of war, a reminder, as is all Saddell, of the half tragic, half splendid history of Scotland.

Work done In 1973 the castle, which had not been inhabited for many years, was all but a ruin. Substantial trees were growing from the roof, all the windows had gone, and the walls were saturated with rain and the timber floors were rotten.

Firstly the vegetation was removed and the roots poisoned. Three horizontal delta bars were drilled into the south-west corner and grouted in to hold a two-inch crack that ran down the height of the castle. The stone-paved battlement walkway was fully repaired and damaged slabs were replaced. All the flooring was replaced with second-hand pitch pine, except in the dining room where second-hand stone paving was

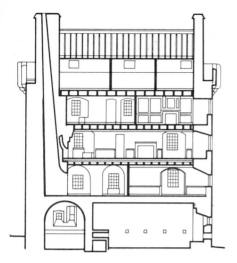

1. North-south section looking east.
2. First floor plan.

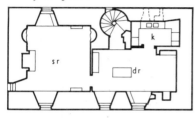

laid. New sash and casement windows were installed and the roof was overhauled. Water, drainage, a septic tank and electric services were provided. Original doors, panelling and architraves were retained in a few rooms. All loose plaster was removed and a pitch-impregnated material to hold new plasterwork was fixed to all external walls. An old-established plastering firm was given the job of reproducing the original mouldings throughout. Stone fireplaces were preserved, three in working order. A fire-alarm system was installed, a rope handrail fixed around the walls of the spiral stair and finally the castle was painted throughout.

Accommodation Basement—stores.
Ground floor—bathroom.
First floor—dining room, kitchen and sitting room.
Second floor—bedrooms.

3. The dining room on the first floor.

Third floor—bathroom and bedrooms.
Fourth floor—attic space.

Date of completion 1978

Cost £130,000. Part of the cost was met by a grant from the Historic Buildings Council and part by a grant from the Scottish Tourist Board.

4. View from the south (PHOTOGRAPH: COURTESY LANDMARK TRUST).

PRINCE-BISHOPS' SUMMER PALACE, EICHSTÄTT, BAVARIA

New use Administrative centre for the local polytechnic

Architect Karljosef Schattner

Client The Federal Ministry of Education and the Land of Bavaria in association with the city of Eichstätt.

Site On Ostenstrasse, on the eastern side of Eichstätt, Northern Bavaria.

History In the early eighteenth century, the Prince-Bishops left the castle of Willibaldsburg and returned to Eichstätt. They had two homes, one near the cathedral, and a summer palace on the edge of the city. This palace, by the Italian master-builder, Gabriel de Gabrieli, was substantially completed by 1735. With secularisation at the beginning of the nineteenth century, it passed into other hands and by 1857 it was standing empty. In 1872 it was acquired by the State and turned into barracks. The Church, which took it back in 1899, used it as a library, but with the building of a new library in 1964, the palace stood empty once again and in need of a new use. In 1969 the authorities concerned agreed to its conversion into the administrative centre of the local polytechnic.

Character This long two-storey building consists of a central block flanked by two narrow wings, only 6m in depth. The main entrance, flanked by pilasters, leads into a square hall divided into bays by columns. Large windows punctuate the stuccoed and painted façades; in the side wings they are handsomely arched with decorative pilasters on the first floor and supported on small columns on the ground floor.

The roofs are pitched over the wings and mansarded over the main block.

Work done On the ground floor, the side wings were cleared of dividing walls and made into open offices. The windows on the south side were removed, leaving an open arcade, with the new glazing fixed in a steel frame behind. In the centre block the high ceiling made it possible to insert two additional levels—a platform 1·15m above the entrance level, which also avoided what would have been excessively high window sills, and a gallery 2·30m above the entrance level.

The windows on the first floor of the side wings were unblocked and glazed in traditional wood frames. The floor space was divided into small offices for lecturers. These are 4 × 4m self-contained studies, each furnished with a desk, a seating arrangement and bookshelf. A wardrobe with a built-in washbasin acts as a dividing space between every two such studies. On the same floor are housed two conference rooms, as well as the chancellor's, the vice-chancellor's and the dean's personal offices. At each end of the two wings a circular escape stair has been freely inserted into the existing structure. Additional offices have been obtained by the conversion of the roof space.

Accommodation Ground floor—entrance hall with reception desk, offices, lavatories.
First floor—assembly hall, conference room, offices, lavatories.
Second floor—lecturers' room with anterooms between.

Date of completion 1974

Cost 3,342,248.79 DM

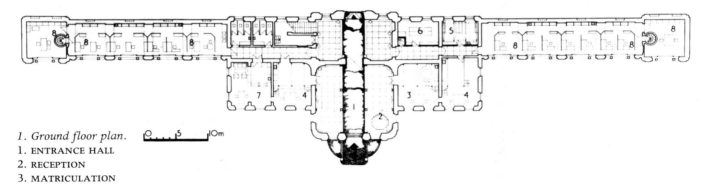

1. Ground floor plan.
1. ENTRANCE HALL
2. RECEPTION
3. MATRICULATION
4. SUPERVISOR
5. REGISTRATION
6. TELEPHONE EXCHANGE
7. DIRECTOR
8. OFFICES

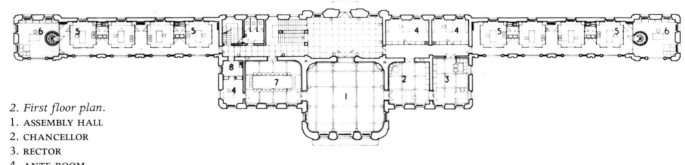

2. First floor plan.
1. ASSEMBLY HALL
2. CHANCELLOR
3. RECTOR
4. ANTE-ROOM
5. LECTURES
6. DEAN
7. MEETING ROOM
8. TEA PREPARATION

3. South front from the unrestored formal garden. (PHOTOGRAPH: SIGRID NEUBERT).
4. The ground floor open offices in the side wings.
5. On the ground floor the centre block has a 4·5m high ceiling which has been divided horizontally by podia and galleries.

6. The first floor offices for lecturers in the side wings—small rooms within the longer, vaulted space.
7. Inside one of the lecturers' offices. (PHOTOGRAPHS: SIGRID NEUBERT).

WILLIBALDSBURG, EICHSTÄTT, BAVARIA

New use Natural history museum and archives

Architect Karljosef Schattner

Client The Federal Ministry of Education and the Land of Bavaria in association with the city of Eichstätt.

Site The castle is situated in open countryside on an acropolis outside Eichstätt in the Altmühl valley about 100km north of Munich.

History In the fourteenth century the prince-bishops of Eichstätt left their palace near the cathedral and took up residence in the newly-built Willibaldsburg on the *castrum montis* S. Willibaldi, outside the city. In the second half of the sixteenth century Martin von Schaumburg greatly enlarged the castle and in the first decade of the following century Bishop Konrad von Gemmingen, with the master-builder Elias Holl, applied the Renaissance style and created the building which survives today. Abandonment and ruin followed secularisation and the break up and sale of the castle in

separate lots. Although the State acquired the castle as early as 1829, no comprehensive restoration work was undertaken for another 140 years. In 1968 the local polytechnic's natural history faculty, originally a part of the Bishops' Seminary, was closed down. A long tradition of natural history and botanical studies at the Seminary had resulted in an important collection which required exhibition space. It was decided, therefore, to convert part of the castle, the Gemmingensaal, into a natural history museum.

Character The massive castle is roughly rectangular on plan, with three ranges and a wall on the fourth side surrounding an internal courtyard. Two crenellated towers adorn the corners of the front façade of the Gemmingensaal, and regularly-spaced windows pierce the upper parts of the thick walls. The roof is of timber construction and has a characteristic mansard form. The structure is of stone and brick and the ground floor rooms of the Gemmingensaal were originally vaulted, but this has now almost entirely vanished.

Work done The Gemmingensaal, the front of the building, was the only part

to undergo conversion, and the work included the restoration of the vaulting in the entrance hall and angle towers. Elsewhere insufficient remains prompted the construction of flat reinforced concrete coffered or beamed ceilings at a higher level, enabling galleries to be inserted. The steel posts which support these galleries also provide fixing points for the cross-slatted timber exhibition panels and display cases. Where this support is not available, panels are suspended from the concrete ceiling on tensioned cables which are also fixed to the floor. Because the exhibits had to be protected from daylight, the museum is lit artificially, mainly by adjustable flood lights and spots fixed to a continuous suspended track.

Accommodation Ground floor—entrance hall with reception desk, lecture hall with projection facilities, galleries with exhibits of natural history, geology, paleontology, etc, aquarium. First floor—archives.

Date of completion 1976

Cost 813,107.34 DM (building work); 588,548.51 DM (fitting out).

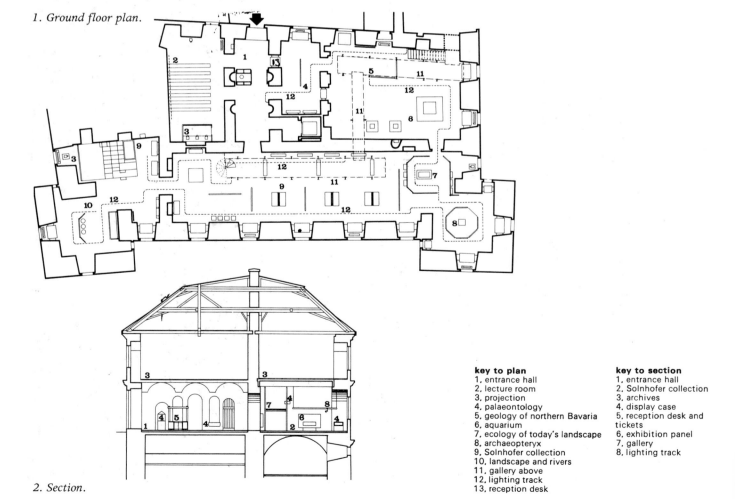

1. Ground floor plan.

2. Section.

key to plan
1. entrance hall
2. lecture room
3. projection
4. palaeontology
5. geology of northern Bavaria
6. aquarium
7. ecology of today's landscape
8. archaeopteryx
9. Solnhofer collection
10. landscape and rivers
11. gallery above
12. lighting track
13. reception desk

key to section
1. entrance hall
2. Solnhofer collection
3. archives
4. display case
5. reception desk and tickets
6. exhibition panel
7. gallery
8. lighting track

200

3. View east over the Altmühl valley, with the Renaissance Willibaldsburg standing proud on its acropolis. The converted Gemmingensaal is in the northern part flanked by the two towers. (PHOTOGRAPH: GERHARD NITSCHE).

4. View into the north-eastern tower with the 'Landscape and rivers' exhibit. No attempt has been made to reconcile the new ceiling with the old. (PHOTOGRAPH: IN-GRID VOTH-AMSLINGER).

5. Looking down the length of the gallery in the room with the Solnhofer collection. The cylinder in the foreground houses a spiral stair which leads to the gallery. (PHOTO-GRAPH: SIGRID NEUBERT).

CLYTHA CASTLE, NEAR RAGLAN, WALES

New use Holiday house

Architect Alan Miles

Client The Landmark Trust

Site Clytha Castle stands on the summit of a low hill, at the edge of a small wood, mostly of old Spanish chestnuts.

History 'Erected in the year 1790 by William Jones of Clytha House . . . it was undertaken with the purpose of relieving a mind afflicted by the loss of a most excellent wife. At the suggestion of the National Trust, the Landmark Trust have taken a long lease of the castle which, due to lack of funds, had earlier been allowed to fall into a state of decay and much disrepair.

Character Despite its name, the castle is in fact a folly in the form of three towers which are linked together, giving the impression of a much larger building. The walls are substantially constructed of random coursed brickwork with a pink stucco finish externally. The castellated battlements, arrow-slit windows and heavily nailed door all contribute to the illusion of a fortified castle. Vertical circulation internally is by means of a circular stone staircase rising through both floors to give access to the roof which affords splendid views over the surrounding countryside.

Work done The object of the restoration was to provide three-bedroom family accommodation which could be let furnished for short periods. The building had suffered from many years of neglect and decay was well advanced before construction work began. The suspended floor above the living room, the roof over the first floor bedroom and bathroom, the roof over the passage link and the roof to bedroom 3 were all renewed. A new damp course was installed and the building re-plastered internally. Stone restoration and replacement was carried out externally together with considerable areas of re-rendering. Most of the windows and all the fittings were replaced. Water was connected to the site and a new drainage system installed.

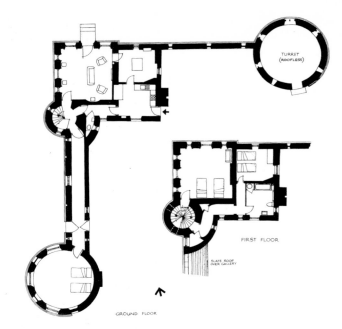

1. Ground floor plan.

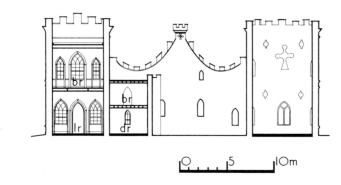

2. Section.

3. The rectangular 'keep' with its corner tower.

202

Accommodation Ground floor—living room, dining room, kitchen, hall, cloakroom and a large bedroom. Also at this level is an empty 'play' tower.
First floor—two bedrooms and a bathroom.
Second floor—roof terrace.

Date of completion September 1975

Cost Approximately £36,500. The local authority contributed £675 and the Welsh Office contributed a grant of £3,750.

4. The living room on the ground floor.

5. A bedroom in one of the towers.

203

PARNHAM HOUSE, BEAMINSTER, DORSET

New use Workshops, school, exhibition centre and residential accommodation for the John Makepeace School for Craftsmen in Wood, and for John Makepeace himself.

Architect None, except for the conversion of the pump house by John Prizeman.

Client John Makepeace

Site The house is situated in its own grounds, half a mile south of the town of Beaminster, in Dorset, and 7 miles from the coast. The river Brit runs close by the house and the grounds are laid out as beautiful gardens.

History The first house known to have occupied this site was built in 1350. Sir Robert Strode, knighted by Elizabeth I, inherited Parnham in 1585 and built a manor house for himself.

During the Civil War, the Strodes were staunch Royalists; and this resulted in Lady Anne Strode being murdered in the Great Hall by one of Cromwell's soldiers. Charles II was an early guest at Parnham after the Restoration of the monarchy. When the last of the Strodes died in 1764 the house and estate passed to Sir John Oglander, a relation by marriage. As he already had an estate on the Isle of Wight, Parnham was left empty and fell into disrepair. In 1810 it was inherited by Sir William Oglander, who commissioned John Nash to restore it. For the first time, in 1896, Parnham was sold. Vincent Robinson, the new owner, died in 1910, after which Parnham was bought by Dr. Hans Sauer, who owned it for only four years but made major improvements to the house and grounds. He built an impressive drive and lodge, landscaped the gardens, planted the yew terrace and reinstated the Tudor interior of the

Great Hall. In 1914 Parnham became the home of the Rhodes-Moorhouse family, and during the war it served as the United States Army's headquarters in south-west England.

John Makepeace moved here in 1976, together with his skilled craftsmen. He has always had close links with this part of England, having trained in Dorset with the furniture maker, Keith Cooper, and later having his own workshop in Banbury, Oxfordshire.

Character The house is built of Hamdon Ashlar stone, now mellowed to a soft yellow. The walls rise three storeys to a crenellated parapet adorned with pinnacles at the gable corners and crests. Mullioned windows, crowned with hood moulds and divided into two or more arched lights, pierce the walls at frequent and irregular intervals. Chimneys are grouped in ornamental clusters on the ridge of the pitched roof.

The original Tudor manor house followed the convention of the time—a Great Hall with a screens passage to the north and a solar to the south. The Great Hall is still the heart of the house, with its minstrels gallery, heraldic stained glass windows and the crest over the fireplace with the motto 'jamais abattu'. The first major extension of the house, the section to the north of the porch, was built early in the seventeenth century, originally to provide a kitchen but converted to a dining room in the eighteenth century. Now it is called the Oak Room and contains linenfold panelling brought from Sir Walter Raleigh's bedroom at West Hawsley Place. There is an eighteenth-century wing to the west and a dining room adjacent to the Great Hall added by John Nash in 1812; on the north side are nineteenth-century stables and coach houses.

Work done The house was developed in four clearly defined stages, each with a clear and separate purpose. Over the

years these had become blurred and the house run as a rambling whole. Now the parts have been clearly re-defined, each with a particular, but related function. The plan clearly expresses the relationship between the various sections of the 'community'.

Building works have included the conversion of the stables and coach houses into workshops and offices, the introduction of new stairways in the student house for fire escape, conversion of the former pump house into staff accommodation, the restoration of the public rooms, the construction of open-sided seasoning sheds and a car park.

Accommodation The Great Hall is used for a display area for John Makepeace's furniture, the drawing room as a gallery for exhibitions of painting and sculpture, and the library serves as a museum of antique tools and the work of both ethnic and designer craftsmen working in wood. The Oak Room—originally the kitchen—together with its adjacent facilities is used as a tea room, or when the house is closed to visitors, is hired out for meetings and celebrations. The West Wing is a self-contained house for students at the School for Craftsmen in Wood, including bedrooms, refectory, studies and recreational facilities in the cellar. The North Wing—formerly the stables and coach houses—now contains the timber seasoning sheds, machine shops workshops and offices.

Completion 1979

Cost £100,000

1. The entrance front of the private residence with the student accommodation to the right (PHOTOGRAPH: LIESA SIEGELMANN).

2. The Great Hall, now an exhibition gallery. (PHOTOGRAPH: FREDERICK WATSON & SON).

3. Ground floor plan.
1. GALLERY
2. LIBRARY
3. DRAWING ROOM
4. KITCHEN/DINING ROOM
5. THE OAK ROOM
6. STUDY
7. BED-SITTING ROOM
8. REFECTORY
9. KITCHEN
10. MILL
11. STUDENT WORKSHOP
12. DRY TIMBER STORE
13. WORKSHOP
14. SPRAYING WORKSHOP
15. DRAWING OFFICE
16. MANAGEMENT OFFICE.

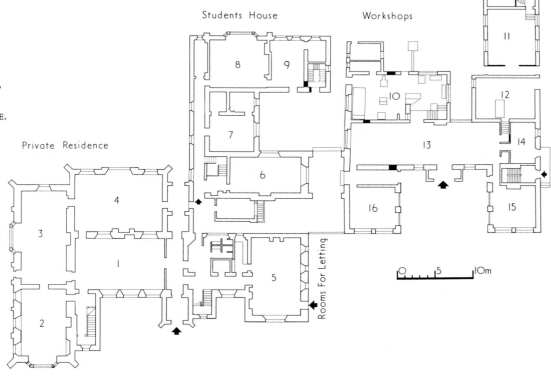

4. First floor plan.
1. BEDROOM
2. BATHROOM
3. LIVING ROOM
4. STUDY
5. BREAKFAST ROOM
6. FINISHED AND PART-FINISHED GOODS STORE
7. LEATHER WORKSHOP
8. COURSE DIRECTOR'S OFFICE
9. STUDENT WORKSHOP

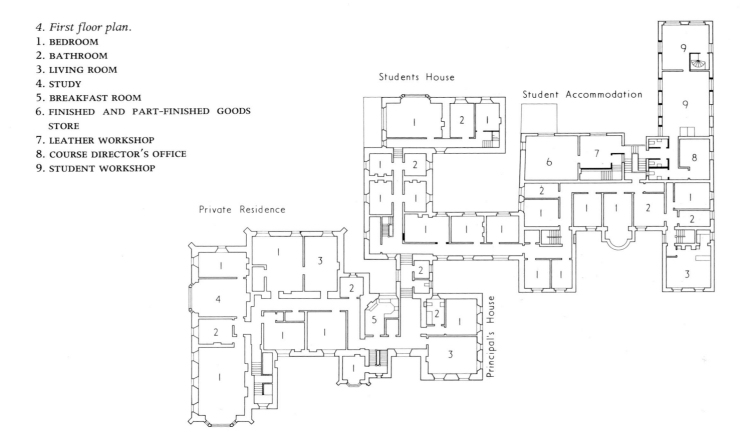

STABLE BLOCK, GREAT FOSTERS, EGHAM, SURREY

New use Conference centre

Architect John Cresswell-Turner

Client Great Fosters (1931) Limited

Site The house is set in open country $1\frac{1}{2}$ miles from Egham in Surrey. Egham is a prosperous town to the west of London about 6 miles from Heathrow airport.

History The main house was probably first built as a hunting lodge in the Great Forest of Windsor, once a favourite place for monarchs and their courtiers to hunt. Its first inhabitants are unknown, but records show that Judge Dodderidge took up residence here in 1620 and in 1631 a Thomas and Mary Bennett built the stable block, which bears their insignia over the door. They were followed by Sir Robert Foster, also a judge, in 1639. The house and its buildings remained a private residence, passing from hand to hand until the present century, when its owner decided first to convert the house into an hotel (1931), and subsequently the stable block into a conference centre.

Character The house was built in 1550 on an older site (probably Anglo-Saxon) in typical Elizabethan style. The outbuildings resemble a type of Anglo-Saxon homestead where livestock and implements were protected within a U-shaped moat, with the buildings and a stockade on the open side. The stable block, a large two-storey brick and tiled building, is situated close to, but quite apart from the main house. Above the heavy oak centre doors to the stable block is a motif in rubbed brick with the initial T over BM, referring to Thomas and Mary Bennett, who occupied the house in 1631. It contained workshops and stables, later garages on the ground floor, with staff bedrooms in what was originally the hayloft. At the south-east corner a wing was added in 1930 to provide further staff quarters. To the south, a tarmac yard with a brick wall formed its southern boundary.

Work done The main house and its surrounding buildings are listed Grade 1 as of architectural and historical interest, so the external appearance of the stable block had to be maintained in its conversion into a conference centre.

The clients' brief was to provide a small purpose-built residential conference centre with the most up-to-date facilities for use by top managerial and international conferences. The brief included instructions to landscape the

1. *Site plan.*
1. HOTEL
2. TITHE BARN (DINING ROOM)
3. PROPOSED EXTENSION TO TITHE BARN
4. CONFERENCE CENTRE
5. PROPOSED NEW STAFF WING
6. DOWER HOUSE
7. MANAGER'S HOUSE

2. *Ground floor plan of conference centre.*

1. RECEPTION
2. BAR
3. CONFERENCE ROOM
4. SUB-STATION
5. PLANT ROOM
6. BOILER HOUSE
7. EXISTING STAFF WING
8. WATER GARDEN

3. *First floor plan of conference centre.*

4. *Cross-section and part elevation of existing staff wing.*

surroundings, form a water garden, and within the building, to design and select all furniture and fittings.

The building was completely gutted and the floors, roof and oak trusses were removed. As the whole building was leaning northwards (with the brickwork at eaves level 9in out of true) it was necessary to provide positive cross-bracing to prevent total collapse. This was done by using the new semi-circular concrete staircase and the new room partitions at first-floor level as stabilising elements.

The clients required the maximum possible number of bedrooms, but no new window openings at first-floor level were permitted by the Historic Monuments Committee. By extremely tight planning, nine bedrooms, each with its own bathroom, were provided at first-floor level, and another five in the roof space. The staircase was placed almost centrally to cut down the length of the necessarily narrow first-floor corridor.

Each bedroom door was set back 6in and no two doors were placed opposite one another, thus giving interest and width to the corridor.

At ground-floor level to the south-west of the building, a single-storey extension and covered way were constructed. This provided space for two offices to the west and increased the width of the main building from 20ft to 26ft, to give a conference area large enough to seat 40 to 60 people. By using sound-proof sliding screens, it can be converted into three separate seminar rooms.

The original tarmac yard to the south was turned into a water garden and planted with trees and shrubs. All ground-floor rooms look on to this garden through double-glazed sliding doors and it provides a peaceful sitting-out area in the summer for seminars, drinks or buffet lunches.

The entire building was equipped with fire protection, smoke detection,

air-conditioning and full audio-visual aids. Planning permission has now been granted to convert the south wing for further bedroom accommodation at first-floor level, with recreation rooms and a sauna bath at ground-floor level.

Accommodation Ground floor—conference room (divisible into three), exhibition area, bar, buffet, television and reading room, two offices, lavatories.
First floor—nine bedrooms, each with own bathroom
Second floor (attic space)—five bedrooms, each with bathroom, linen room, sitting-out areas for casual seminars.

Date of completion May 1973

Cost £150,000

7. The conference room, looking through to the reception and bar.
8. The conference room seen from the reception area. It can be divided into three rooms with sliding partitions. (PHOTOGRAPHS: BILL TOOMEY).

5. The hotel.

6. The water garden, with the conference room and reception on the left.

207

BARANOV CASTLE, POLAND

New use Cultural centre

Architect Alfred Majewski (Directorate for the Restoration of the Royal Castle in Cracow)

Client The Ministry of Culture and Art and the Ministry of the Chemical Industry

Site The castle is situated in a country park some 90 miles north-east of Cracow and nine miles south of Tarnobrzeg, the centre of the sulphur basin. The landscape is flat and dotted with clumps of trees and settlements on the banks of the broad, winding Vistula.

History The castle was built between 1591 and 1606 by Andrzej Leszczynski to a design attributed to the Florentine Mannerist Santi Gucci. It was altered in 1695 by Jozef Karol Lubomirski to the designs of Tylman van Gameren, was twice devastated by fire in the nineteenth century, and was severely damaged during the Second World War. As a result of the discovery in 1955 of extensive sulphur deposits in the neighbourhood, and the consequent exploitation of several mines, Baranov castle was taken over by the sulphur industry and converted into a cultural centre with guest rooms for officials and a geological/archeological museum of the sulphur mining industry.

Character Rectangular on plan, its corners are marked by turrets crowned with cupolas and lanterns. The walls are stuccoed and the four ranges are topped with elaborate Mannerist parapets. In sharp contrast the inside is a beautiful Italianate *cortile*, with two storeys of

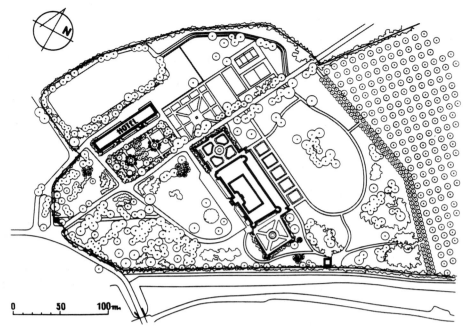

1. Site plan.

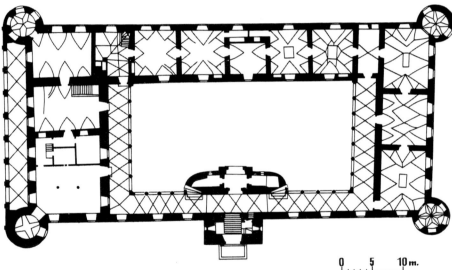

3. The entrance front.

2. First floor plan.

4. The staircase in the cortile *leading up to the first floor arcaded loggias.*

arcaded loggias on three of its sides. The inner walls of these loggias have extravagantly carved door surrounds and pediments—a foretaste of the rich plaster decoration of the interior. The ground floor preserves its Renaissance

5. The elaborately sculpted door pediments in the loggias.

vaults, but the first floor has flat ceilings which date mostly from the last restoration.

Work done In the grounds a small tourist hotel has been built and the castle's basement and ground floor were turned into a café and a museum of the sulphur mining industry. The first floor

was turned into office space and guest rooms for officials of the sulphur industry.

Accommodation Basement—café and museum.
Ground floor—museum and reception rooms.
First floor—offices, reception rooms and guest rooms.

Date of completion 1957

NIEDZICA CASTLE, POLAND

New use Conference centre, guest house, museum

Architect Alfred Majewski (Directorate for the Restoration of the Royal Castle in Cracow)

Client The State Conservation Society for Historic Buildings

1. The irregular plan follows the contours. The oldest and highest part is in the bottom left-hand corner.

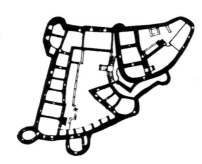

2. The castle seen from the entrance side.

Site The castle stands on the borders of Slovakia and dominates the beautiful Dunajec valley. This was once a corner of Hungary, hence its other name, Nedeczvar.

History The castle has a long and chequered history. It was built in 1325 probably in place of an earlier earth and timber fort. It was sold or captured several times over the ensuing centuries. In the fourteenth century it was enlarged by the Zapolyi family and in the late sixteenth century it was sold to George Horvath of Palocsy who added the central part and completely rebuilt the lower castle. There is a crest which testifies to this work over the main entrance doorway. In 1636 the upper part of the castle was rebuilt. It passed once more from hand to hand until 1945 when the state authorities took it over. Restoration was begun in 1949.

Character On plan the castle is a triangle at the apex of a larger triangle. It has an irregularly shaped courtyard, following the contours. In the highest and oldest part (the triangular apex), there is a chapel and, on a lower level, a prison area which has been preserved complete with its guard house and torture chamber. The walls are of random stonework and the roofs are of shingle.

Work done The castle has been restored and made into a conference centre and guest house for tired academics. The stonework and roofs were repaired where necessary. New timber gutters and down-pipes were fitted. Electricity and sanitation were installed. The oldest part of the castle has been kept as a ruin, with the remnants of the frescoes in the chapel protected. The prison quarter now houses two small museums, one of the castle, the other ethnographic.

Accommodation Reception rooms, bedrooms, dining room, administrator's flat.
Museum of the castle, ethnographic museum.

Date of completion 1956

3. The courtyard, looking towards the oldest and highest part.

FARM BUILDINGS, CULZEAN CASTLE, AYRSHIRE

New use Country park reception centre

Architect The Boys Jarvis Partnership

Client The Culzean Country Park Joint Committee

Site A cliff top a quarter of a mile north of Culzean Castle, overlooking the Firth of Clyde with view towards the mountains of Arran.

History John Bulley, the farm manager for Thomas Kennedy, the 9th Earl of Cassilis, said in 1775, 'I have not a proper farmyard nor a house nor shed for feeding cattle or for the convenience of raising near so much dung as might be made; but these things will come in due course. Lord Cassilis has an extensive and very commodious plan of offices which he intends to build soon'. The Home Farm of the estate was in fact built in 1777 and like the rest of the Cassilis estate, was designed and the existing castle re-developed by Robert Adam.

In 1945 the 5th Marquess of Ailsa offered Culzean Castle and 531 acres to the National Trust for Scotland. In 1969 Culzean Country Park was formed, with adjoining local authorities taking responsibility and the National Trust for Scotland providing the administration. Miss Elisabeth Beazley, the consultant for the country park, suggested that the Home Farm buildings would make an ideal reception centre. Conversion work began in 1971.

1. Ground floor plan.

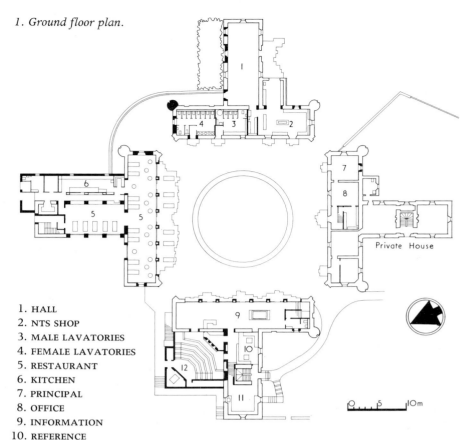

1. HALL
2. NTS SHOP
3. MALE LAVATORIES
4. FEMALE LAVATORIES
5. RESTAURANT
6. KITCHEN
7. PRINCIPAL
8. OFFICE
9. INFORMATION
10. REFERENCE
11. SCHOOLS
12. AUDITORIUM

2. The south-east archway, with the hall on the right and the private house on the left. (PHOTOGRAPH: HENK SNOEK).

Character Four T-shaped buildings facing the central square courtyard are joined at the corners by tall arches surmounted by turrets. Two sides of the courtyard are arcaded, to allow access to farm carts. The downstrokes of the Ts

211

3. The hall is a wet weather shelter of a general purpose. (PHOTOGRAPH: WILLIAM MCCALLUM).
4. The restaurant.

5. The courtyard with the restaurant wing in the background and the information centre on the left. (PHOTOGRAPH: HENK SNOEK).

6. The ground floor of the information centre. The wing was formerly the cart shed. (PHOTOGRAPH: WILLIAM McCALLUM).

are two storeys high with crow-stepped gables. Two of these were lived in—one a house, and one the ploughman's bothy. They were built in solid stone from Swallowcraig, a nearby quarry. The stone is a lovely warm yellow ochre with a touch of pink. The roofs are of West Highland slate.

Work done Because the stone was in a very weathered state, many stones were replaced or dressed back to a sound surface. All the arches facing the courtyard had to be re-faced. Ten new arched openings, principally in the restaurant, were formed. The corbels supporting the many turrets have been largely replaced, as have badly eroded mouldings. New windows were inserted, and former unsympathetic alterations removed or blocked up. All the roofs except one were stripped; the roof timbers were examined, repaired, re-lined, insulated and re-slated. Many of the beams, floors and access stairs are completely new. All the doors were renewed to comply with building regulations.

A new mains water supply with cold and hot-water storage was provided. A completely new drainage system and outfall with a modern aerated sewage treatment plant has been constructed. Electric lighting and heating were provided, with a new substation hidden behind a high garden wall. Electric underfloor heating was installed beneath the new Caithness slab floor of the reception area and the quarry tile floor of the restaurant.

Robert Adam's conception has been added to and altered over the years; for instance, the 3rd Marquess extended the east wing to house his boat building activities (removing one of the main towers). There was a blacksmith's shop extension, iron hay barn, large concrete silage pit and a brick toolhouse. These have been removed. Arches which were blocked up have been opened up again. It was found necessary to build a kitchen and an auditorium on to the original structure. Both are well provided with equipment and are sympathetic in style and materials to the original.

Accommodation West wing—reception and information centre, exhibition space, lecture rooms, auditorium.
North wing—restaurant.
East wing—National Trust for Scotland shop, lavatories, wet-weather shelter.
South wing—administration, Ranger's office; the house in this wing remains in residential use.

Date of completion 1973

Cost £256,800, including stonework repair, main contract, demolition and siteworks, auditorium and exhibition area.

WORTHAM MANOR, LIFTON, DEVON

New use Holiday house

Architect Pearn and Proctor

Client The Landmark Trust

Site Wortham Manor, which is a very unusual example of a late medieval house, nestles in a fold in high ground to the north of the village of Lifton. It stands about 400ft above sea level on a windswept plateau which gently slopes towards the north-east and the water-shed of the River Tamar.

History Wortham Manor remained in the possession of the Wortham family until William Wortham died in the reign of Richard III, leaving his six daughters as his co-heirs. One of these, Agnes, brought Wortham to her husband Otho Dinham, a scion of one of the great Norman families of Devon. It has re-mained in residential use until recently.

Character It seems that alterations were made to the house in the first quarter of the sixteenth century, probably by the first John Dinham when the upper room was formed by the insertion of a floor whose cross beams, wall bearing and joists are moulded and end-stopped with richly carved motifs at the junctions. Since that time the house has been left unaltered in every respect, successive owners being neither too rich nor too poor. Many of the features of the Manor are similar to those found at Cotehele on the other side of the Tamar Valley, particularly the slight ogee curve in the window tracery, the tympanum of the granite doorway in the north elevation and the moulded, intersecting arched windbraces of the roof of the upper hall.

There are no passages in the house, all the rooms leading out of each other.

Work done In acquiring this beautiful building the Landmark Trust wanted to restore it without changing its architectural features but at the same time reinstating the gable and roof forms shown in Edmund Prideaux's sketch of 1717. In order to retain its setting, the disused farm buildings on two sides of the house were also purchased.

The work took five years and can be divided into the following phases. The west and south walls were shored up, the foundations were underpinned and drains were laid around the perimeter walls. An electro-osmotic damp-proof system, a damp-proof membrane and electric underfloor heating were in-stalled.

The west wall, which had bulged and

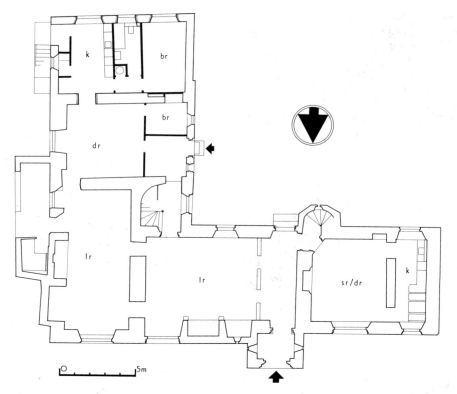

1. Ground floor plan.

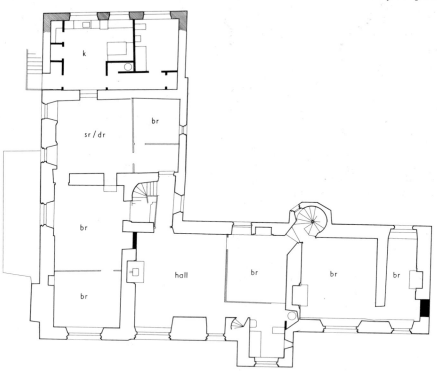

2. First floor plan.

moved outwards, was strengthened by inserting reinforced concrete tie beams between the gable walls and injecting cement grout. The gable walls and chimneys were rebuilt, the roof trusses were repaired and new trusses were rebuilt over the east wing. The parapet on the north elevation was replaced, and finally the whole roof was re-covered with small slates.

The work included a completely new electrical installation, water supply and plumbing, drainage and septic tank disposal system.

Work on the windows included re-pairing spalled granite to heads, mul-lions, jambs and cills, both internally and externally, re-leading and glazing lights and providing and fixing new opening lights. Floor beams, lintels and

213

joists were repaired and renewed where necessary. Carved beams, ceiling bosses and decorative rubs and panelling were cleaned. All timber was treated against woodborers and fungus attack.

External walls were re-pointed and internal ones plastered and limewashed. The existing timber newel staircase was replaced by a new one and the old hardwood balusters were refixed.

Garden walls and the pond were cleaned and renovated.

Date of completion December 1974

Cost Approximately £100,000

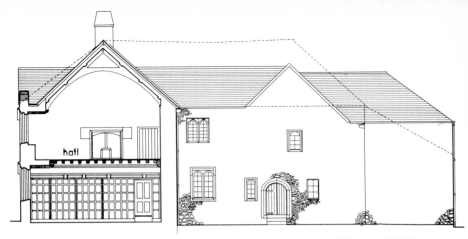

3. *Section through hall and west elevation.*   4. *(Above) View from the south.*

5. *The exposed trusses and braces of the original medieval roof over the first floor hall.* (PHOTOGRAPH: ROBERT CHAPMAN).

6. *The north front.*

7. *The east front before and, 8, after restoration and reinstating the gable and roof forms shown in Edmund Prideaux's sketch of 1717.* (PHOTOGRAPH: ROBERT CHAPMAN).

Appendix: Found space

Found space

In a report from Educational Facilities Laboratories[1] entitled *Found Spaces and Equipment for Children's Centres*[2] found spaces are defined as 'the discarded, overlooked and inexpensive spaces . . . of an abundant and sometimes wasteful society (transformed) into useful places . . .'. Although the report is specifically about educational facilities, the definition can be applied more widely. This chapter, which bridges the two halves of the book—the city and the village— looks at redundant barns, warehouses, television studios and railway stations, simply and cheaply converted for the use of the general public or local community and, in the case of the warehouses, to a basic commercial use which is intended to make floor space more easily available to small and impecunious organisations.

The Vale and Downland Museum Trust at Wantage in Berkshire, under the inspired and energetic direction of Dr. Richard Squires, has three remarkable projects in hand. The Trust was formed to set up the Vale and Downland Centre, a meeting place, art centre and museum of local life, in the old surgery building at Wantage. This project, which is now well advanced, will eventually include the re-erection of a barn at the end of the garden to house large exhibits.

The second project, the conversion of Tulwick Barn at Grove near Wantage, was completed in 1975 and is also administered by the Trust. There are in fact two adjacent eighteenth-century barns—each three bays wide. Together with the farmhouse they stand on the site of a medieval hamlet which was deserted in the fourteenth century because of the plague or one of the enclosure acts. By the late 1960s when combine harvesters had taken over from horses, the barns, which were not wide enough to take the combines, fell into disuse and began to deteriorate. The owner wanted to pull them down but Dr. Squires, who lives in the farmhouse, persuaded him of their value and offered to find a new use for them.

The work entailed the removal of both roofs and the replacing and splicing in of many new roof timbers. All the unskilled work was

[1]A non-profit corporation in New York established by the Ford Foundation to help schools and colleges with their physical problems by the encouragement of research and experimentation and the dissemination of knowledge regarding educational facilities.

[2]First printing March 1972. EFL, 477 Madison Avenue, New York, N.Y. 10022.

1. *Tulwick Barn: drawing showing the accommodation provided in the two adjacent barns. The left-hand barn is for living and sleeping, the right-hand barn for entertainment.*

2. *Tulwick Barn, Grove, near Wantage.* (PHOTOGRAPH: OXFORD MAIL AND TIMES).

3. *View of the living area in the left-hand barn showing youngsters from London spending the week-end.*

carried out by voluntary labour, though thatching, glazing, electricity and plumbing was in the hands of skilled people who agreed to work at charity rates. Dr. Squires has described how the design of the conversion evolved as the structure was being repaired 'so that we had a living end—the old stable which was thatched with two dormer windows and a glazed triangular gable; and a working end—the larger barn which was left more basic. In the living area we fitted 15 bunk beds upstairs, and downstairs we divided the bays into a cooking area with a simple stove, dresser and sink; an eating area with a long table made out of demolition wood from the motorway; and a sitting area where children can sit around the open log fire which we built. The larger barn was also divided into three areas—the rough stage, made from the floor of the old apple store; a watching area for the audience (the old threshing floor); and a working area in the furthest bay. Using this method of voluntary help, reduced rates and salvaged materials, we have kept the cost of the conversion of the 90ft long complex to as little as £3,500'. The converted barns were an instant success and have been used almost incessantly by local dramatic clubs, youth groups, folk dancers, the local silverband, etc. The type of conversion, though somewhat more elaborate, accords with the Duchess of Devonshire's and the Derbyshire Preservation Trust's idea, referred to in the chapter on the changing village (page 142), of regarding barns as stone, brick or wooden tents in which hikers can stay at weekends and use as a base for exploring an area.

The third project, Lains Barn at Lockinge, is a magnificent group of roadside farm buildings, 1½ miles east of Wantage, on the Portway section of the Icknield Way. It rests on a green sand shelf overlooking the eastern end of the Vale of the White Horse towards Oxford and the

Thames at Abingdon, with the Chilterns forming the distant horizon. Four bays of the large barn were built in the eighteenth century; the other two bays and the L-shaped cow byre enclosing the fold yard were added in the nineteenth century when the property became part of the Lockinge estate. The barn is a classic Berkshire barn with its long axis at right-angles to the slope of the ground, roofs of plain tiles and walls of feather-edge lap-boarded elm on an oak timber frame. It is divided internally into six bays by elm and oak trusses supported both sides on posts and shallow partitions. Two lots of huge double doors facing one another divide the barn unequally, leaving two bays on one side and three on the other. The remarkable feature of the cow byre is its cloistered arrangement of 12 equal open-fronted bays, supported by oak posts and curved braces. Inside there is a 200ft long hayrack and manger which is being preserved.

In 1960 the farmland was sold without the buildings which had ceased to be of any use to the modern farmer. A planning application for residential use was refused and the buildings were later offered to the Trust at a token price on the understanding that they were used principally by the local community. The large barn is now being converted into a basic theatre and concert hall for the use of local and travelling groups. It will have a gallery at one end and a mobile stage which can be erected at either end or in the middle. Besides plays and concerts, the barn will also be available for rehearsals, film shows, barn dances, banquets, lectures, exhibitions and conferences.

One wing of the cow byre will be glazed in and will accommodate a long gallery with a simple kitchen. It will be used for eating, either separately from or in conjunction with the barn, as a small art gallery or as country class-room. The other wing, which will remain open, will serve as a covered way, a picnic area for school parties, a place for craft fairs (in conjunction with some of the interior spaces) and a pen for the two sheep, bred specially to crop the grass of the former fold yard.

As in the case of Tulwick Barn much of the labour has been voluntary, skilled workmen have offered their services at charity rates, and materials have been scrounged or gifts gratefully accepted. Nevertheless up to £20,000 may be needed to cover the purchase price and pay for the installation of electricity, heating and lavatories. To avoid paying interest, no money is borrowed and all of it has to be in the form of gifts.

The problems of raising money and getting the work done cheaply were nothing compared to the difficulties raised by the planning, rating and fire officers. Nothing less than a complete change of heart is needed to persuade these officers to waive regulations which were never meant to be applied to the buildings and circumstances under discussion. Dr. Squires begged the planning officer to regard his barns as beautiful shelters which would have been destroyed had he not found a new use for them. 'Think of them', he wrote, 'in the same light as the Scottish mountaineering huts . . . providing shelter and simple facilities—a permanent tent, not a building having to comply with modern housing regulations. If a cow wants to live in one part of the building so much the better. She needs shelter too, provides more atmosphere for the children and is certainly not a health hazard'.

The rating officer at first wanted to increase the rates on Tulwick Barn on the grounds that the sleeping accommodation constituted a change of use. Dr. Squires pointed out that the barn had always been used by the 'weekly boarding' type of farm workers who would live in the barn and then walk 20 miles home at week-ends. As a private citizen, moreover, who had asked for no improvement grant, who had

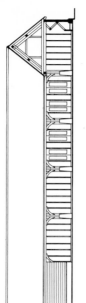

4. *Lains Barn: section on BB through the covered way and picnic area, and the elevation of the glazed-in gallery.*

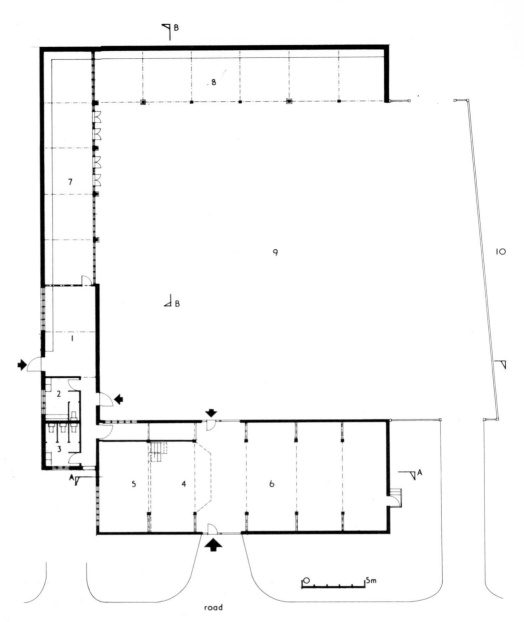

5. *Lains Barn: ground floor plan showing the conversion of the barn into a community centre for the arts.*

1. FOYER AND BAR
2. MALE LAVATORIES
3. FEMALE LAVATORIES
4. STAGE
5. GALLERY OVER BACK-OF-STAGE AND DRESSING ROOM AREA

6. AUDITORIUM
7. GLAZED-IN GALLERY
8. COVERED WAY AND PICNIC AREA
9. FOLD YARD
10. CAR PARK

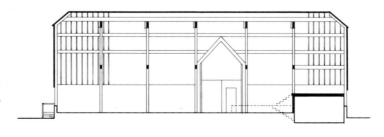

6. *Lains Barn: section AA showing the stage (dotted line) and the gallery over the back-of-stage and dressing room area.*

218

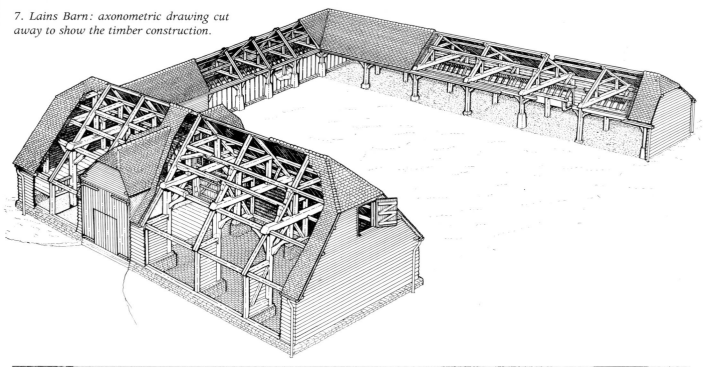

7. Lains Barn: axonometric drawing cut away to show the timber construction.

8. Lains Barn from the road before conversion.

9. The interior of Lains before conversion to an auditorium.

219

spent his own money to save barns which the council would have been quite happy to see pulled down and who had then offered them as a community asset, was he to be penalised by being made to pay the council?

Fire, on the other hand, is a serious matter and it is essential to discuss the problems with the fire officer on the site before any plans are made. He will want to divide the building into a series of sealed compartments with fire-doors and will insist on alternative means of escape and fire extinguishers. At Tulwick Barn Dr. Squires was able to persuade him to accept the red staircase floating elegantly in space and not to insist on having it cased in. But in other respects the fire officer's requirements were met, though not without difficulty and extra cost.

The next group of 'found space' has the theatre and the arts in common. It consists of some old BBC studios converted into a local arts centre, a project to turn a multi-storey warehouse into a centre of Afro-Caribbean arts and culture, and a railway station and single-storey warehouse converted into theatres.

The Riverside studios at Hammersmith in fact began life in the 1920s as a foundry. The subsequent conversion into BBC studios left it a warren of small spaces which will gradually be rehabilitated as money becomes available. At present only part of the building is in use—the foyer, the two studios, the rehearsal room on the first floor and a number of dressing rooms and offices. But the rehearsal room would make an excellent cinema if public access could be provided, and the two studios require complete sound separation if they are to be usable simultaneously. There are plans to provide an exhibition gallery and to take advantage of the spectacular position on the Thames by opening a riverside restaurant and terrace.

The idea of creating an arts centre out of these studios is only a year or two old and began with Hammersmith Borough Council's inviting a group of people to form an independent trust. The council, which has been behind the project from the beginning, has provided the studios rent free, as well as generous grants towards building costs and revenue subsidy. More recently the Arts Council (£12,000), the Baring Foundation (£2,000) and the City Parochial Foundation (£1,500) have made it possible for a bookshop to be built, equipped and stocked (architects: Will Alsop and John Lyall) thus fulfilling a considerable need in this area of London. Fullers, the brewers, paid for the cooling equipment, though it proved possible, with the exception of the electrical equipment, to re-use and adapt the mechanical installations which the BBC had left behind. Most important of all, the Department of the Environment has given a grant of £150,000 enabling Riverside Studios to buy their own stage lighting equipment and a permanent but flexible seating system, thus saving heavy hire charges.

The architects, Michael Reardon and Associates, were given only a very general brief. The two large studios were to be made usable for public performances of some sort and preferably of every sort. Peter Gill, as Artistic Director, was particularly determined that the development of Riverside Studios as an arts centre should not be restricted by the way in which the building was planned. The building to him was simply one of a number of factors which would shape the policy of the arts centre and he begged everyone to 'beware of architects bearing plans'. So the building work was started on the basis of a general plan without anyone knowing the uses to which many of the rooms would be put.

The architects derived some of their ideas from an appreciation of

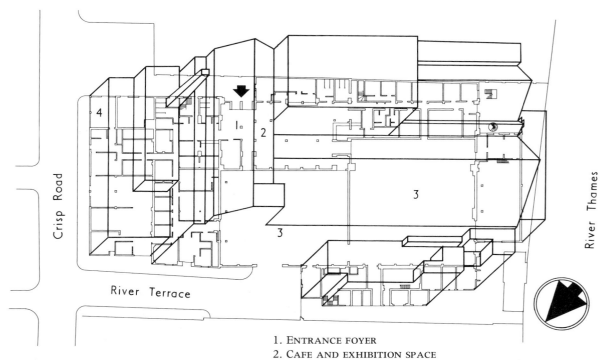

10. *Riverside Studios, Hammersmith: ground floor plan.*

1. ENTRANCE FOYER
2. CAFE AND EXHIBITION SPACE
3. STUDIOS
4. BOOKSHOP

11a. *Riverside Studios from Crisp Road.* (PHOTOGRAPH: RAY ABBOTT).
11b. *The new bookshop at Riverside Studios.* (PHOTOGRAPH: WILL ALSOP & JOHN LYALL)

12. *Riverside Studios: the café.* (PHOTO-GRAPH: CHRIS J. ARTHUR PHOTOGRAPHY).

13. *Riverside Studios: a performance for children in one of the studios.* (PHOTO-GRAPH: JOHN HAYNES).

the building's labyrinthine nature which was even more marked before the muddle of offices was cleared to make the new foyer. Rather than design the main entrance on the Crisp Road frontage, they deliberately chose to bring the public in at the side in a rather secretive way, (though this will no longer be the case if the new plan, by Will Alsop and John Lyall, is put into effect). The practical advantage is that it lands people in the heart of the building from which they can move outwards to different areas and activities.

In executing the work Riverside Studios as employer wished to take maximum advantage of the Government's Job Creation Programme whereby unemployed labour is recruited and engaged outside the contract by the employer under the supervision of an experienced building foreman and all costs of such labour are reimbursed by the Manpower Services Commission. Whenever possible, priority was to be given to young and inexperienced persons and some training was to be provided during the period of employment. Since the scope and extent of the works were not fully defined at the outset, the architects recommended a Fixed Fee Form of Prime Cost Contract which was modified to make the contractor responsible for selecting and recruiting the necessary M.S.C. labour and to prohibit the use of his own sub-contracted labour, except where suitable un-employed labour could not be found.

The contractor selected was one of only two who submitted tenders. Most firms who were approached were reluctant to risk the use of M.S.C. labour. After interviewing some 150 applicants, the contractor arranged for the employer to engage a suitable labour force, which reached a peak of 16 to 18 and was employed throughout the contract period. This system worked well as long as the need was mainly for unskilled labour. When towards the end of the job skilled men were required, they came from the contractor's labour force because the employment agencies, despite claims to the contrary, were quite unable to provide them. During the work the architects established an office on site for close direction and supervision. Each section of the work, which formed part of the generally defined 'prime cost' contract, was the subject of an 'architect's instruction' as the work proceeded—a flexible method of working which is becoming more common in the field of conservation and restoration.

Hammersmith used to have two theatres, both of which closed 20 years ago or more. Until Riverside Studios opened in 1978 it had no theatre at all. Such a cultural injection is perhaps less important for Covent Garden, an area of London already peppered with theatres and art galleries. Ever since the market moved out and the area was saved from the Greater London Council's redevelopment proposals, Covent Garden has been attracting new residents as well as new commercial and artistic activities. The trend has been for the rehabilitation of existing property, among which the Central Market building (see Chapter 2), restored and converted to commercial use by none other than the GLC, ranks as the most important.

The Drum Arts Centre is a project by Rock Townsend for a warehouse in Macklin Street on the north-east fringes of Covent Garden. With more than half the black population of Britain living in Greater London, it is well situated for black artists to come and perform, learn to perform or offer their work to the public. Founded as a charitable trust in 1974, with office premises only, Drum sees itself as having five functions: to co-ordinate, to educate, to act as a catalyst, to provide a platform and to create maximum opportunities for employment. The new building will provide a centre for all these

14. Warehouse in Macklin Street which Drum would like to acquire for its arts centre. (PHOTOGRAPH: RICHARD BRYANT).

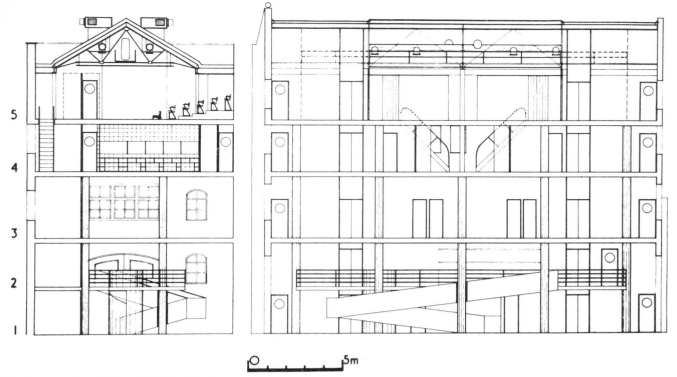

15. Cross-section of the Macklin Street warehouse.

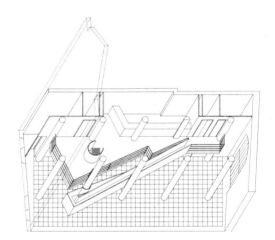

16. Axonometric of levels 1 and 2 (entrance foyer, exhibition area and bar).

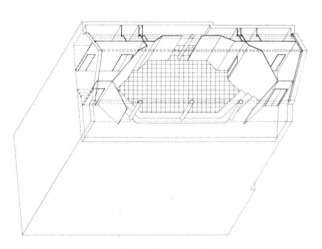

17. Axonometric of level 5 (theatre).

activities which have hitherto taken place at other institutions. Its conversion deserves and needs the funds it is seeking from central and local government, and from private sources.

Nos. 9–11 Macklin Street is a late nineteenth-century brick warehouse with stone features around the windows and parapets. The street façade is wholly symmetrical with a projecting central pedimented feature of large timber windows above a double-height door, flanked by smaller arched windows and doors. The building is on five floors with each floor a simple rectangle on plan. The concrete floor structure is supported on twin beams which rest on elegant cast-iron columns. The proposal is to put the theatre on the top floor, whose high ceiling follows the profile of the roof structure. New lifts and staircases at front and back give on to small foyers, which lead up to double doors and into the back of the 155-seat auditorium. Large props can be hoisted up the outside of the building and pulled in through the central window. The back-stage area contains straight flights of stairs which lead down to the green room. The public functions are at ground and mezzanine level—an entrance foyer linked by a diagonal ramp to the bar, which overlooks the double-height exhibition area. Library and administration are on the next floor; and technical workshops, studio training and dressing rooms are immediately below the theatre. Services have been concentrated on one side of the building to leave as much free space as possible on each floor.

If Macklin Street demonstrates the potential of a multi-storey warehouse, Pakhus 13 in the harbour district of Copenhagen has already proved itself in its exemplary use of a single horizontal space. The single-storey warehouse stands on the waterfront on Larsens Plads. Built around 1870 and originally used to store goods transported by ferries to and from Oslo, it has a structure of cast-iron columns and iron roof trusses. Its arched roof is covered, like its façade, with corrugated iron. Over the wide doorways is an attractive fanlight with different coloured glass panes set into a cast-iron lattice-work, a motif echoed in the two round-headed windows on either side of the door.

In 1975 the dancer and choreographer Eske Holm received a grant from the Danish Ministry of Culture to start his own ballet theatre and obtain suitable premises. He found the warehouse and took his name from it—Pakhus meaning warehouse. Renovation was carried out quickly and cheaply, and the group gave their first performance in September 1975.

Because of the group's limited budget and the temporary nature of the accommodation (the warehouse is scheduled for demolition) the conversion work was kept to a minimum. Both the stage and the seating were built up of wooden beer boxes fastened together and covered with chipboard. The existing trusses were used for hanging stage lights. Spaces were walled off on either side of the entrance, one for cloakrooms and the other for a bar. At the far end of the warehouse dressing rooms, lavatories for performers and areas for props and scenery storage were provided.

Very different in size and character, but also on the waterfront, is the monumental Gare d'Orsay in Paris. Designed as a railway station and hotel by Victor Laloux and completed in time for the 1900 exhibition, it was vacated by the SNCF in the early 1960s and stood empty for some years. In 1977 the Compagnie Renaud-Barrault rented part of the building and gave performances in a tent pending the erection of a more permanent structure, just like the Royal Exchange Theatre Company in Manchester (see page 30). They were soon followed by the Salle Drouot, the famous auctioneers whose right-bank premises were being rebuilt and who came temporarily to occupy another part of the station. They established their administrative offices on the first floor level, overlooking the river, and they erected on the station floor a bubble-shaped structure of salerooms to the designs of the Fromanger Partnership.

The Renaud-Barrault company's more permanent structure was built in three-and-a-half months to the company's own designs and cost £300,000. It consists of a tent-like timber structure, seating 900 people and suitable for all types of staging including theatre in the round. There is also a more intimate theatre upstairs, seating 180, and a foyer, exhibition area, bar and buffet downstairs.

The most important thing about the Gare d'Orsay at this time was the fact that it was in use. For an ambitious project, in 1973, by Patrick

18. Pakhus 13 in the harbour district of Copenhagen: plan and sections of the conversion to a modern dance theatre.

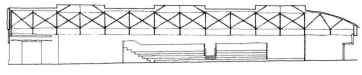

19. Pakhus 13: view of the waterfront.
20. The interior with a rehearsal in progress. (PHOTOGRAPH: ESKE HOLM).

O'Byrne and Claude Pequet, to convert the building into a museum of the nineteenth century, had run aground for lack of funds at a time when the construction of the Centre Pompidou was beginning to make heavy demands on resources. This project has now been revived and the days of the station's temporary uses have inevitably ended. Money is again available for the 43,000m² complex, and the museum is officially expected to open in 1983.

5 Dryden Street, a derelict Edwardian printing works in Covent Garden, and the original Sanderson's wallpaper factory in Barley Mow Passage, Chiswick, are the brainchild of one man, the architect David Rock of Rock Townsend, who were responsible for both conversions. 5 Dryden Street, with some 1700 sq ft of space, was begun in 1972 and completed a year later. When the leasehold was acquired, the building was in poor condition and had a questionable future. By the time it had

21. The Gare d'Orsay from the river front. (PHOTOGRAPH: MARTIN CHARLES).
22. The tent-like timber structure within the station shed which is the larger of the two theatres used by the Renaud-Barrault Company. (PHOTOGRAPH: GÉRARD GUILLAT).

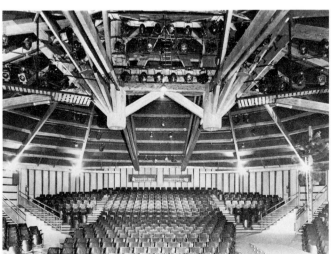

225

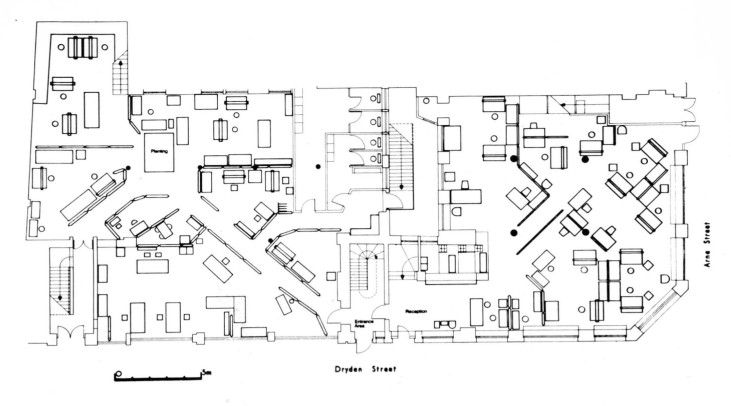

Arne Street

Dryden Street

5m

23. *Ground floor plan of 5 Dryden Street.*

24. *Basement plan of 5 Dryden Street.*

been converted, it was a Conservation Area with most of the block listed Grade III. The intention was to get together a group of firms, in the field of design and construction, working in the same building and managing the building as a limited company. The idea was simple enough: that a number of small firms should be able to retain their individuality, while supporting a higher standard of combined facilities; that such facilities should make it possible to provide a base in London for overseas firms; that the presence of many allied skills

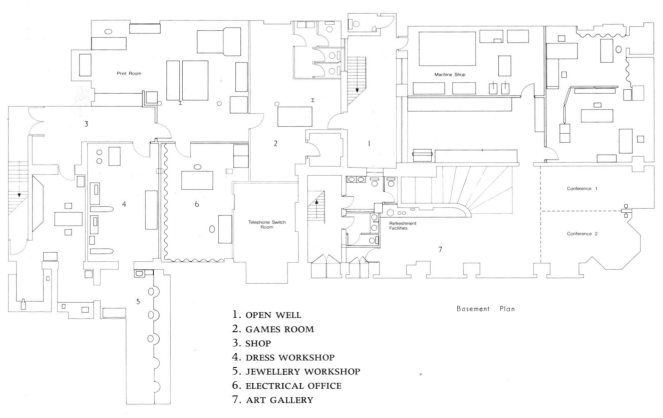

Print Room

Machine Shop

Conference 1

Conference 2

Telephone Switch Room

Refreshment Facilities

Basement Plan

1. OPEN WELL
2. GAMES ROOM
3. SHOP
4. DRESS WORKSHOP
5. JEWELLERY WORKSHOP
6. ELECTRICAL OFFICE
7. ART GALLERY

25. *View of 5 Dryden Street looking down Arne Street. The corner window at ground level used to be two large timber doors. The loading doors and hoists on the second and third floor have been preserved. The glazing at pavement level has re-placed cast iron grilles which ventilated the stable in the basement.* (PHOTOGRAPH: RICHARD BRYANT).

26. *The communal area in the basement which is also used as an exhibition gallery open to the public. The conference rooms which join on to this area can become part of it for lectures etc, with the audience sitting on the wide staircase which horses used to descend when the basement was a stables.*

27. *The ground floor area which used to be a garage and store. The floor under the plants is removable and could form, as it used to, a well for lowering equipment to the workshops in the basement.* (PHOTOGRAPH: RICHARD BRYANT).

should produce a flow of ideas and a breadth of outlook found only in large, multi-disciplinary firms; that the opportunity should exist for firms to work together on specific projects. Richard MacCormac and Peter Jamieson, architect partners at Dryden Street, believe that the place 'gives the small firm a plausible basis which they could not otherwise afford. It also allows for expansion or contraction without the hassle of moving or sub-letting . . . if it wasn't for Dryden Street we might well be working from a basement in Clapham without anybody else to talk to'.

With 33,000 sq ft of floor space, the old Sanderson's wallpaper factory is twice as large and concentrates more on workshop areas, to which about one third of the total is devoted. The rest is divided into design studios, office space, conference rooms, showroom and the new

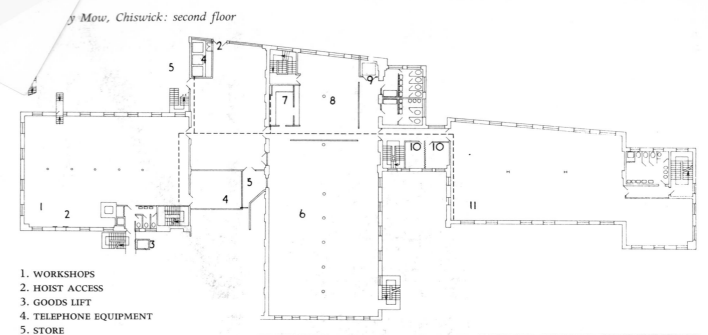

1. WORKSHOPS
2. HOIST ACCESS
3. GOODS LIFT
4. TELEPHONE EQUIPMENT
5. STORE
6. OFFICES AND STUDIOS
7. KITCHEN
8. RESTAURANT
9. PASSENGER LIFT FROM GROUND FLOOR
   ENTRANCE HALL
10. CONFERENCE
11. STUDIOS AND DRAWING OFFICES

29. The former Sanderson's wallpaper factory in Barley Mow Passage, now a community workshop and office centre.

concept of 'office hotel', which is fully serviced office accommodation available on a weekly basis. The factory is situated in Barley Mow Passage, a quiet pedestrian way just off the busy Chiswick High Road, opposite C. F. A. Voysey's famous Sanderson's warehouse. Unlike Dryden Street, where the lessors provided the limited company with the money to repair and renovate the building, at Barley Mow it was the architect John Morton, who acted as co-partner in the scheme with David Rock and John Townsend, and was able to negotiate a loan with an insurance company because of the successful Dryden Street precedent. Barley Mow Workspace, as it is called, was opened in 1976 and cost approximately £220,000, or one third of what it would have cost to build the same area at £20 per sq ft.

With the exceptions already mentioned, Dryden Street and Barley Mow are essentially similar. In both, the priorities were sophisticated services and simple finishes. Space is subdivided by screens supporting shelves, cupboards and desk tops, a system which allows

30. *Typical arrangement of offices and studios on the warehouse floor.* (PHOTOGRAPH: COLIN MAHER).

31. *The restaurant on the second floor.*

32. *The new mezzanine which has been suspended in the roof space.* (PHOTOGRAPH: COLIN MAHER).

the layout to be altered freely as firms leave to change size. Equally flexible are the exposed overhead services which carry telephone and electrical cables, with facilites for plugging in fluorescent light fittings and desk lamps.

The limited company, of which everyone renting space in the building is a member, provides heating, lighting, telephones, photocopying, teleprinting, cleaning, waste collection and maintenance. In Barley Mow there is also a dining room and kitchen run on a concessionary basis. To run these services there is a small staff that includes a company manager, a receptionist-cum-telephonist and a company secretary. Individual members or firms pay a fixed rental sum related to the amount of space they occupy and its location; all overheads are shared; and there exists a reserve fund for contingencies. The whole organisation is non-profit making, with any surplus returned to, or deficit made up by, the individual firms.

Both Dryden Street and Barley Mow are fully let and show that there is a demand for this kind of accommodation. There is after all an age-old precedent in the market hall, which is nothing more than the open market brought indoors, a number of independent stalls under one roof. More recently antique dealers have tended to come together in this manner and, in the professional field, there are examples of doctors', solicitors' and accountants' group practices. With $1\frac{1}{4}$ million small firms in the country accounting for one-third of the total employed population there is clearly room for more experiments of the Dryden Street kind.

If the barn is the building type with the highest redundancy rate in the countryside, its equivalent in the inner city is the warehouse. In Greater London it is reckoned that there are some 23 million sq ft of empty factory and warehouse space. As Covent Garden has already shown, the rehabilitation of some of this space would have a positive effect on the regeneration of the inner city. But Dryden Street and Barley Mow are not just examples of rehabilitation and putting buildings to new uses. They demonstrate a significant change of attitude, away from the purely commercial values of the property market towards a belief in the individual and a more human scale.